BETRAYAL

BETRAYAL
Developmental, Literary, and Clinical Realms

Edited by

Salman Akhtar

KARNAC

First published in 2013 by
Karnac Books Ltd
118 Finchley Road
London NW3 5HT

British Library Cataloguing in Publication Data

A C.I.P. for this book is available from the British Library

ISBN-13: 978-1-78220-015-4

Typeset by V Publishing Solutions Pvt Ltd., Chennai, India

Printed in Great Britain

www.karnacbooks.com

To
STEVEN SAMUEL
in friendship

CONTENTS

ACKNOWLEDGEMENTS

An invitation to speak on the topic of betrayal from Elizabeth Thomas became the impetus for my putting this book together. To my delight, she agreed to contribute a chapter herself. Eight other distinguished colleagues devoted much time and effort to writing original works for inclusion in this book. They responded to my editorial suggestions with the utmost grace. My assistant, Jan Wright, prepared the manuscript of this book with her characteristic diligence and good humour. My dog, Majnun, taught me much about loyalty, the obverse of the topic of this book. To him, and to all the individuals mentioned here, my sincere thanks indeed.

Salman Akhtar
Philadelphia, PA
December 11, 2012

ABOUT THE EDITOR AND CONTRIBUTORS

Anne J. Adelman, PhD, is a clinical psychologist and psychoanalyst with the Contemporary Freudian Society. She completed her doctoral studies in clinical psychology at the City University of New York, and later trained at the Yale Child Study Center in New Haven, CT. She joined the faculty there in 1995, providing training, teaching, and supervision along with her clinical practice. Dr. Adelman relocated to Chevy Chase, MD in 1999, and graduated from the Baltimore Washington Institute for Psychoanalysis in 2004. She has published in the areas of children and violence, trauma and the Holocaust. She is the co-author of *Wearing My Tutu to Analysis and Other Stories: Learning Psychotherapy from Life* (Columbia University Press, 2011). She has also co-edited *The Therapist in Mourning: From the Faraway Nearby* (Columbia University Press, 2013). She graduated from the New Directions Program of the Washington Psychoanalytic Institute in 2010 and is currently a faculty member of the New Directions Writing Program. Dr. Adelman maintains a private practice in Chevy Chase, MD.

Salman Akhtar, MD, is professor of psychiatry at Jefferson Medical College and a training and supervising analyst at the Psychoanalytic Center of Philadelphia. He has served on the editorial boards of the

International Journal of Psychoanalysis and the *Journal of the American Psychoanalytic Association*. His more than 300 publications include fourteen books—*Broken Structures* (1992), *Quest for Answers* (1995), *Inner Torment* (1999), *Immigration and Identity* (1999), *New Clinical Realms* (2003), *Objects of Our Desire* (2005), *Regarding Others* (2007), *Turning Points in Dynamic Psychotherapy* (2009), *The Damaged Core* (2009), *Comprehensive Dictionary of Psychoanalysis* (2009), *Immigration and Acculturation* (2011), *Matters of Life and Death* (2011), *Psychoanalytic Listening* (2013), and *Good Stuff* (2013),—as well as forty-one edited or co-edited volumes in psychiatry and psychoanalysis. Dr. Akhtar has delivered many prestigious addresses and lectures including, most recently, the inaugural address at the first IPA-Asia Congress in Beijing, China (2010). Dr. Akhtar is the recipient of the Journal of the American Psychoanalytic Association's Best Paper of the Year Award (1995), the Margaret Mahler Literature Prize (1996), the American Society of Psychoanalytic Physicians' Sigmund Freud Award (2000), the American College of Psychoanalysts' Laughlin Award (2003), the American Psychoanalytic Association's Edith Sabshin Award (2000), Columbia University's Robert Liebert Award for Distinguished Contributions to Applied Psychoanalysis (2004), the American Psychiatric Association's Kun Po Soo Award (2004), the Irma Bland Award for being the Outstanding Teacher of Psychiatric Residents in the Country (2005), and the Nancy Roeske Award (2012). Most recently, he received the Sigourney Award (2013), which is the most prestigious honour in the field of psychoanalysis. Dr. Akhtar is an internationally sought speaker and teacher, and his books have been translated in many languages, including German, Turkish, and Romanian. His interests are wide and he has served as the film review editor for the *International Journal of Psychoanalysis*, and is currently serving as the book review editor for the *International Journal of Applied Psychoanalytic Studies*. He has published seven collections of poetry and serves as a scholar-in-residence at the Inter-Act Theatre Company in Philadelphia.

Jennifer Bonovitz, PhD, received her doctoral degree in social work from Bryn Mawr College School of Social Work and Social Research. She is currently a training and supervising analyst in both the Child and Adult Programs of the Philadelphia Center of Psychoanalysis. Her areas of special interest are early childhood trauma and cross-cultural issues in psychoanalysis. She has co-authored (with Jeffrey Applegate) the book *The Facilitating Partnership: A Winnicottian Approach for Social Workers and Other Helping Professionals* (Aronson, 1995). Dr. Bonovitz has also published important papers on diverse psychoanalytic topics, including the impact of childhood migration, Freud's omission of the maternal in God, and racial issues as they emerge in the course of psychoanalytic treatment.

Calvin Colarusso, MD, is a clinical professor of psychiatry at the University of California at San Diego and a training and supervising analyst in adult and child psychoanalysis at the San Diego Psychoanalytic Institute. He is the author more than fifty peer-reviewed articles and book chapters. An expert witness in more than 100 cases of child sexual abuse, he has treated both victims and perpetrators. Dr. Colarusso has co-authored two major texts on adult psychological development: *Adult Development: A New Dimension in Psychodynamic Theory and Practice* (1981), and *New Dimensions in Adult Development* (1990). In addition, he has authored many books of his own, including: *Child and Adult Development: A Psychoanalytic Introduction for Clinicians* (1992), and *The Long Shadow of Sexual Abuse: Developmental Effects across the Life Cycle* (2010).

Christine Kieffer, PhD, is a psychoanalyst and clinical psychologist who serves on the faculties of the Chicago Institute for Psychoanalysis as well as Rush University Medical School, Chicago. Dr. Kieffer is the author of numerous papers and three co-edited books: *Breast Cancer: A Psychological Treatment Manual* (1994), *Psychoanalysis and Women* (2004), and *Into the Void: Psychoanalytic Perspectives on Gender* (2005). She has edited special issues of *Psychoanalytic Inquiry* on fathers and daughters (2008), Psychoanalysis and Cyberspace (2012), and Psychoanalytic Perspectives on Bullying (2013). She serves on the editorial boards of the *Journal of the American Psychoanalytic Association*, *Psychoanalytic Inquiry, The International Journal of Self Psychology, and PSYCHcritiques*. Dr. Kieffer is currently at work on a monograph, *Mutuality, Recognition and the Self* (Karnac Books, expected 2014), that will elaborate upon her integration of relational and intersubjective perspectives on psychoanalytic theory and treatment. Dr. Kieffer is the recipient of the 2013 Ticho prize given by the American Psychoanalytic Association. She has a dual specialisation in child/adolescent as well as adult psychoanalysis and psychotherapy, and also provides group psychotherapy and couple counselling. She is in private practice in Chicago and Winnetka, IL.

Eugene J. Mahon, MD, is a training and supervising analyst at the Columbia Psychoanalytic Center for Training and Research and at the Contemporary Freudian Society. He is a member of the Center for Advanced Psychoanalytic Studies, Princeton, NJ. He won the Alexander Beller Award at the Columbia Psychoanalytic Institute in 1984. He has been on the editorial boards of the *International Journal of Psychoanalysis*, the *Journal of The American Psychoanalytic Association* and he is currently an editorial reader for the *Psychoanalytic Quarterly*. He has published in all the major psychoanalytic journals on a wide variety of topics that include mourning, screen memories, prejudice, humour, the golden section, and several papers on dreams: "The Dissolution of the Oedipus Complex", "Play and Working Through", "Anna Freud and the Evolution of Psychoanalytic Technique", and "A 'Good Hour' in Child Psychoanalysis and Adult Analysis". He has written applied psychoanalytic essays on the golden section, and Coleridge, and several articles on Shakespeare. He has also published a number of psychoanalytic dramatic dialogues between Shakespeare and Freud, Freud and Fliess, Beckett and Bion, Sigmund Freud and Anna Freud, and a play based on Beckett's "Waiting for Godot", called *In the Company of Ghosts*. He has written a psychoanalytic fable entitled *Rensal the Redbit* (1960). Several of his poems have been published; and one poem, *Steeds of Darkness*, was set to music by the American composer, Miriam Gideon.

Mark Moore, PhD, is the director of psychological services at the Joan Karnell Cancer Center at Pennsylvania Hospital in Philadelphia, and a recent graduate of the Psychoanalytic Center of Philadelphia. In his clinical work over the past ten years he has developed expertise in the psychodynamic treatment of cancer patients and in the use of hypnosis for palliative care. He teaches and supervises clinical psychology interns and post-doctoral students on issues relating to working with cancer patients. Dr. Moore is frequently invited to lecture to health professionals on the topic of psycho-oncology. His contributions to psychoanalytic literature include many book chapters, including those on the concept of harmony in Japanese culture and sociocultural aspects of dishonesty. He has also published papers on the topics of domestic violence in cancer populations, outcome research and times-series statistics, preparing patients for therapy, and the empirical status of clinical hypnosis.

Ann Smolen, PhD, is a supervising and training analyst in child, adolescent, and adult psychoanalysis at the Psychoanalytic Center of

Philadelphia. Dr. Smolen graduated summa cum laude from Bryn Mawr College and received her master's degree in social work from Bryn Mawr College School of Social Work and Social Research. She received her doctorate in philosophy from the Clinical Social Work Institute in Washington, DC. Her first profession was as a member of the New York City Ballet. Dr. Smolen has won several national awards for her clinical work, which she has presented both nationally and internationally. Dr. Smolen has published several articles including 'Boys Only! No Mothers Allowed', published in *The International Journal of Psychoanalysis* and translated into three languages. Dr. Smolen is the author of *Mothering Without a Home: Representations of Attachment Behaviors in Homeless Mothers and Children* (Aronson, 2013). She maintains a private practice in child, adolescent, and adult psychotherapy and psychoanalysis in Ardmore, PA.

Elizabeth H. Thomas, MTS, MSW, PhD, is a clinical social worker on the faculty of both the New Directions program and the Close Attention program of the Washington Center for Psychoanalysis. Dr. Thomas's professional writing focuses largely on work with couples and on supervision for clinical social workers. She is organising a national conference on the topic of betrayal to be held in Washington, DC in spring 2015. She has been both presenter and respondent at professional conferences, including the International Psychotherapy Institute and the Psychoanalytic Research Consortium in Washington, DC. Dr. Thomas maintains a psychotherapy practice for individuals and couples in Chevy Chase, MD and in Bluemont, VA.

Richard Waugaman, MD, is a training and supervising analyst, emeritus, at the Washington Psychoanalytic Institute. He is clinical professor of psychiatry and faculty expert on Shakespeare for media contacts at Georgetown University. He has written more than 100 publications; fifty of them are on Shakespeare and on the psychology of pseudonymity. Since 2004, he has done archival research at the Folger Shakespeare Library. There he discovered one of the largest previously unknown literary sources for Shakespeare's works, in Edward de Vere's copy of Sternhold and Hopkins's *Whole Book of Psalms*. De Vere's annotations showed his unusual interest in some of these psalms, which are echoed repeatedly in Shakespeare's plays and poems. This discovery has unlocked new levels of meaning in Shakespeare's works, and has helped validate Freud's theory that it was Edward de Vere who wrote the works of "William Shakespeare".

INTRODUCTION

Betrayal is an integral component of all psychic trauma. Whether it is sexual abuse or profound neglect, violence or treachery, extramarital affair or embezzlement, hurting others invariably involves a dimension of breaching their trust in us. When we betray others, we violate their confidence in us. When others betray us, they pierce the veil of our innocent reliance. Betraying and feeling betrayed are ubiquitous to the scenarios of trauma and yet surprisingly neglected as a topic of specific attention by psychoanalysis.

The book in your hands aims to fill this void. Graciously responding to my invitation, nine distinguished psychoanalysts offer their thoughts on betrayal from differing perspectives.

Jennifer Bonovitz (Philadelphia) notes that while the experience of betrayal might be ubiquitous in childhood, its lack of recognition by the parents is what leads to fixation upon it and, often, to the tendency to inflict similar trauma upon others when one becomes an adult. She offers five poignant clinical vignettes to support her hypothesis and, more important, addresses treatment implications, including the emergence of betrayal behaviours and fantasies in the transference-countertransference axis.

Ann Smolen (Philadelphia) presents the account of a young woman who had been an "Oedipal victor" during childhood but—as invariably happens in such cases—felt terribly betrayed by her father once she became an adult. Tracing the vicissitudes of a seductive father-daughter relationship from childhood through adult development to the course of analytic treatment, Smolen illuminates the deception that lurks underneath the "beautiful" formative years of such children and the toll it takes upon their psychic lives.

Christine Kieffer (Chicago) provides a sophisticated review of adolescent development and painstakingly deconstructs the intricacies of drive upsurge, relational challenges, shifting loyalties, peer group tensions, superego alterations, and identity formation during this phase. She differentiates feelings of betrayal during early adolescence from those during late adolescence. The former are spurred by and utilised in the service of identity consolidation. The latter arise in the context of reworking Oedipal conflicts and involve the struggles for making an appropriate romantic choice. Deftly weaving a vignette from her own adolescence, Kieffer gives us a thoroughly satisfying account of the ebb and flow of trust-betrayal in the turbulent setting of this developmental phase.

Mark Moore (Philadelphia), a psychoanalyst with considerable experience with terminally ill cancer patients, provides an account of situations where our bodies betray us. Dividing his discourse in three sections, Moore addresses the realms of body image betrayal, body self betrayal, and the body's ultimate betrayal via physical death. He provides many evocative clinical vignettes while also touching upon the technical handling of the dilemmas presented by such situations.

Richard Waugaman (Washington, DC) opens the literary section of the book and elucidates the myriad ways in which the theme of betrayal appears in Shakespeare's writings. Characteristically thorough and multi-layered in his conceptualisation, Waugaman carries his earlier Shakespeare studies a step further in a dual-pronged manner. Microscopically, he focuses on one small piece of the Bard's voluminous output, namely Sonnet 21, to tease out his insights on betrayal. Macroscopically, he addresses the problematic question of the identity of Shakespeare and demonstrates the preponderance of betrayal-related scenarios in the life of Edward de Vere, the actual man who is known to us as the pseudonym "William Shakespeare".

Eugene Mahon (New York) contributes the second literary essay in this book. He takes Oscar Wilde's poem "The Ballad of Reading Gaol" as his topic and in step-by-step fashion brings the pain of betrayal implicit in it to our attention. Mahon never misses a beat when it comes to an anguished sigh of a word, a shy retreat of a phrase, a sly interlocution of irony, and so on. Setting his literary deconstruction in the context of the puritan sexual values of a given historical era, Mahon suggests that a sense of betrayal was actually the creative force behind Wilde's writing this poem. The dehumanising confines of a prison and the public hanging of a fellow inmate round out the accoutrements of this throbbing lexical journey.

Salman Akhtar (Philadelphia) writes about the compulsion to betray others and the unconscious need to be betrayed. He notes that the two constitute a psychodynamic and structural pair. They invariably coexist even though one might be more manifest than the other in a given instance. The compulsive need to betray others is seen in the setting of narcissistic and antisocial personality organisation and the unconscious need to be betrayed exists in the setting of masochistic personality organisation. Two detailed case histories help illustrate these points and show how an essentially similar trauma of betrayal during childhood can lead to different phenotypical outcomes in adult life.

Calvin Colarusso (San Diego) brings us back to the clinical realm by detailing several clinical cases of childhood sexual abuse. These involve both incestuous and non-incestuous violations and also the reporting of such abuse at various subsequent stages of life. Colarusso offers glimpses of what actually went on, how these tragic scenarios unfolded, what really was said and done, and in how many ways trauma of such sort traversed far beyond childhood and continued to have effects throughout the rest of the victims' lives. Vivid, convincing, and often painful to read, Colarusso's case histories are bound to be highly instructive. They prove, beyond any doubt, that the betrayal of the sacred trust a child puts in caregiving adults has lifelong deleterious consequences.

Elizabeth Thomas (Washington, DC) takes us inside the closed chambers of marital life and lets us taste the bitter bile of being betrayed by a spouse. She provides verbatim material from her sessions with a couple, picking up the shards of their broken bond, one minute hopeful of gluing this back together and the next minute pricked by this or that sharp edge all over again, bleeding. Thomas anchors her clinical understanding in a laudable amalgam of object relations and relational approaches and shows how the betraying and betrayed partner come full circle back to resuming a meaningful dialogue of relatedness between them.

Anne Adelman (Washington, DC), in the last chapter of the book, addresses the harrowing topic of the psychoanalyst's betrayal of his patients. She notes that when an analyst loses his existential moorings and defiles the transitional envelope of the clinical space by his instinctual temptations, severe damage occurs not only to himself, to the particular patient whose boundaries he has violated, but also to other patients who hear about the transgression from the "grapevine". Adelman gives us the gift of her trust by describing the devastation she experienced upon learning of a sexual boundary violation by her analyst. The resulting difficulties of sustaining an analytic dialogue with that analyst or, for that matter, with any analyst, is a topic of her worried but altruistic and nuanced concern. Her contribution is a "mustread" for all training institutes and especially their ethics committees.

These thumbnail sketches of the book's chapters are intended to whet the reader's appetite. Obviously, there is more texture, more substance, and more heuristic and technical material in their individual entirety than I have been able to summarise here. What is certain, however, is that being betrayed causes mental pain and the awareness of having betrayed others leads to remorse. Both emotions are difficult to bear. The fact that we psychoanalysts and psychotherapists, at times, get the opportunity to help ease these emotional burdens is the proverbial silver lining in this otherwise dark cloud of despair.

PART I

DEVELOPMENTAL REALM

CHAPTER ONE

Betrayal in childhood

Jennifer Bonovitz

B etrayal is contextual. It occurs within a trusted relationship with a person who has established a history of reliability and faithfulness, especially in times of need or uncertainty. Confident expectation of trustworthiness is a developmental achievement acquired incrementally, as the infant interacts day in, day out with a mother who is consistently emotionally available, predictable, attuned to her infant's communications, and responsive in a timely way (Beebe, 1986; Tronick, 2003). Erikson (1950) regards trust as the infant's first social achievement. It is manifested by a willingness to "let the mother out of sight without undue anxiety or rage, because she has become an inner certainty as well as an outer predictability" (p. 147). This "inner certainty" grows out of a myriad of affective exchanges which enable the infant to form a prototypic, stable, internal representation of himself with his mother. Erikson links the capacity of trust in others with confidence in the ability to control one's own urges to hurt beloved objects.

Betrayal, in the sense of disappointed hopes or expectations, presents itself in many forms in the life of every child. It is one of those ubiquitous, unavoidable narcissistic slights, which if acknowledged empathically by the offending parent or caregiver, can be mourned, forgiven, and repaired, without the need to resort to compensatory vengeance. Included here are ordinary life events: a parent's unexpected absence, a painful but necessary medical procedure, or the birth of a sibling. The child's cognitive and psychosexual stages of development will colour the meaning given to a particular external event. For example, the arrival of a newcomer into the family requires sensitive handling by the offending mother. Sam, aged four, and at the height of an intense Oedipal attachment to his mother, felt betrayed by the birth of a brother. "What did you have to go and do this for, wasn't I enough?" His mother, unable to acknowledge her treachery, had tried to convince him that she had given him a great gift, a little playmate. Sam, not to be fobbed off with a falsehood, proceeded to exact his revenge by pooping in his pants at the most inopportune moments. His mother recognised that something had gone awry, sought help to understand Sam's behaviour, and quickly repaired the rupture in their relationship.

This chapter focuses on betrayal experiences which went unrecognised by the caregiver, and were not repaired. I first delineate some of the developmental factors which make children vulnerable to experiencing betrayal at the hands of their parents. I then describe a number of factors which inhibit empathic responses from previously "good enough" (Winnicott, 1953) mothers. Data from the analyses of adults and children are used to illustrate how the early betrayal experience may have longstanding adverse effects upon the individual's subsequent capacity to trust himself and others, to develop the capacity for empathy, for mentalisation, and, ultimately, to enjoy and sustain mutually satisfying intimate relationships. Throughout the clinical material, I will address some treatment implications, including the emergence of betrayal behaviours and fantasies in the transference, as well as countertransference challenges, and the handling of the propensity for the defensive use of vengeful behaviours and fantasies to maintain a sadomasochistic object tie.

Developmental factors

Several characteristics of young children render them exquisitely vulnerable to the subjective experience of betrayal:

- total dependence for their physical and psychological well-being on their caregivers' empathic attunement to their nonverbal cues;
- immaturity of cognitive and perceptual equipment makes them prone to misinterpret both internal states and external events, leaving them at the mercy of their primitive, persecutory fantasies which may be seen as an attempt at meaning making; psychic structures, including representations of self and other, ego and superego, develop over time, not only from the infant's drive endowment, but as a product of the dynamic interplay between the child's and caregiver's affective experiencing of one another;
- affect regulation, and mentalising capacity, in the sense of being able to label internal states and discriminate them from the internal states of others, require a stable relationship with an empathic partner for optimal development; immaturity of defence mechanisms render the young child almost totally dependent on the caregiver for management of anxiety in fear-producing situations.

On the parental side of the dyad, a number of factors may inhibit well-intentioned, devoted parents from acknowledging and responding empathically to a child's subjective experience of betrayal. These include:

- temporary preoccupation with their own painful affect states which interferes with attunement to the child's pain;
- guilt around having been unable to prevent a child's painful experience blocks empathy;
- temporary ego regression with loss of mothering functions during illness or bereavement;
- failure to appreciate the child's profound need for physical proximity with his caregiver in fear-producing situations and the handing of this role over to professional caregivers.

Intergenerational betrayal trauma

Two definitions found in *Webster's Dictionary* articulate important aspects of betrayal at the hands of a trusted caregiver. These are: (i) to prove faithless, or treacherous in time of need, and, (ii) to deliver into the hands of the enemy by treachery or fraud. Both betrayal themes played out in the previous generation of the following patient.

Clinical vignette 1

Mrs. A., a forty-one-year-old computer programmer, called in a state of panic upon discovering that her husband was having an "online affair" with one of his colleagues. She made the discovery after hacking into his e-mail account. While she felt contempt for her spouse most of the time, she was afraid that if he left her she would be unable to find a replacement. In the initial session, Mrs. A. presented a laundry list of her husband's failures over the span of five years of marriage. She had recognised some of his imperfections early in the courtship, in particular his passivity, but hoped that he would make good on his Ivy League education and enable her to climb the socioeconomic ladder. At the end of the hour, I noted to myself that my sympathies were with the husband. I had slipped quickly into the role of betrayer.

Her grandmother and most of her immediate family had been hidden from the Nazis by close friends, who eventually became too fearful and turned them over to the Gestapo. They were transported to a concentration camp where many of them were murdered, including Isaac, grandmother's youngest brother. Mrs. A. was the first grandchild, greatly treasured by her survivor grandparents who made her the centre of their universe and became her primary caregivers for the first three years of her life, until a baby brother arrived. Grandmother, in particular, abruptly shifted her time and affection to baby Isaac, who represented the brother murdered by the Nazis. Mrs. A.'s care was handed back to her mother who welcomed her with open arms but Mrs. A. was too pained to accept what her mother had to offer. Instead, she focused her energies on winning her grandmother back by disparaging Isaac. She handled her envy by belittling him for his dependence on their grandparents and took pleasure in his grief when the grandmother died during his late adolescence.

The painful scenario of betrayal was subsequently repeated in many different forms with Mrs. A. alternating between active and passive in the re-enactments. She endeared herself to her teachers in elementary school but gradually alienated them by her mean, sneak attacks on any younger child who received attention. Eventually the hitherto beloved teacher "would turn on me" and take up for the victimised child. Similarly, in adulthood she wooed her husband and his family with acts of extreme consideration and kindness, and then was shocked and outraged by their "sudden coldness". Careful exploration revealed that Mrs. A. could not tolerate that her husband and his siblings had a past history she had not shared, and she was envious of their enjoyment of one another. She began to respond with contempt to the overtures the family made to her. For example, when a sister-in-law offered to lend her a beautiful family heirloom necklace to wear on her wedding day, she accused her of deliberately offering something that would make her modest gown look shabby. As time went on, she did everything she could to keep her husband from spending time with his family and belittled him for his closeness with them. She then felt betrayed when he began to sneak away without her, to spend time with them.

As a mother, Mrs. A. did well with Sam, her first child, but she could not tolerate his ordinary, expectable upset after she had a little girl. With total lack of awareness that she was repeating her own betrayal experience, she turned his care over to a kind and nurturing babysitter. When the babysitter became Sam's primary attachment figure, she accused the woman of undermining her as a mother, and fired her. This retaliation and directing of rage outward served as a powerful defence against an empathic understanding of Sam's pain at losing his mother, and more significantly, of her own anguish over losing Sam to the babysitter. Both were unbearable reminders of her plight as a child.

In the analytic relationship, Mrs. A. initially expressed gratitude that I was "taking her in" at an affordable fee. She could not believe that I would want to meet with her four times a week. She looked me up on the internet and told me how lucky she felt to have such a successful analyst. Later, she used the same flimsy evidence to point how little I had accomplished in my career. Things began to change between us when she allowed herself to know that she was not my only analytic patient. She began to wonder if other patients paid higher fees and would be given preferential treatment. On one occasion, she "accidently" locked the waiting room door so that my next patient could not get in. A week later, I returned the favour and "forgot" to unlock the waiting room door on a day that she was my first appointment. The low fee became a source of her contempt for me. "You must not be doing very well, if you're willing to go that low."

Mrs. A.'s most provocative act of betrayal, one which almost destroyed the treatment, occurred two years into the analysis, just after I had handed her the monthly bill. She lingered in the waiting room after her session and waved the bill in front of my next patient telling her, "I can't believe she is so generous. She charges me less than half fee." All manner of angry, resentful, hurt feelings were stirred up in the second patient who undoubtedly had been selected because her expensive clothes and car suggested that she probably paid full fee. I felt a strong push in the countertransference to punish Mrs. A.'s vindictive behaviour by telling her we were finished, that I could no longer treat her but would help her find another analyst.

Apart from the strain of containing and metabolising my own rage and sense of betrayal, I now faced some difficult technical issues. How could I confront Mrs. A. without betraying the confidentiality of the patient she had victimised? Ironically, in seeking consultation with a trusted colleague, I was fulfilling one of Mrs. A.'s worst fears that I would talk about her unfavourably behind her back. At the time this gave me considerable satisfaction.

In the session following her egregious behaviour, Mrs. A. was outwardly calm, perhaps a little warmer in her greeting. She seemed relaxed as she chit-chatted on the couch. Apparently having deposited her toxic rage, envy, and destructiveness via projective identification (Klein, 1946) into my other patient and me, she felt temporarily relieved of the persecutory panic they engendered in her. I, on the other hand, had dreaded seeing her and was reduced to impotent silence in my efforts to restrain myself from retaliation. It was extraordinarily difficult to allow myself to engage in the flood of revenge fantasies which shocked me with their level of primitiveness. I struggled against self-loathing and the guilt-ridden destruction of all sense of my goodness as a human being, let alone as an analyst. Helped by my colleague's containment, I sat quietly in the room with Mrs. A., tormented by the inner turmoil she had brought to me, and although I was not entirely neutral, in that I was quieter than usual, I was able to resist discharging the intensity via a ferocious counter-attack.

After a week of what felt like a deadly impasse, Mrs. A. reported the following dream. She was a small, lost puppy whose owners had moved and could not take her with them. The puppy was taken in by a kindly old woman. One day while the woman was feeding her some delicious food from her own dinner plate, the puppy was so ravenous she lost control and bit her benefactor's hand, causing great pain. The old woman withdrew her hand and angrily ordered a servant to throw the puppy out into the cold. Mrs. A. awoke in a state of panic and was relieved to find that her husband was in bed beside her and had not slipped off to work without saying good-bye. She felt the need to be close to a warm body.

Analysis of the dream went slowly. Mrs. A. had difficulty asso-ciating and wanted to see the dream as simply indicative of her insecurity in her marriage. She next shifted to the foolishness of the old woman feeding the puppy by hand. It was unsanitary and she got what she deserved. I had to curb my impulse to assault Mrs. A.'s defences with an enthusiastic interpretation of last week's biting of my hand that fed her. I stayed with the opportunity to empathise with the hungry, abandoned, desperate puppy, parts of Mrs. A. that she disowned, projected into others, and then attacked. She was able to accept her desire to be found, taken in, and taken care of, as well as the terror she felt that she would do something to hurt the loving object and be cast out. We were gradually opening the way for her to confess to me what she had done in the wait-ing room. It was difficult for her to own that her act of aggression had hurt and betrayed me. She tried to stick to her fantasy that she was merely letting others know about my generosity. I had never told her to keep quiet about the reduced fee: that was my problem not hers. She accused me of thinking unkind thoughts and won-dered if she could forgive me. To her credit, and mine, she was able to stay with the analysis and a year later, on the anniversary of her betrayal, she asked me to forgive her. The intensity of the affective experience of having been betrayed and then my strong wish to retaliate by betraying my patient with her worst fear, that of being handed over to someone else, presented both an enormous challenge and an opportunity in the analytic work. It was essential that I survive her attacks so that she could gradually develop the capacity to recognise, contain, and metabolise destructive impulses which threatened to destroy all the goodness in her and in her objects (Winnicott, 1971). Eventually we were both able to empathically understand what had transpired between us, meaning not only to have compassion for one another, but also a tolerance for the mutual anger, hurt, and wish for revenge. It was only then that forgiveness could be given and received (Akhtar, 2002). The injury and repair cycle in the analytic dyad led to repair of internal object relations with the abandoning grandmother. My responsiveness to Mrs. A.'s enactments opened the way to our being able to reconstruct how her own repetitions of this painful experience maintained an unconscious bond with her grandmother, one which persisted long after the old woman's death. (Sandler, 2003)

The small child's experience of betrayal in time of need

The following case illustrates how feeling betrayed by parents during childhood, especially when one is sick and in greater than ordinary need of attention, can become the basis of betraying others (even unconsciously when one grows up).

Clinical vignette 2

Mr. B. came for help with a deeply unhappy marriage and a turbulent relationship with his drug-addicted eighteen-year-old son. He had been married for thirty years, viewed himself as a devoted husband and father, and could not fathom why both wife and son were constantly angry and unappreciative. In the four session weekly analysis, he told me story after story of appealing to them to treat him lovingly and of being either rebuffed or ridiculed. I noticed that he often raised his eyebrows and nodded his head in my direction as he told me of their cruelty. It seemed that he was hoping to evoke not only my sympathy but confirmation of their maltreatment. Yet when I did venture an empathic remark that it must be very painful to be trying so hard and getting nothing back, he would dismiss me with a wave of his hand and tell me how much he loved them anyway. Sometimes this sequence between us would bring tears to his eyes, but he could not tell me what the tears signified. It seemed he could not access the more needy and hurting parts of himself.

Mr. B. frequently confided in male friends about how poorly his wife treated him. On more than one occasion the response was, "You have to be a masochist to stay with her."

Careful exploration of the explosive relationships with both wife and son revealed that Mr. B. was an active participant. On a daily basis, he failed to show up when or where he had promised his wife. He attributed this to being "absent minded". Furthermore, he regularly "forgot" to do something she had requested. When confronted he would tell her, "I have memory problems, so shoot me." His cavalier attitude towards his inability to be reliable and "to show up" evoked enraged attacks from his wife. With his son, there was another variation of being untrustworthy. Rather than talk directly with him about his failure to meet his responsibilities at home, school, and his job, Mr. B. would turn his son in to the disciplinarian at his school, his boss at his workplace, or to the boy's angry mother. Interpretation of these behaviours as expressions of some anger he might be feeling were accepted but brought about no change. In retrospect, I see my interpretations as a countertransferential attack in which I betrayed Mr. B. by taking up for his wife and son.

Several months went by before I realised that Mr. B. was repeating the pattern of unreliability in the analysis with last minute cancellations explained by unexpected emergencies in his business, or a flat tyre, or having overslept. He would feel "punished" when charged for the sessions. In the countertransference, I noted anxiously feeling that I could never be sure from one day to the next whether he would show up. In the initial evaluation, he reported no history of early separations, losses, or disruptions in key relationships. It was not until his wife called him from a hospital emergency department asking him to come immediately, that his feeling of panic and reluctance to go gave us access to a flood of early memories about being taken several times to a hospital between the ages of three and four for treatment of recurrent bowel blockages. He recalled his mother's handing him over to emergency medical staff who took him to a small room where a doctor with "a masked face" would either clean him out manually or a nurse would give him an enema. Both procedures were painful and terrified him. His mother could not handle how distraught he became and sometimes lied about where she was taking him. She was so anxious herself that upon arrival at the hospital, she had to be calmed down by the nursing staff while he was whisked away screaming. On one occasion when he was brought back to the waiting room, she was not there and the staff eventually found her in the bathroom throwing up. His father was a top level executive who was reluctant to cancel his business commitments to be with his son at the hospital. Mr. B. was surprised by his intense emotion in the telling of this story. He made a number of connections, one of them being that he avoided regular check-ups with his specialist and did not seek medical care unless he was "at death's door". However, he could not take in any connections I made between his experience of having being "handed over to the enemy" or abandoned in his time of greatest need by his mother and his re-enactments with his son and wife. He thought his mother's behaviour was understandable and that she was only doing what was expected in handing him over to the medical staff. When I empathised with the terror of the little boy and his desperate need for his mother, he shrugged and said it would be disloyal to his dead mother to feel angry with her now. She was not here to defend herself. He resisted any further exploration and said he didn't want to get into anything he couldn't handle before my summer vacation. After the break, he missed his first appointment and then called to say he was doing well and needed no further therapy. When I pressed for him to come in so that we could understand why he needed to end the analysis so abruptly, he said he was worried that if he "dug too deep" he would have to end his marriage. For Mr. B., it seemed a matter of psychic survival to maintain a sadomasochistic relationship with his internal objects. He could not risk disturbing the fragile balance between love and hate he had maintained since early childhood and instead was doomed to repeat the original betrayal trauma. (Joseph, 1989)

When the mother inflicts pain

Child analysts frequently see children who have experienced painful medical conditions or procedures. Where the mother has restrained the child to help the medical staff, or has herself administered a painful procedure, the young child does not have the cognitive capacity to understand why a trusted attachment figure has "joined with the enemy".

Clinical vignette 3

In the case of Emily, a four year old with multiple, severe allergies, the mother assisted the child's doctor by restraining the little girl for weekly allergy shots. In retrospect, the decision to use injections was premature in that Emily did not have the cognitive capacity to understand what was happening. She was in general an emotionally robust child and her terrified reaction took her mother by surprise. Because of her own distress, and guilt that she had "made a bad decision", the mother was unable to talk soothingly to the child, either during or after the doctor's visits. Emily's heightened ambivalence towards her mother (Parens, 1979) at the peak of a passionate Oedipal romance with her father, added to the complexity of her experience. For several months she refused to allow her mother to have any physical contact with her, insisting that either her father, or babysitter, bathe and dress her. At this point, the parents brought her for treatment. Emily insisted on having her mother in the room and very early in the therapy she began to play out the theme of mommies who did not take good care of their children. Her mother needed a lot of support from me to accept the bad mommy role. When I interpreted that perhaps Emily felt that her mommy had not taken care of her and had let the doctor hurt her when she had her allergy shots, the little girl screamed "You helped that bad man hurt me. You are a very bad mommy and you deserve to be punished!" On another occasion, I was enlisted in a re-enactment when Emily charged at her mother with a sharp pencil and I had to restrain her.

Prior to the experience of mother's betrayal by "helping the bad man", Emily had a secure relationship with her and this was quickly restored. One of the key elements in the therapy was mother's being able to tolerate and empathise with Emily's subjective experience of her as a very bad mommy, deserving of punishment. When she spoke softly to Emily about how scared and angry she must have been and how terrible it was that mommy didn't stop the bad man, the little girl ran to her lap and began to sob. The initial rupture of the relationship occurred because the child could not understand why her mother did not respond to her distress, and appeal for relief, when being given allergy shots. The mother's assisting the offending doctor compounded the child's suffering. When her mother could fully empathise with Emily's subjective experience of being abandoned in a time of dire need, and could accept her child's anger, repair became possible. (Settlage, Bemesderfer, Rosenthal, Afterman & Spielman, 1991)

Clinical vignette 4

Ellie was brought for treatment at seven years of age for what appeared to be an insecure attachment with her mother. Both parents had warm, loving relationships with two younger children but Ellie rebuffed their overtures, especially those from her mother. She was aversive to physical affection, was defiant, and refused to accept help from them. Significant in Ellie's history was that at the age of nine months she suffered a couple of episodes of constipation and her paediatrician noted that one of the infant's legs was longer than the other. Ellie was taken to the hospital for abdominal x-rays to determine if she had a Wilms tumour. She was laid on the hard surface of an x-ray table; her mother was draped in a protective vest, and asked to hold Emily still by using two large wooden paddles. This procedure was repeated three times over the next eighteen months.

Ellie had seen two therapists prior to me and refused to talk to either one. She reluctantly agreed to be present, but not to talk, while I met with her mother. During the first two sessions, she sat with her back to us. I encouraged her mother to tell me about the early ordeal in the hospital, especially about how awful she felt that Ellie was so frightened and how she could not hold her in her arms even though she wanted to. For the next session, Ellie asked me to bring in a shoe box. She wanted to make a diorama. To her mother's amazement and mine, she covered the interior of the shoe box with black construction paper and then built a table in the middle. She made two disproportionally huge paddles out of brown cardboard and taped them to the hands of the mother from the doll's house. Finally, she laid the baby from the doll's house on the table and taped the other ends of the paddles onto the baby's body. When she had finished, she took it to her mother and said, "See what you did to me!" Ellie then turned to me and said she would not return. She wanted me to help her mother to be her doctor. Only her mother could help her; she refused to see a stranger. Ellie's insistence was in part a turning of passive into active, but may also be understood as her attempt to repair the injury sustained when her fantasy of omnipotent control of her mother needed to balance the child's dawning realisation that separateness in rapprochement was prematurely and abruptly ended. Mother agreed to see Ellie in "therapy sessions" every day for as long as she needed. I saw the mother once a week to "supervise" the treatment. After just a month, Ellie's relationship with her parents was substantially improved.

Clearly Ellie was too young to have declarative memory (Clyman, 1991) of the traumatic experience of her mother's complicity with the medical staff in the terrifying x-ray procedure. However, her subsequent insecure attachment behaviours indicate that mother as an untrustworthy, hurtful figure was encoded in implicit memory.

Clinical vignette 5

Rebecca was taken to the hospital after she had fallen down the stairs at the age of eighteen months. Her mother restrained her while she was examined, and then again when she was sent for x-rays of a suspected leg fracture, and yet again when the leg was placed in a cast. Subsequently, mother noted that Rebecca was low key and angry with her. Ruptures in the relationship with the mother during rapprochement, a key period for development of psychic structures and for basic mood (Mahler, 1972) are particularly challenging for the dyad. The child was brought for treatment at the age of four because of the parents' concern about her play. She insisted on wrapping her little friends in her jump rope, or directing them to tie the rope around her arms and legs. Rebecca's mother had already connected the play with the child's earlier frightening experience at the hospital. The key elements in her successful therapy were mother's retelling the story over and over and her empathic responses to Rebecca's telling her what a bad mother she had been to let her fall down the stairs and then to tie her up so "those bad doctors could hurt me". When Rebecca demanded a "Say you're sorry!", her mother was able to do so with genuine feeling. By the age of four, this child had sufficient cognitive capacity to rework the traumatic experience and to restructure the negative representation of her mother as having betrayed her by being complicit with "the enemy".

Concluding remarks

These clinical vignettes underscore the young child's vulnerability to experiencing betrayal by caregivers at key stages of psychosocial bio-logical development. In all five cases, the child was subjected, before the age of five years, to painful external events. These were construed by the child's immature cognitive and psychological equipment as abandonment in time of great need, by beloved and trusted primary caregivers. The adults, Mrs. S. and Mr. B., did not receive help as children, and remained unable to fully trust and depend on others, or to be fully trustworthy and dependable for others.

Trust in their caregivers' reliability and capacity to protect them are key for young children's sense of well-being and for the internalisation of a good, loved, and helping object. If experiences of betrayal at the hands of beloved caregivers are not repaired, they interfere with this internalisation process. Fantasies and fears related to the betrayal are not modified; instead, representations of self and other carry an over-load of hostility and destructive aggression. The child is trapped in the intolerable position of having to negotiate both an internal and exter-nal relationship with someone who is at the same time beloved and untrustworthy. If the offending caregiver, usually the mother, is able to empathise with and tolerate the child's subjective experience of hav-ing been abandoned in time of need, or handed over to "the enemy" to be hurt, the child is relieved of having to carry the burden of hate and fear. Children frequently use projective identification in an effort to have the parent understand their internal state, with the hope that their unbearable affects can be metabolised and returned to them in more manageable form. If this does not occur, the child remains vulner-able to unconscious anxiety about depending upon and trusting others, and grows up continuing to dread being overwhelmed by the original unbearable affect state generated during the betrayal by a caregiver on whom there was total dependence.

A notable difference in the technique with the child patients was that of utilising the opportunity for the "offending" parent to partner with the analyst, and to work therapeutically with the child's replay and re-enactment of the original betrayal trauma. This requires that the parent is able to make use of the help of the analyst in tolerating, containing, and metabolising, for the child, the split off, noxious elements of the early subjective experience of a hurtful, frightening, abandoning, "bad" mother. In the work with adults, or with children whose parents are unable to tolerate the intensity of highly negatively charged affects and behaviours, a more traditional approach of facilitating and utilising transferences and countertransferences emerging within the analytic dyad is required. With either technique, it is essential that the analyst can bear the painful affects associated with being both the betrayer and the betrayed.

CHAPTER TWO

A seduced child is a betrayed child

Ann Smolen

Bella, a leggy, seventeen-year-old beauty, slid gracefully into my office for her initial session. Her large luminous eyes hurriedly scrutinised her surroundings as she settled herself into the chair. Even though she was quite tall, she gathered her gazelle-like legs under her and appeared as if a small child, bewildered to find herself in this place. Bella, an accomplished musician on full scholarship to a renowned music school, wanted to quit, giving up the dream of a promising professional career, a dream she had aspired to and wished for since she was a very young child when she first fell in love with her instrument.

At first Bella was wary of me and of therapy, especially psychoanalysis, because a friend had told her that analysis was a terrible hoax, where the analyst "seduced" you into a "dependent" love, only to "abandon" you. "This", she emphatically exclaimed, "is the ultimate betrayal!" This provocative statement enticed me, and I began to feel seduced by her as her story unfolded.

Seduction

In one of his aetiological hypotheses, Freud (1895d, 1896b) proposed that all neuroses were caused by sexual seduction of children by adults.

This could vary from overstimulation, visually and/or verbally, to physical sexual abuse. Freud's seduction hypothesis proposed that when a child was overstimulated sexually (verbally, visually, or physically) by an adult, the result was anxiety and repression. Later, these repressed memories are triggered by an event, which leads to symptom formation. Freud believed, for example, that all his hysterical female patients had experienced sexual trauma as children. As a result, their hysterical symptoms symbolised and communicated repressed traumatic sexual memories. Over time, Freud came to doubt his seduction hypothesis and replaced it with a theory of intrapsychic causation. He purported that his hysterical female patients' "memories" of seduction were intrapsychic fantasies, which in turn were remnants of unconscious childhood wishes (Person & Klar, 1994).

This striking (although gradual) change from seduction in reality to intrapsychic childhood fantasies was pivotal in the evolution of psychoanalytic theory and technique. From then on, psychoanalytic ideas were grounded in the study of wishes and fantasies that derive from the unruly and anachronistic unconscious. In other words, exploring unconscious conflicts was the focus of psychoanalytic thinking and practice. Traumatic events in the lives of patients were no longer of consequence, which in turn diminished the significance of reconstructing childhood memories. Until recent years, most American analysts emphasised unconscious mental contents and their transformations as the chief interest of psychoanalysis. The focus has been on how these fantasies impact reality, but not the other way around. This is undoubtedly a one-person psychology (ibid.). However, Freud (1940a) continued to think of actual seduction as one possible cause of adult symptom formation and never gave up entirely on his seduction hypothesis (Blum, 2008).

As psychoanalytic theory evolved, some analysts gave up trying to reconstruct the past and accepted psychoanalysis as a hermeneutic science, while many others took the position that unconscious fantasies are impossible to differentiate from repressed memories. We know that memories are condensed and altered over time and are multiply determined as well as multi-layered with meanings. We also understand that prohibited fantasies and real experiences often merge, but nevertheless, actual trauma needs to be addressed. It is a painful reality that many children are seduced by their parents (Colarusso, 2011; Gartner, 1997; Kramer & Akhtar, 1991; Shengold, 1989). This is a sad and disturbing truth, which works to fortify the effects of the child's forbidden Oedipal fantasies (Greenacre, 1956). For this contribution, I will not address actual sexual abuse or incest, but instead will focus on the girl who has ostensibly won her Oedipal struggle. This is the girl who feels she is preferred over her mother by her father; the girl who feels she is given greater adoration than the mother. The girl who is *seduced* and *betrayed*.

Introducing Bella

Bella was the youngest of three girls. Her two sisters were ten and twelve years older than her. Both were married and highly successful in professional careers. Bella's father enjoyed acclaim and fame in his field, while her mother never worked outside the home. Bella was clear that she was a "mistaken pregnancy", born to parents in their mid-forties. She described her mother as "exhausted", taking frequent naps throughout her childhood. She was a lonely little girl who retreated into elaborate make-believe play as her mother slept away the day. Bella longed for physical closeness with her mother, which she felt she had to "steal" from her while she slept. Bella told me in an early session: "I would tiptoe into her room because if I woke her she would chase me down the hall, so I was terrified of waking her. I would lie next to her and wrap my leg over her back while she slept. I loved that." As Bella's story unfolded, it became clear that she had been a creative, bright little girl who figured out that the only way to be close to her depressed, ineffectual mother was to join her in slumber. She turned to her father for emotional support, and he to her. In both of their eyes, she was the most special daughter.

The role of the father

Freud did not deem the role of fatherhood particularly significant until the child reached the Oedipal phase of development. For Freud, it was the father's responsibility to establish the incest barrier (1909b, 1924d); almost a decade later he emphasised the father's role as that of protector (1930a). There was little interest in the role of fathers among psychoanalytic theorists until Loewald (1951) introduced the idea that the father must step in to prevent engulfment by the mother. Mahler and Gosliner (1955) "further elucidated the father's role in the development of the child's ego as well as his superego precursors" (Akhtar & Powell, 2004, p. 76). A decade later Mahler (1967) underscored the father as different from the mother in that he was more playful, while Benedek (1970), focused on the father's role on its affect on the child's personality development, and Abelin (1971) emphasised the important function the father has in helping the pre-Oedipal child separate from the mother (Akhtar & Powell, 2004). Following Abelin, Mahler, Pine, and Bergman (1975) also declared that the father's job was to rescue the infant from her symbiotic bond to the mother. Mahler demonstrated, through child observational research, that as the child developed from infancy to toddlerhood, the father is differentiated from the mother and is seen as mystifying and stimulating. However, as much as the father is enjoyed, the "practising" infant returns to the mother when in need of comfort or when upset, hungry, or tired. During the rapprochement subphase (sixteen months to thirty-six months), the father becomes more important to the toddler who begins to experience ambivalent feelings towards the mother. In this way, the father is essential in helping the toddler separate and individuate from the mother (Mahler, Pine & Bergman, 1975). More recent theorists explain that during rapprochement, the little girl and her father share a mutual admiration. The child has a wish to identify with the father, which he supports and encourages (Benjamin, 1991).

Bella had no memories of playing with her mother or of being read to or held except when bathed. She came alive when she spoke of her father, describing him as funny, loving, and extremely physical. In one particular session, eighteen months into her analysis, Bella was despondent over her career and her love life. She felt her musical career and her current boyfriend were lacking, frustrating, and unfulfilling. Bella had had a series of men whom she easily seduced, but just as quickly her feelings turned to abject disdain and she rejected them. Her thoughts went to her father as she worried that he was disappointed in her. She longingly reminisced about her early childhood: "He was the best father. I know I was his favourite when I was little. When we went out to eat, he would tell the waitress that my mother was *his* mother and that I was *his* wife. It embarrassed me a little when I got older, but when I was really little I loved it. He said to me almost every day, 'Let's kill your mother and run away and get married!' It was a silly joke, but he said it all the time. I loved it. I would laugh. It was exciting. But now as I tell you about it, I'm embarrassed and I feel sad. I feel bad for my mother. It's sad."

As far back as Bella's memories go, she found herself in a predicament. She was an "Oedipal victor".[1] Because of her mother's depression and emotional unavailability, she was unable to identify with or idealise her. She was forced to turn to her father. In response, her father encouraged this relationship, as Bella provided the emotional closeness that he was not able to get from his wife. In such situations "… fathers often turn to their daughters as surrogate spouses or mothers and then re-enact the separation-individuation conflicts of their own childhoods" (Kieffer, 2004, p. 76). For Bella, there seemed to be a pre-Oedipal narcissistic quality to her need to replace the mother.

Bella's Oedipal conflict

Let us imagine Bella from the age of three on. Her mother is asleep, passive, and depressed, uninterested in, or unable to engage with her bright creative little girl. Her somewhat narcissistic father playfully seduces her into believing that she is favoured over her sleeping mother. He jokes about killing off mother and marrying Bella, often calling her his "wife" in public. In addition, Bella described her home environment as a "naked house" where bathroom and bedroom doors were left open, and baths and showers were shared. Bella often showered with her father until well into her latency years. Blum (1973) states: "Parental seduction and exhibitionism undermine and corrupt superego development. There can be paradoxical permission and prohibition of sexual gratification by a superego modeled after contradictory parental behavior" (p. 67). Clearly Bella's overstimulating (father) yet depressed (mother) home environment affected many aspects of her development.

Back to theory

According to Freud (1908c), "penis envy" occurs when the pre-Oedipal girl discovers anatomical differences, feels inferior, and desires to have a penis. Because of her lack of a penis, the little girl turns away from her mother and takes her father as a libidinal object. This gives way to the Oedipal complex, which is resolved when the little girl no longer wishes for a penis but instead wishes for a baby. Only then can she identify with her mother as a woman.

Not everyone agreed with Freud as to the little girls' entry into the Oedipal phase of development. Horney (1924, 1926) felt that penis envy was a "flight from womanhood" and was pathological, not a normal phase of development. In her view, penis envy develops when the Oedipal phase goes awry and the girl runs away from her libidinal connection to the father, fearing competition with her mother. In Horney's view, this is why the girl desires a penis as she identifies with the father (ibid.).

Jones (1927, 1935) also disagreed with Freud stating: the "girl's attitude is already more feminine than masculine" (Jones, 1935, p. 265) as her "femininity develops progressively from the promptings of an instinctual constitution" (1935, p. 273). Jones did not understand female sexual development to be based on a girl's disappointment in her genitals (Zetzel, 1960). Thompson (1954) spoke of a psychology of women that was not based on penis envy as the bedrock of female psychosexual development. Several other psychoanalysts understood the little girl's desire for the penis as a reaction against the fear of engulfment by the all-powerful, omnipotent pre-Oedipal mother (Chodorow, 1978; Dinnerstein, 1976; McDougall, 1980). The term "penis envy" came to be associated with the idea that women are psychologically inferior to men which in turn altered psychoanalytic thinking, as many analysts no longer viewed conflicts of identity, narcissism, and aggression as "merely 'penis envy'" (Barnett, 1966; Ewens, 1976; Grossman & Stewart, 1976). Lerner (1976), spoke of "parental mislabeling of female genitals" as a cause of grave psychological consequences resulting in the girl feeling like she has something less than the boy which contributes to the girl's penis envy. Lerner reasons that "[P]enis envy is not really a wish for a penis … but rather may reflect the wish to validate and have 'permission' for female sexual organs" (1976, p. 269).

Parens, Pollock, Stern & Kramer (1976) take a different theoretical pathway into the Oedipal complex for little girls. From their mother/infant research, they observed that the girl's "wish to have a baby during the first genital phase does not necessarily follow upon or depend on the prior wish to have a penis" (p. 102). They further postulated that the little girl does not need to experience castration anxiety in order to enter into the Oedipal phase and that biological and maturational forces "thrust the girl into her Oedipal complex" (p. 103).

Freud described the Oedipus complex as occurring between three to five years of age, when the child copes with a multitude of confusing feelings in association with his or her parents. Most pronounced are erotic feelings for the opposite-sex parent, and rivalrous feelings with the same-sex parent. At the same time, the child is fascinated with the mysteries of pregnancy and childbirth. "Successful negotiation of passage through the Oedipus complex results in the creation of the incest barrier, acceptance of generational boundaries, entry into the temporal dimension of life, respect for the value of waiting and effort, and formation of the superego" (Akhtar, 2009, p. 197). In addition, the child also needs to identify with the superego prohibitions of the "forbidding oedipal parent" (Davies, 2003, p. 3). Loewald (1977) asserted that the child needed to be able to mourn what he or she must relinquish and not repress these feelings. He stressed that when Oedipal guilt is repressed, a relentless pursuit of punishment results and enters into future relationships.

As stated above, with successful negotiation of the Oedipal phase, the incest barrier is established; however, this does not mean that all declarations of attractiveness between parents and children are eliminated. Akhtar (1994) spoke of an "oedipally-optimal distance that is neither incestuously intrusive nor oblivious of cross-generational eroticism" (p. 443). It seems clear that Oedipal development as well as its resolution is affected by both intrapsychic dynamics, and the outside environment (Gill, 1987).

The child enters the Oedipal phase of development already influenced and shaped by her pre-Oedipal years (Abend, 1988). From memories as far back as the age of three, we know that Bella's mother was depressed and for the most part, uninterested in her child. We can easily speculate that perhaps Bella's first three years were also with a very depressed mother. In Bella's early phase of her analysis, she was constantly afraid that she was boring me, stating that she worried I would fall asleep while she spoke. In the second year of her analysis, Bella became depressed and described her emotional needs as "disgusting". She worried that I would be repelled by her needs and turn my back to her as her mother did when she was young. After many difficult months, she was able to call my message machine, gaining comfort in hearing my voice and accepting a return call from me when needed. This transference of the depressed mother was excruciatingly painful, as Bella often spent sessions silently weeping. It became clear that she needed me to speak to her at these moments to assure her that I had not fallen asleep. It was during this time that Bella lost the ability to maintain the "as-if" quality to our relationship. When the mother is emotionally unavailable or rejects and ignores her child's requirements, the child is unable to develop an efficient and adaptive method of communicating his or her needs. Very quickly, a system of gross misattunement is set up which sets the stage for dysregulation and distress (Slade, 1998; Stern, 1985). As the mother recognises and finds meaning in her child's affects, the child is then able to see herself as a thinking, feeling, separate self. When the mother is unable to contain and reflect her infant's affects, the infant then becomes unable to self-regulate and normal development is at risk (Slade, 1998).

Stern (1985) defines attunement as the "intersubjective sharing of affect" (p. 141). Several developmental and attachment theorists (such as Bowlby, Ainsworth, Winnicott, Stern and Karen) all consider attunement to be critical to the psychological and physical development of the infant. As the infant cries and demands to have his needs met, the mother responds and thus gives meaning to the infant's signals. Eventually the infant begins to know what he wants and how to signal with intent. This harmonised mother/infant *pas de deux* is a form of mutual regulation, and as a result the infant learns to regulate himself. First, the infant is able to self-regulate biological functions such as sleep patterns, elimination, and eating. Gradually, as the mother/infant dance continues to develop, the baby learns to self-regulate on a psychological level as well. Shared social experiences (such as playful interchange and mirroring) give the child a sense of being appreciated and cared for. His emotions and affects are accepted and validated. He feels approval. These early social experiences usher the child into the richness of object relations and what it means to relate to another person.

A depressed or otherwise compromised (e.g., battered, ill, drug-addicted) parent who does not have the capacity for self-reflection is unable to reflect on the inner states of her infant. This child will, in turn, be unable to relate to his or her own inner world. Attachment research has shown that insecurely attached adults tend to persist in strategies and schemas that they first learned from their own rejecting parent. In an effort to avoid an empty inner world devoid of objects, people incorporate malevolent inner objects. This loyalty to the early depriving caregiver causes a parent to continue rejecting patterns in her own interaction with her own children (Eagle, 1995; Karen, 1998). The infant who does not experience attunement and mirroring may experience her emerging preverbal self as defective. She is left to feel empty, helpless, and perhaps in severe cases, even without hope.

In order to navigate the Oedipal experience, the child needs to have experienced good-enough pre-Oedipal years. This "requires a unified self with the capacity for intentionality, and objects which are experienced as distinct from oneself and towards whom ambivalence can be tolerated" (Akhtar, 1994, p. 443). Luckily, Bella's father was able to step in for mother, but at a cost, for while he was attentive, and loving, he was also highly seductive and overstimulating. Davies (2003) writes that the parent's love for the Oedipal child is steeped with healthy narcissistic adulation that she describes as "primitive" and "boundariless". She portrays the parent's love for the Oedipal child as "… simply different; it is of a different order and type than love for the partner. It is more idealizing, more narcissistic, more visceral" (p. 9). Long before this, Fenichel (1931) stated that the parent's unconscious sexual feelings and attachment for his child may become exceptionally strong when his sexual and emotional relationship with his partner is ungratifying. It seemed that Bella's father's own unsatisfied needs to be adored took over as he seduced Bella into thinking she was loved and desired more than her mother, which in turn had crucial consequences for her future development.

Unconscious Oedipal fantasies influence later life as they have an effect on symptom formation, character traits, and preferential means of gratification. "Love, jealousy, possession, envy, rivalry, rejection, ecstasy, disappointment, betrayal, power, helplessness, self-esteem, procreation, sexual roles, identity, triumph, defeat, guilt, revenge, restitution—preoccupy us for all the rest of our lives" (Abend, 1988, p. 502). Oedipal fantasies make the child vulnerable as her infantile narcissism is in full force. She wishes for the parent to pledge much more than he is realistically able to provide. "[T]he implicit parental promise is that sexually competitive wishes to win an exclusive, possessive relationship with the desired parent will be gratified if only the child wins the competition by playing by the imagined rules of the game" (Josephs, 2001, p. 705). Eventually the child realises that at the end of the day, daddy drives off into the sunset with mommy, while she is left to go to bed alone in her own room. This is met with terrible disappointment but she comes to understand that no matter how flirtatious she is or how hard she tries to win the game, she will lose. From the child's perspective, the "oedipal situation represents the tension between the child's first traumatic experiences of sexual/romantic exclusion from the parental relationship" (Davies, 2003, p. 9). The child must be able to cope with the realisation that her fantasy of blissful romantic perfection with her parent of choice is a myth. It is at this time that the child begins to see and understand that her parents are loyal to one another and they share intimacy and sexual passion from which she is excluded. As this is realised, the child may have a "sense of being small, sexually and romantically impotent, even insignificant" (Davies, 2003, p. 10).

Talking of Bella again

From Bella's narrative, I surmise that she did not experience the necessary painful disappointments that accompany Oedipal resolution but instead continued to believe that she had won her daddy while mommy slept. Within the "father" transference, Bella demonstrated a feeling of entitlement as it was not uncommon for her to demand to change her appointment time, expecting me to comply. At these times, she became enraged, insisting that her needs should come first, ahead of all my other patients. While Bella was not sexually abused, I would speculate that she experienced a type of sexualised seduction that left her feeling emotionally betrayed and affected her development.

Bella's post-Oedipal years—latency and adolescence—were also complicated. Now, we know that one of the main goals of post-Oedipal development is to be able to tolerate imperfections in oneself and in others. This requires a "mutual relinquishing of both the idealized other and the idealized self, in return for the experience of more deeply knowing and being known, being accepted for who one is, and discovering in oneself, the capacity to love in spite of, and because of other's imperfections" (Davies, 2003, p. 12). Because of the trauma of having a depressed mother in her pre-Oedipal years creating narcissistic impairment and unresolved pre-Oedipal developmental conflict, Bella seemed to be stuck, never achieving the complex organisation of tolerating ambivalence; simultaneously loving and hating the people she loved and depended on. In addition, post-Oedipally comes the ability to tolerate disappointment in ourselves and others and, most important, the capacity for intimacy through mutual vulnerability.

Bella's latency years were difficult as she struggled academically. She experienced difficulties with learning how to read, describing feelings of embarrassment and humiliation. Because of her high intelligence, she compensated for what could have been an undiagnosed learning difficulty and figured out ways of "fooling" her teachers. It is also possible that Bella's overstimulating home environment prevented her from being able to sublimate as her latency stage of development seemed delayed. She was an outgoing little girl and made friends easily, although in late latency and pre-teen years, she was bullied by a group of "mean" girls. These years were miserable, causing her to withdraw from friendships. She found comfort in her music but at the cost of isolation. The loneliness she described as a five year old remained and was still present when she began her analysis. Bella would find her mother napping every afternoon when she returned home from school and she disappeared into her pretend world. In her sessions, she often worried that others would discover that she was "stupid", especially me, and she had a recurring dream where her professors accused her of not belonging: "They were not fooled by my As."

When she was seven years old, she was given a violin and it quickly became apparent that she was talented. By the time she was ten years old, she was practising more than three hours per day and began to dream of a performance career. The music woke her mother (both literally and metaphorically) as Bella realised that when she played her mother was animated and attentive. Her music brought her mother back to life and for the first time she felt special in her mother's eyes. From that moment on Bella knew that as long as she played the violin, her mother would love her. It is interesting to note that while Bella struggled in school, playing a difficult instrument and learning the intricacies of music theory came easily to her. At the age of seventeen, when she first sought treatment, she struggled with not only giving up her own identity as a musician, but she faced the threat of losing her mother's love once again. Bella was fearful that if she did not become an accomplished violinist, her mother would once again turn away from her and fall asleep.

The loneliness that filled her earliest years was quasi-replaced with a passion and drive for her music and a quest for "perfection". Her pretend play of her childhood that had filled her afternoons developed into daydreams and fantasies of fame and success as a violinist but also of the "perfect" man who would adore her. Bella described herself as "boy crazy", always in love, always a flirt. She became sexually active at fifteen years old. Bella spoke lovingly of her first boyfriend. Their relationship seemed innocent and pure. She wanted to be with him constantly, missing music lessons, practising with less interest. Bella longed to be a "normal" teenager. She wanted to "hang-out", go to football games, and other perceived normal activities that were denied her. Both of Bella's parents were disturbed by this sudden change. Her mother made her feel guilty. Bella cried silently as she recalled this time: "She didn't really say anything. She just looked as if I had killed her. That if I didn't become this great violinist, she would be mortally wounded." Bella's father's reaction was strikingly different from her mother's. He withdrew all physical contact and became cold and distant. Many fathers experience discomfort when their daughters enter puberty. It is a known phenomenon that fathers may feel discomfort in managing their erotic feelings towards their adolescent daughter and may result in the father's withdrawal (Kieffer, 2004).[2] At the time, Bella thought his behaviour was a reaction to her lack of interest in her musical career; however, in her analysis she came to understand his cold distancing as a reaction to her budding sexuality with her boyfriend.

As stated above, Bella fell in love at fifteen. He was her first kiss as well as the boy she lost her virginity to. They had been together for eight months when they first engaged in sexual intercourse. It was soon after that Bella lost interest in him and broke his heart. From then on she had sex with a succession of boys and men much older than her. She spoke with contempt about the men she conquered. "It's so easy! It is just way too easy and they ALL say the exact same thing in bed [she mimicked and imitated her numerous lovers]. As soon as it is over, I just want them gone forever. I no longer have any interest. They disgust me … I think because of the mere fact that I can fool them. But the sad part is that I don't know any other way to feel close to them." Bella exhibited a grandiose omnipotent self as she described her badly chosen sexual entanglements. Her grandiosity can be understood as a "defense against awareness that oedipal victory is false" (Kohut, 1996, p. 318). I hypothesise that Bella's lack of an internalised "good-enough mother" (Winnicott, 1960) resulted in her difficulties in tolerating frustration, poor impulse control in her interactions with men, fragile self-esteem, and unneutralised aggression (Blum, 1981). This left her inclined to develop sadomasochistic relationships as noted within the transference and in her relationships with men.

Why is the "seduced child a betrayed child"?[3]

The act of seduction can have an overwhelming destructive effect on a child's intrapsychic stability and development. Greenacre (1956) warned that if the child's Oedipal fantasies are reinforced by a reality experience, the disorganising effect is immense. The child may experience conscious and unconscious rage towards her seducer as well as feelings of guilt. The defence of repression is commonly induced which protects the individual from the incestuous meaning of the seductive behaviour (Williams, 1987). When Bella began treatment, she was unaware of her anger towards either of her parents, but instead was acting out in a sadomasochistic way with men and by threatening to destroy her musical career. Because betrayal at the hands of her father was experienced as a narcissistic injury—first his unfulfilled seduction of her as a little girl and then his withdrawal from her when she became sexually active—her turning her back on her musical talent may also be viewed as an act of revenge. Perhaps this was a way of finally winning although she would ultimately harm only herself. "To the extent parental betrayal remains a narcissistic injury, the child wishes to turn the tables on the parents by seducing and betraying them in revenge, thereby attaining a vindictive triumph" (Josephs, 2001, p. 706). I believe this behaviour also served to help alleviate and cope with overwhelming depressive feelings.

When Bella became sexually active her aggression/anger was directed towards the men she seduced. This could be understood as identification with the aggressor but also an attempt to feel intimacy and to be loved. Bella's seductive fantasies, which she acted upon, seemed to be ego-syntonic as she rationalised and hoped that her sexual conquests would provide the ultimate bliss of winning the forbidden man for herself. One could imagine that this is a type of psychological agony, as this behaviour seemed to be driven by shame, jealousy, and envy. We can further surmise that as Bella identified with the aggressor, she developed a "seductive superego", which "unconsciously arranges a tragic downfall for those who possess the hubris to believe that they can triumph in transgression" (Josephs, 2001, p. 702). Bella's defensive structure was to seduce and betray over and over again before these men could seduce and betray her.

Bella began her analysis with the strong conviction that I would grossly disappoint her. She claimed I would seduce her into dependency and then abandon her, leaving her feeling only disappointment and betrayal. Her presenting problem when she sought treatment was an overarching disappointment in everything in her life, specifically her romantic relationships and her music. In other words, there was an air of non-fulfilment about Bella that seemed to be both defensive and aggressive. Many people feel a sense of disappointment when life experiences do not meet wishes and expectations.

Bella often spoke of her experiences as not living up to her expectations. Her performances were never good enough; she never played well enough in rehearsal or in her private sessions with teachers. Most striking, her relationships with men were never what she had imagined or hoped for. She entered her analysis profoundly steadfast to the idea of being disappointed in her analyst and her analysis as a whole. Throughout the early years of treatment, she tried again and again to seduce me into loving her, whereby she would quickly turn me into a disappointment who could never meet her expectations. She either saw me as her father who promised her everything and delivered nothing, or her mother who turned her back and fell asleep. In both of these scenarios, she worked hard to bring out the worst in me, as I became the bad object who always let her down. Bella's dilemma was that if she became vulnerable and allowed herself to experience intimacy with her analyst she ran the risk of engulfment, yet to reject me left her alone.

I understood Bella's use of disappointment as a defence against very early memories of recurrent disappointments and loss. After all, her father promised her daily that they would "kill her mother and run away together". When she became interested in boys and entered into an age-appropriate relationship, her father rejected her by demonstrating displeasure and withdrawal of physical contact. The emotional abandonment by her depressed mother was extremely damaging as she was insecurely attached, had difficulty developing object constancy, and suffered from separation anxiety. In addition, Bella carried the guilt of winning her father's admiration away from a depressed sleeping woman. Schafer (1999) notes: "Many patients who develop fixed, hardened attitudes of disappointment have suffered prolonged, severe deprivation and pain in their early object relations" (p. 1095).

Psychoanalysis thinks of the superego as the compass of an individual's moral development and manager of affects and behaviour. The development of the superego has long been understood as a by-product of progressing through the Oedipal phase of development. It is also thought that the superego is shaped by the attachment dynamic: "What is 'permissible' and 'good' is determined as much by the vicissitudes of the need for security as by rivalries and regulations of the oedipal triangle" (Holmes, 2011, p. 1228). Certainly, a major job of the superego is to oversee limits and boundaries. Early on in development the superego is harsh and is limited to *good* and *bad*. However, as the individual matures and moves through developmental phases, the mature superego is more subtle and forgiving. Holmes adds that the development of a healthy, mature superego is dependent on an "internalized parent-child relationship that maintains safety" (p. 1238). As noted earlier, Bella was insecurely attached to her mother, which set up "narcissistically derived ego ideals—doomed to disappointment when confronted with reality" (p. 1229).

A seductive superego is defined as a "superego that rationalizes the gratification of prohibited impulses and renders them ego syntonic. This is, however, followed by humiliating punishment" (Akhtar, 2009, p. 257). It seemed that Bella had developed a seductive superego, which served to re-traumatise her as she set up seductions and betrayals in almost all her relationships. Akhtar calls this phenomenon a "betrayal trauma upon the self and repeats similar betrayals by parents during childhood" (p. 257).

Some final remarks

For Bella, winning an "Oedipal victory" was a great disadvantage as her father's special treatment of her was both misunderstood by her and not genuine, given its base in his narcissism, leaving her with a sense of betrayal. She received a great deal of admiration from her father, but at an enormous cost to her development. When she entered her analysis at the age of seventeen, she was unable to enjoy a mature sexually gratifying relationship, nor was she able to pursue her career. She expected to be disappointed in everything she did: her relationships, her career, and especially her analyst and analysis. I believe this was directly related to the loss of her seductive relationship with her father whom she idealised. Kieffer (2004) suggests, "that the favored daughter's position is maintained only by a continued dependence on father as a source of self-esteem" (p. 73). Bella identified with her father as she re-enacted seduction and betrayal in every romantic relationship. I speculate, supported by her analytic material, that Bella felt such overwhelming guilt by winning her father's love at the expense of her depressed mother that she brought about her own punishment in her love life and also by attempting to destroy her musical career.

Bella longed for a mother who would love and nurture her, while she was simultaneously riddled with guilt, blaming herself for her mother's lack of engagement. Only when she played music did her mother seem to see her. Bella came to realise that she worried that she was somehow hurting her mother by playing so beautifully, for being successful. She came to understand that by becoming a successful musician, she was competing with her mother once again. Earlier in this paper, I commented that Bella identified with her father. It became clear in our work together that she was also very much identified with her mother. Within this identification with mother, Bella often devalued herself as seen in her music and in her relationships. This was played out within the transference as she denigrated and demeaned herself in an effort to punish herself, while keeping me interested.

Bella's analysis was terminated prematurely when she accepted an offer to join an orchestra in Europe. While it was clear to both Bella and myself that we had further work to accomplish, we were both satisfied that she was in a much better position to move forward with her life. Just as normal development is never linear, neither was Bella's development into mature love. When it felt we might be entering into a post-Oedipal transference, she would once again idealise me and demand undying attention and love. I became the idealised love object only to disappoint her with my shortcomings. Slowly, Bella was beginning to cope with and accept the unattainability of her wishes, and she no longer had to seduce and betray others.

Notes

1. The term "Oedipal victor" refers to the child who seemingly wins the affections of the same-sex parent away from the other parent in fantasy or reality. "This is seen as a tragedy, as it was in the tragedy of Sophocles' Oedipus Rex. The tragedy is seen in the consequent disturbances in sexual function and object choice, inhibitions in achievement of any

sort, and incomplete coalescence and consolidation of the superego" (Auchincloss & Samberg, 2012, p. 182).

2. In fact, the presence of a daughter might exert a "civilizing influence" (Akhtar, quoted in Kieffer, 2008, p. 80) upon the father. Five factors account for this. (i) First of all is the delicateness with which the father handles his female baby; cultural expectations, injunctions from the baby's mother, and his own psychobiological intuition impel a greater amount of aim-inhibition of aggression in the father. In learning to be gentler with his girl than he is with his boy, the father altruistically gives up the satisfaction of his assertive-aggressive impulses. (ii) A second factor is comprised by the greater distance the father takes from his daughter's naked body from early on; in this process, there is suppression, repression, and actual renunciation, via mourning, of dormant voyeuristic impulses (that were, at least in part, a reactivation of his boyhood curiosities about his mother's body). (iii) A third factor is comprised by the daughter being a female who (like mother and, to a lesser extent, sister) is a combination of an object and a selfobject; this increases cross-gender knowledge and empathy. (iv) Teaching ego skills to a girl imparts a sense to the father that execution of tasks is not a so-called phallic prerogative. This diminishes his masculine narcissism and makes him humbler. (v) Finally, having to renounce sexual gratification, while retaining a modicum of the erotic resonance, in response to the girls' Oedipal overtures (both during her childhood and later when she is blossoming into a young woman), strengthens the incest barrier in the father's mind.

3. The epithet "A seduced child is a betrayed child" is a paraphrase of Chasseguet-Smirgel's (1984) declaration that "A seduced child is a fooled child" (p. 16).

CHAPTER THREE

Betrayal, shifting loyalties, identity, and love in adolescence

Christine C. Kieffer

In this contribution, I will examine the impact and meanings of betrayal in adolescence with particular attention to early adolescent girls. I will explore the process of betrayal, reparation, and forgiveness, and their creative possibilities in furthering psychological development, particularly with respect to the tasks of separation-individuation and the formation an autonomous identity. To give what we are about to consider an "experience-near" quality, I will open my discourse with a personal experience.

The betrayal of Elaine

This happened when I was in year nine and I and my fellow students were poised on the threshold of high school. Elaine, a classmate of mine, had been disdained by the other girls in my class, including those among the subgroup of my friends, referred to as the "smart kids", by others in the class. I was friendly with everyone in this subgroup, although through the years, there were formations and reformations of dyads who described themselves as "best friends". One dyad went so far as to dress exactly alike, calling one another each morning to find out what accessories and hairstyle to wear for that day, even though the heavy, woollen, and itchy uniforms at our Catholic school provided little opportunity for variety.

While Elaine had been on the periphery of this group, I became interested in befriending her as we became aware of mutual interests—in books, the arts, and in sociocultural ideas. This was not a perfect match, however, since Elaine was a staunch Republican among fervent Democrats in our Irish Catholic (and some Italian) Bronx neighbourhood. Her mother had supported Barry Goldwater with what had bordered on an almost cult-like adoration. While spending time with Elaine, I became aware that she had admitted me into a very cramped circle of two: she and her mother. She harboured intense and apparently deathless feelings of narcissistic rage towards the other students, feelings that Elaine tried to cover up with grandiosity and contempt. My mother noted that I seemed to have become Elaine's first friend, adding that she had long wondered why no one seemed to like her.

One morning, Elaine had asked me if I would like to come over to her house after school, and I demurred, adding that I had some chores to do. Three o'clock rolled around, however, and as the dismissal bell rang, a girl name Linda (towards whom I felt equally close) asked me to come over to her house and I agreed. As we reached the street, amidst a swarm of uniform-clad, laughing girls, all eager to spend a few hours in the springtime sun, Elaine, who had been walking behind us (unbeknown to us) and who had heard every word of my exchange with Linda, loudly and angrily confronted me about what she had experienced as a betrayal. "I asked you over to MY house *first* and so you MUST come with me!" By this time, Elaine was shouting at the top of her lungs. A crowd began to form around the three of us, eager for the excitement—perhaps even a fight—that seemed about to begin, and I felt my cheeks aflame with embarrassment. Linda coolly said, "So, what are you going to do?" with a disdainful toss of her curls. She and Elaine hated one another. Elaine repeated her demand, insistent upon the righteousness of her position; she again insisted that I come with her. *Now!* It had felt to me in that moment as though the only way in which I could retain a shred of my own dignity would be to go with Linda, which I did. Linda seemed triumphant, and later asked me why I would even want to be friends with Elaine: "We all have been wondering what you see in her. Look at what she did today. What an idiot!" As the afternoon wore on, however, I felt a growing sense of unease. I had felt cornered by Elaine in a public setting, taken aback by the intensity of her response, and had felt—in the pressure of the moment—that the only way in which I could maintain a sense of autonomy had been to walk away with Linda. But later, I began to feel badly about hurting her feelings.

When I spoke about this situation with my parents, however, each of them told me that it would have been wiser—less hurtful and more politically astute—to choose neither friend and go home alone. I agreed, although that option had not occurred to me at the time. All that had seemed to matter in that moment had been a desire to avoid ridicule and to maintain my freedom. My father marvelled at the combustibility of the relationships of teenage girls and maintained that this would not have occurred—at least not in the same way—among adolescent boys. "Why not just all go out together?" he wondered, mystified.

While I tried to remain friends with Elaine, she was unable to recover from the sense of injury—and the unwavering conviction—that I had betrayed her. Repeated apologies from me, along with attempts to convey sincere remorse, were met with condescension and sarcasm. Elaine's sense of victimhood only increased over time. Finally, at the end of the summer, Elaine marched up to me and declared, "I have decided to drop you as my friend." I felt sad about losing my friend as well as regret about having hurt Elaine so grievously. I also felt a sense of guilt: while Elaine was still an excellent student in high school, reports of her drinking binges and indiscriminate trysts with boys— all new and unexpected developments in a girl who had formerly been quite prim—had reached me, and I also knew that Elaine had formed no new friendships. These symptoms turned out to have been fairly short-lived, and may have represented an alternative attempt at separating-individuating from her mother; however, at the time, I felt partly culpable. I had let Elaine down.

Interestingly, I had rather too quickly dropped any attempt to convey to her my own sense of unfair treatment as it had unfolded in the street. After all, I had been caught off-guard and publicly humiliated, enduring the gaze of an adolescent crowd eager for drama and gossip. To have capitulated in that moment would have felt as though I was surrendering all autonomy and an independent identity of my own. However, Elaine's emphatic (and loud) insistence upon the enormity of her betrayal had seemed to fill all available intersubjective space, and my own sense of injury soon faded. I began to feel sorrow that I had hurt her so grievously and was helpless to make reparations. It was only later that I became more cognisant of the bind that had been created: I had been set up to bring about the betrayal that Elaine had expected from others all along, the betrayal that her mother had predicted would befall her if she strayed from their reliable twinship selfobject relationship.

I now recalled that in year seven, when I and another girl, Eileen, were class monitors, and while our teacher had stepped away from the classroom, there had been some contretemps between Elaine and Eileen that had resulted in Elaine tearfully running into the washroom. Eileen and I ran after her, imploring her to come out. Elaine had locked herself in a stall, and, in response to our entreaties, finally said, in a voice choked with tears, "What do I have to live for?" We felt a rising sense of panic. Eileen suggested that Elaine consider her family. I suggested that Elaine could live for her art. She was a wonderful painter, determined that some day she would be a world-famous artist. I reminded her of this aim. Elaine then laughed bitterly. While I do not recall the details of what happened immediately after that moment, soon after, Elaine made overtures of friendship to me. In retrospect, I have wondered whether my response to her despair—to think of herself and her own aspirations—had been more empathically in tune with her than Eileen's suggestion that she consider others. This friendship had lasted until I refused to choose her—had refused to do what she required of me in a public proclamation of loyalty to our singular friendship. I continue to wonder what became of Elaine. I also have reflected much upon what actually transpired between us when we were young girls. Before delving into it further, I would like to make a foray into our theoretical understanding of adolescent development.

Adolescent development

Early contributions

Most psychoanalysts are in agreement that adolescence is a distinct developmental phase that is characterised by a steady, sometimes even simultaneous, forward and backward movement as teenagers strive to individuate from their first love objects, loosening early identifications (or at least, moving them into the background), as they strive to form an expanded identity that that enables them to form new object ties and permits the attainment of adult life goals. Many of the paradoxical aspects of this phase—for example, the insistence upon individuality while adhering strictly to absolute conformity, the oscillation between self-definition and exaggerated focus upon the opinions of others— reflect these strivings.

Anna Freud (1936) has been recognised as one of the first psychoanalysts to acknowledge the importance of this phase of life, describing adolescence as a distinct and definable developmental phase heralded by the onset of puberty and leading to a reawakening of the struggle to bolster a compromise formation between the ego and the id. This "truce", first brought about in latency, eventually gives way to a struggle driven by physiological forces in which the more firmly consolidated ego must now contend with superego conflicts as well. Anna Freud observed that adolescent upheaval is but an external indication of the many internal adjustments that are underway, noting that, while adolescent acting out of these conflicts often receives more attention, neurotic symptoms may also result in withdrawal into excessive amounts of anxiety and inhibition. While Anna Freud observed that adolescence recapitulates infantile strivings, she also noted that adolescence may also be a time of unusual creativity, and others have observed (Erikson, 1950) that many artists and scientists make their most important contributions in late adolescence and early adulthood.

Subsequent psychoanalytic writers also have described adolescence as a time of reworking infantile conflict, notably Kaplan (1984), who wrote of a "farewell to childhood", and Blos (1962), who described the essence of adolescence as centred around a second individuation process which can result in firmer boundaries and greater stability of both self and object representations, with a corresponding resistance to shifts in cathexis. Mahler, Pine, and Bergman (1975) also have written about adolescence as offering a second opportunity to work through conflicts around separation and individuation.

Psychoanalysts, developmental psychologists, and other social scientists alike—along with most casual observers, and certainly *parents*— tend to agree that inconsistent and unpredictable development is one of the hallmarks of adolescent development. One analyst has even described adolescence as a "borderline" state (Blos, 1976) but Anna

Freud would emphatically disagree with this view.[1] She maintained that the "upholding of a steady equilibrium during the adolescent process is in itself abnormal" since "... adolescence is by its nature an interruption of peaceful growth" (A. Freud, 1958, p. 164).

Contemporary perspectives

While psychoanalysts have tended to view development as a linear sequence in which previous steps must first be filled in or worked through as a scaffolding for later stages, there are an increasing number of contemporary psychoanalytic theorists who have applied the axioms of non-linear dynamic systems or applied chaos models to explain normal growth, psychopathology, as well as therapeutic action; they include Galatzer-Levy (2002); Harris (2005); Piers, Muller, and Brent (2007); and Seligman (2005). Other writers have demonstrated that chaotic models may be particularly apt in understanding adolescent development (Jaffe, 2000; Kieffer, 2007).

Chaos theory, while initially developed to explain phenomena in the physical sciences, has come to be seen as having particular applicability to the social sciences, and Thelen and Smith (1994) were leading researchers in the application of non-linear dynamics systems theory to solving problems in development. In studying infants learning to walk, they disproved the old dictum that one must learn how to crawl before learning to walk. In fact, the thousands of infants they studied all seemed to have unique patterns of learning to walk, some never crawling at all. They were able to demonstrate Von Bertalanffy's (1968) principle of "equifinality"—that is, that there are multiple pathways to a common developmental outcome.

Thus, chaos theory might be useful in helping to explain the particularly uneven developmental process of adolescence. The psychological phenomena during this time tend to unfold erratically, often with rapid oscillation between reflective thought and non-reflective action. However, over time, there is usually a shift towards adaptation and a movement towards increased capacity for self-regulation, an internalised sense of agency as well as a more realistic set of goals and ideals (Kieffer, 2007). This, too, is consistent with Von Bertalanffy's (1968) principle of equifinality, in which he demonstrated that all biological systems self-organise and self-regulate, with multiple paths towards a common developmental outcome. That is, we can think of people as "self-systems" which organise around "attractor states" or a "momentarily stable, equilibrated place, a preferred topology or a particular behavioral mode" (Harris, 2005, p. 85). Therefore, early objects may be thought of as attractors around which infants self-organise, and later, "strange attractors" such as the influx of hormones and the peer group impel the adolescent forward in a move towards autonomy and an expanded sense of identity. Another systems principle that is particularly relevant to development is that of "emergence", which refers to a situation of synergy that is more than the sum of its parts—one in which "… something novel or surprising appears from a situation that is not even suggestive of this novelty—something that arrives out of the blue" (Galatzer-Levy, 2002, p. 710). This phenomenon seems particularly dramatic during early adolescence in which seemingly dormant periods can suddenly and unpredictably shift into periods of rapid change and growth. Emergence can be especially useful in helping us to understand the process of play and creativity, elements which can be particularly salient in adolescence (Kieffer, 2011).

Cognitive aspects

The adolescent must integrate rapidly developing capacities not only for physical functioning but also cognitive and emotional functioning as well. These new capacities can foster creativity which enables some adolescents to make novel contributions to science and the arts in young adulthood—or, at least, help them to manage the developmental hurdles that multiply during this phase of life.

Blakemore (2008) has presented persuasive research on adolescent brain development which demonstrates that behaviour related to social cognition changes dramatically during human adolescence. This is "paralleled by functional changes that occur in the social brain during this time" (p. 267), specifically in areas that highlight face recognition and mental state attribution. Blakemore observed that her findings are consistent with those of social psychological studies which indicate that adolescence is characterised by a heightened state of self-consciousness along with the increased importance of peer relationships. Gradually, the adolescent develops a greater understanding of how others think and feel, with greater skill in "attribution of mental states" (Steinberg & Morris, 2001), which psychoanalysts regard as an increase in the capacity for "mentalization" (Fonagy, Gergely, Jurist & Target, 2004) or empathy.

Blakemore interprets the confluence of these findings to mean that it is not the increased capacity for mentalisation that is significant so much as the improvement in the modulation of mentalising by the executive functions of the brain that leads to the development of social judgment and improved interaction in adolescents. This adds credence to the view that complex influences, such as the combined impact of physiological and psychological domains as each influences the other realms, cannot be adequately explained with reference only to a linear model of development. Moreover, this finding is likely to be one that Anna Freud would acknowledge: she anticipated chaos theory in developing her theory of "developmental lines" particularly with respect to how their confluence or discordance (or unevenness) may impact development and character.

Piaget (Piaget & Inhelder, 1958), of course, also had taken up the question of the adolescent thought process, maintaining that the fundamental problem of adolescence is not puberty *per se* but rather the cognitive and emotional challenge of having to take on adult roles, which vary in timing and complexity cross-culturally. Piaget also observed that the organisation of formal operations, which has the capacity to develop in adolescence, is dependent upon the social milieu in which the adolescent finds him- or herself. While between the ages of eleven and twelve the brain may reach a state of readiness to attain formal operations, its development is highly dependent upon formal education as well as a sociocultural environment that promotes a future-orientation as well as one that creates the conditions that will promote a *capacity for self-reflection*. Inhelder and Piaget (1958) maintain that the essence of formal operations is "thinking about thinking" (p. 438). That is, there is a development of a capacity for abstraction both in thought and in social relationships which can come to fruition beginning at thirteen to fifteen years of age. Therefore the onset of formal operations facilitates the acquisition of complex, adult social roles, but a crucial element of that process entails the *integration* of thought and affect, along with the capacity to differentiate between both processes, an important developmental task of adolescence.

These preceding research paradigms offer considerable convergence with respect to the development of the capacity for abstraction as well as the potential for play—with ideas, emotions, and with others—a capacity which increases in both kind and sophistication in adolescence. Thus, a further task of adolescence, and one for which play and playfulness is a particularly apt medium, is the integration of affect with cognition (Kieffer, 2011). Blum (2005) has noted that affects have come to acquire a place of central importance in psychoanalysis, having mutually determined neurophysiological as well as psychological influences throughout life, but affects can be particularly challenging to adolescents and their families. Blum has emphasised the transactional nature of and influence of affect exchange between infant and caregiver, noting that the "modulation and taming of affects begins very early" (p. 4) and that affect co-determines both motivation and inhibition. The acquisition of language, bringing with it an increased range and subtlety in nuance, serves to radically alter the regulation of affects, with language coming to co-determine both the sociocultural context and the evolving parental-child relationship. Thus, language is a crucial developmental achievement since it can facilitate the integration of affects and ideas with emerging systems of memory and fantasy. Blum has noted further that while anxiety has been utilised in theorising about the role of affect as a signal, it is not a central paradigm for the significance of the positive affects, which provide signals to proceed rather than retreat.

The research of Tomkins (1962) and Stern (1985), as well as the work of Lichtenberg, Lachmann, and Fosshage (2001), has provided evidence for the independent importance of the primary affect of curiosity and interest in promoting exploration of novel situations as well as aiding in the mastery of negative affects.[2] Thus, the further development and refinement of a capacity for play and playfulness in adolescence serves to facilitate problem-solving in the development of both autonomy and the acquisition of new roles and an adult identity, two of the main tasks in adolescent development.

Striving for autonomy

Strivings towards separation and individuation are undertaken with renewed force and passion as early adolescence commences. Friendships, in particular "best friend" relationships often come to occupy a place of particular importance in early adolescence, both in a search for twinship that will serve as a bridge between reliance upon parental alliances and as a foreshadowing of the romantic relationships that come to the fore in middle and late adolescence. Even before the advent of cyberspace,[3] adolescents have found ways to distance themselves from family ties in the interest of forming intense, all-encompassing ties with peers. Many of us have observed the irony in which adolescents protest that they want to express their individuality and yet eagerly seek the acceptance of peer groups to which they must pledge fealty in which absolute conformity to dress, activities, and attitude is demanded.

Other social critics have observed, with bemusement, the rise of the "helicopter parent" (Cline & Fay, 1990) who seems to encourage parent-child enmeshment, even after the child goes to college, assisted by many of the devices provided by cyberspace as avenues for ongoing connection. What these pundits sometimes miss is the bi-directional, intersubjectively constructed aspects of this phenomenon: both parent and adolescent use the domain of cyberspace in the interests of expressing the ambivalence of letting go while creating ways to gradually attenuate and transform intimate connections.

Mahler's theory (Mahler, Pine & Bergman, 1975) positing the centrality of separation and individuation in human development has been challenged by self psychologists who have questioned the desirability of autonomy—even its very existence, maintaining that the use of selfobject experience and selfobject responsiveness remains a feature of healthy development and adult functioning throughout the lifespan (Galatzer-Levy & Cohler, 1993; Kohut, 1971, 1981). Intersubjective psychoanalysts (Orange, 1995, 2002; Stolorow, 2007; Stolorow & Atwood, 1992) have rigorously deconstructed the idea of the autonomous self, arguing for the still radical notion that the self is continuously developed within the intersubjective context.[4] All these theorists argue in various ways that secure attachment permits a gradual individuation process, one that permits a *relative* separation from "essential others", but one in which the end goal is the maintenance and elaboration of mutual interdependence. Moreover, some of these researchers question the view that conflict and turbulence need be a hallmark of adolescence, maintaining that Mahler and Anna Freud may have been overgeneralising from their own personal struggles in their youth (Galatzer-Levy & Cohler, 1993; Stolorow & Atwood, 1992).

However, there are other self psychologists and intersubjectivists who have expanded their theories to include a dimension of relative autonomy: that is, motivational systems theory, the third "branch" of self psychology, developed by Lichtenberg, Lachmann, and Fosshage (2001, 2010). Deriving these basic motivational systems from research with infants and their primary caregiver, Lichtenberg, while agreeing with Kohut that autonomy is illusory, expanded his theory to include motivations such as aversion/withdrawal and assertiveness/reactive aggression that posit a basic need for a relative degree of autonomy. One of Kohut's original group of seven disciples, Wolf (1988) expanded Kohut's set of three basic selfobject needs (mirror, idealising, and twin-ship) to include adversarial selfobject needs as well as a need for self-efficacy.

Wolf described adversarial selfobject experiences as a "need to experience the selfobject as a benignly opposing force who continues to be supportive and responsive while allowing or even encourag-ing one to be in active opposition and thus confirming at least partial autonomy; the need for the availability of a selfobject bond of asser-tive and adversarial confrontation vis-à-vis the selfobject without the loss of self-sustaining responsiveness from the selfobject" (p. 55). The origins of adversarial selfobject needs first appear in toddlerhood, and then become prominent again in adolescence as the teen becomes more aware of parental deficits, accompanied by a de-idealisation that is gradually replaced by a more realistic and nuanced appraisal in young adulthood. Or, as Mark Twain (1874) noted, "When I was a boy of four-teen, my father was so ignorant I could hardly stand to have the old man around. But when I got to be twenty-one, I was astonished at how much he had learned in seven years" (p. 554). Wolf (1988) emphasises the importance of a gradual rather than sudden and traumatic de-idealisation as facilitating the adolescent's transition into adulthood; thus he incorporates a universal striving for autonomy into the psy-chology of the self.

Identity formation

The "second individuation" of adolescence brings into the foreground the striving to attain autonomy from the family in the service of developing a more mature identity, which is facilitated by the adolescent's emerg-ing capacity for more complex thinking, an increased capacity for abstract play, and a more creative use of transitional space. Blos (1967) has observed that the adolescent often engages in "play-acting"—in various bodily self-presentations as well as in trying on different modes of relating to others. Lemma (2010) has noted that, under conditions in which adolescents encounter particular difficulty in individuating from early relationships, the marking and piercing of the body may represent a primitive attempt at self-definition.

As a further spur to this second individuation, the adolescent's locus of attention increasingly shifts from the family to the peer group, seeking new sources of idealisation, emulation, and identification. This leads to the adolescent's attraction to glorified images of sports figures, pop singers, and actors, who represent temporary role models—but role models that they may safely worship from afar, without becoming vulnerable to the demands of an accessible romantic object. Blos (1967) also has noted that adolescents not infrequently seek a quasi-merger with the larger peer group—in large musical arenas and crowded dance floors—while they watch singers and dancers on stage, thus attaining "ego states of quasi-merger … (which) … serve as safeguards against total merger with the infantile, internalized objects" (p. 175). Contemporary adolescents are also attracted to various forms of group internet participation, such as social networks and alternative living spaces (such as *Second Life* and *SimCity* and probably others by now) which offer the experience of merger and identification with a large group, as well as the opportunity to try out different identities and modes of relating.

Perhaps the most difficult task that faces the parent of an adolescent is the sometimes almost paradoxical process of being available while simultaneously getting out of the way of further development. Adolescents may be thought of as having a heightened need of transitional space in which to play with aspects of identity and new modes of relating to others, and must maintain the illusion of complete autonomy even while continuing to sense and covertly rely upon the background of a responsive, protective environmental milieu. While, as with toddlers, adolescents insist upon letting us (and themselves) know, "I can do it all by *myself!*", the emergence of new cognitive capacities can contribute to a heightened sense of awareness—and hypervigilance—about acknowledging intersubjective embeddedness. This is the other side of the coin of mentalisation and empathy, as previously noted. Thus, adolescents may be quick to bridle at any hint of manipulation.

At the same time, adolescents, while suspicious of adults' motives, need to experience essential others as authentic. Those they idealise must be genuine and allow themselves to be known—including friends, parents, and psychoanalysts. Markman (1997), Billow (2004), and Kieffer (2007) have observed that adolescents tend to monitor their analyst's countertransference reactions particularly closely for signs of inauthenticity, readily experiencing technical interventions as evidence that the analyst is simply "playing at being an analyst". This scrutiny may stem from adolescents' "anxiety of influence" as well as concerns about their own authenticity as they try on different roles as part of consolidating their own identity.

Betrayal and early adolescence

I will now examine the impact of betrayal in early adolescence as the confluence of physical, cognitive, and affective changes first makes itself felt (which is often itself experienced as a kind of betrayal), as the early adolescent begins to loosen ties to the family of origin and is captivated by the peer group and the "best friend". While my vignettes have focused in particular on how this phase of life affects early adolescent girls, many of my comments pertain to adolescent boys as well.[5]

Twinship mergers and narcissistic rage

As previously noted, the adolescent peer group often plays a pivotal role in promoting separation, individuation, and adult identity. But an adequate separation-individuation process also requires a stalwart and present parent against whom one may define oneself.

Elaine had been encouraged by her mother, with whom she was in an alter ego selfobject merger, to be contemptuous of her father, whom her mother regarded as having been an unworthy match. While Elaine revered her mother and often quoted her (particularly her political and rather racist views), she seldom spoke of her father, of whom she felt ashamed. In an attempt to separate and individuate from the twinship merger with her mother, Elaine sought a similar type of twinship in her relationship with me and felt betrayed when I exhibited an independence of desire and attitude. (There undoubtedly were echoes of negative Oedipal strivings as well as a displacement of Oedipal conflicts, but that is beyond the scope of this paper.) And what of my role in this betrayal? The choice of Linda represented a move towards an interest in boys (about whom Linda talked constantly) as well as a move away from the suffocating aspects of a continuing demand for twinship, which I had begun to outgrow. Moreover, the conflict posed by the two girls represented for me, I suspect, some of my own unresolved feelings about my parents' divorce, and the conflicting loyalties it had generated. Hence, the perhaps excessive guilt concerning the "betrayal".

In my clinical practice, I have encountered several adult female patients who have displayed similar reactions of betrayal when a twinship selfobject merger was disrupted. I had been conducting a psychotherapy group for women for about a year when I became pregnant. One woman, who had made the decision to stay at home with her children, became outraged when she learned that I intended to return to work after a two-month leave. It became evident that my announcement of a return to practice disrupted her sense that she and I were exactly alike and that she felt betrayed by my choice. She then abruptly left treatment. During the same group, another patient, a lesbian, became increasingly disturbed as the evidence of my pregnancy began to intrude into the analytic space, and had a dream (written about more extensively in Kieffer, 1996) in which I was an unwelcoming, rather grouchy short order cook/waitress who served a very limited menu to her customers at the snack bar: only hot dogs. Upon further examination, the patient associated to the customers as members of the group, and expressed a sense of betrayal towards me: my pregnancy had interfered with this patient's fantasy that I, too, was homosexual. She, too, had needed to make a premature departure from treatment, but only after I returned and she was reassured that I was okay, that is, had survived the birth and her narcissistic rage. The first patient in particular (the stay-at-home mother) had reminded me of my friend, Elaine, in her vehement self-righteousness and icy hauteur. The other patient was able to make therapeutic use of her experience and was able to forgive me to some extent. In each case, there had been a history of a struggle to emerge from a controlling twinship bond with a parent, and a lack of adequate peer relationships in adolescence.

Betrayal, forgiveness, and psychic growth

Four years after our graduation from grade school (elementary school), I had the occasion to drop by my former high school to obtain a transcript for college. I encountered Elaine at the bus stop. Despite the fact that much time had passed, she still treated me as though the episode of betrayal had occurred only yesterday. Upon seeing me, she seemed to fill once again with narcissistic rage, behaving towards me with renewed hauteur and contempt, despite my warm greeting. No longer remorseful, I marvelled at the continued intensity of her sense of injustice. From the cooler standpoint of greater separation from our relationship and relative maturity, I wondered, had she not played a significant role in bringing about this public humiliation herself? And had not I been humiliated sufficiently before the remorseless gaze of the adolescent crowd that day? (Although, to be sure, public sentiment had been on my side: perhaps nothing arouses adolescent scorn more than a loss of "cool".). I realised that I, too, had had something to forgive and perhaps my forgiving attitude may have even contributed to the intensity of Elaine's reaction, evoking some element of the sentiment expressed in Oscar Wilde's witticism to always forgive your enemies because nothing annoys them so much (Heider, 1958).

The psychoanalytic literature, as Akhtar noted (2002), has not had much to say about the notion of forgiveness, and little more has been written since his groundbreaking paper. In his paper, which delineates aspects of pathological states of betrayal and forgiveness (and much more), Akhtar links the inability to forgive with severe psychopathology, including borderline, paranoid, and narcissistic personality disorders. He describes the contributions of object relations theorists such as Klein (paranoid-schizoid and depressive positions, reparation), Winnicott (surviving hatred and the capacity for concern), and Mahler (the need for parents to tolerate the vicissitudes of the rapprochement phase) as providing a scaffold from which to understand the phenomenon of both betrayal and forgiveness. Kohut (1971) has described vividly the states of narcissistic rage that may dominate the minds of those with significant narcissistic psychopathology. I maintain that the insistence upon twinship in adolescence as a strategy for separating and individuating from parental ties may sometimes erupt in an intense sense of betrayal when the friend fails in mirroring functions, and, in the extreme case, proves not to be under one's omnipotent control. This may help to explain some of the tempestuousness of early adolescent relations, with its shifting alliances, particularly in the lives of teenage girls. While Elaine's reaction certainly was extreme, this sort of behaviour is far from uncommon during the upheaval of early adolescence. What was different was the undying commitment to the sense of betrayal. While her reaction to me four years later may have been suggestive of an unforgiving nature that one associates with the severe psychopathology described by Akhtar, there is insufficient data available about her later life. Moreover, many adolescent psychoanalysts have noted that the lack of cohesion of early adolescence, which is particularly prone to uneven development, often gives way to integration and maturation in later adolescence and early adulthood. A chaotic model of development may be more explanatory in this period than one that is more linear.

Just as adolescents must learn to forgive their peers and tolerate differences, so to must they forgive their parents, a process that Klein (1937) believes comes about, not only due to an identification of the kindness of one's parents, but also from a desire to make reparations for the injuries done to them in fantasy when the parents frustrated the infant's desires. As Kaplan noted (1984), adolescence is a "farewell to childhood", providing an opportunity for revisiting and reworking the conflicts that had been repressed in latency, now reawakened by the press of maturational processes, both physical and psychological.

Akhtar (2002), as well as Cavell (2003) and Siassi (2007) have all observed that holding on to grievances and an inability to forgive represents a strategy for avoidance of mourning and a failure to accept limitations both in others and oneself. I would add that the underside of a twinship selfobject merger, particularly in the case of early adolescents who are struggling with the integration of multiple influences—both internal and external—is that traumatic idealisation and abrupt awareness of its illusion may contribute to the more tempestuous relations of early adolescence, with its shifting loyalties and sensitivity to a host of betrayals.

Cavell (2003) explicitly links freedom and forgiveness, although Akhtar (2002) also alludes to this in his account of a story of Buddha, who teaches a grieving father angry at the perceived failure of the Buddha to save his son, to consider the role of holding a grudge as part of the illusion of controlling time passing, as well as a form of self-bondage. Akhtar, Siassi, and Cavell also note that sadomasochism is often a prominent feature in the failure to forgive, as it can lock both parties into a to-the-death struggle, a phenomenon that they have observed both in the consulting room as well as outside it.

Betrayal and later adolescence

Betrayal in the latter part of adolescence is more often centred around romantic disappointment in content, and may flounder upon poorly worked-through conflicts from the Oedipal period, but may also reflect pre-Oedipal dimensions as well. I would like to focus briefly upon two phenomena characteristic of this period: (a) excessive and/or prolonged reactions to romantic betrayals and, (b) excessive involvement in a romance to the exclusion of other investments.[6] But sometimes, these "old married couples", who spend high school as a tightly bound duo, can be making a retreat from the risks of making new relationships and negotiating encounters, including conflictual ones with peers. In each situation, however, the individual is completely single-minded.

Before further discussion, I would like to review briefly those two of Erikson's (1950) stages that span adolescence: "Identity vs. Identity Confusion" and "Intimacy vs. Isolation". Erikson describes the stage of a search for identity as encompassing much of adolescence, with the onset of puberty as providing a crisis that is the harbinger of many new roles and experiences. While Erikson delineates the search for intimacy and the simultaneous fear and solace of isolation as the hallmark of young adulthood, most researchers think of this stage as beginning in late adolescence as many teens leave home either for college or some other form of preparation for work, such as the armed forces or vocational training. As Stephen Mitchell and Margaret Black have noted (1995), one of the most compelling and useful aspects of Erikson's positing of opposing poles in his stage theory, is that it highlights the dialectical tension between both endpoints. It also suggests that the manner in which the individual negotiates the tension between the two poles is one of the aspects that can serve to propel ego development forward. Erikson further demonstrates in his classic book, *Childhood and Society* (1950), that the negotiation of each new stage is either facilitated or hindered in turn by the manner in which earlier stages have been resolved (or, at least, traversed). Perhaps it is no coincidence that Erikson's book has been particularly beloved by adolescents and young adults since its publication, because its depiction of a fluid and dynamic tension between opposite poles is particularly characteristic of the adolescent's predilection for extremes. I will now provide two brief clinical vignettes that will highlight developmental conflicts from both of these stages.

Clinical vignette 1

Sophia, as her mother described her in the initial consultation, seemed to be "in love with love", flinging herself headlong into romances and then becoming inconsolable when they ended, although many consisted essentially of admiration from afar.

An academically gifted fourteen year old with many artistic talents, Sophia would find it impossible to concentrate after she experienced what she considered to be a romantic betrayal, and her mourning was intense and prolonged. The betrayal could entail either a de-idealisation or involve a real or imagined slight, and Sophia would then spend endless hours dissecting the incident with her friends, many of whom had grievances of their own to share and compare. During the course of treatment, however, it soon became apparent that Sophia's romances all contained a sequence in which she received a flurry of attention and was then summarily dropped by her suitor. We soon began to recognise that this echoed Sophia's experience of her relationship with her mercurial father, who had divorced her mother when Sophia was eight. Sophia tearfully recounted a memory in which her father had visited the family at their country house one summer and then walked down a long road towards the train station, turning to wave occasionally as Sophia stood at the gate, keeping vigil, her eyes fixed on her departing father's back as he dissolved into the horizon. In that moment, it had felt as though he might be leaving forever. As Sophia recounted the details of her latest failed romance in each hour, we began to notice together how this narrative seemed similar to the way in which during custodial visits, her father might first shower Sophia with attention (sometimes tinged with flirtation) and then would abruptly drop her to return his attention to the business pressures of being a rising executive. He then seemed to regard his daughter as a hindrance. Sophia, too, began to articulate a sense, originally experienced as that bereft eight year old, confused about her parents' separation and divorce, that she must have done something wrong to make her father leave *her*. During one session, Sophia made a slip in which she referred to *her* divorce. When Sophia reached the age of thirteen, and her father's new wife had just given birth to a daughter of her own, it became evident that Sophia's preoccupation with romances had permitted her to avoid experiencing the pain and loss evoked by these relatively recent events in which two new competitors for her father's attention had arrived on the scene. Moreover, it had distracted Sophia from a more direct encounter with disavowed Oedipal wishes that had been reawakened by her stepmother's pregnancy and birth just as Sophia was entering puberty. The analysis permitted Sophia to mourn and move forward. Eventually, she formed a more long-term and stable relationship with a beau who was more constant and loving, and Sophia was able to focus more fully on planning for her future, working up to her potential in school, and also making enduring friendships.

But teenage "love-sickness" is not the only solution to psychosexual and relational problems in adolescence. Among mid- and late adolescents, one encounters the not infrequent phenomenon of the "old married couple" in high school who cling to one another exclusively to the detriment of other social relationships, and, sometimes, even intellectual development, since they may not be able to tolerate a prolonged interruption when one or both partners may have to choose a separate university. (This phenomenon is particularly surprising to many contemporary adolescents who are more accustomed to "hooking up" and who have replaced dating with going out in groups.)

Clinical vignette 2

After transferring from a high school in which she had been bullied mercilessly, and having felt particularly betrayed by one who had been her best friend, sixteen-year-old Cora successfully transitioned to another school in which she immediately became involved with a boyfriend, Todd, with whom she spent time to the exclusion of deep investments in other friends, and to the detriment of her studies. At the new school, Cora was popular and made friends easily, but her relationship with Todd seemed to buffer her against the slings and arrows of the lunchroom milieu, and, while she developed several friendships of some depth with girls, she acknowledged that she had consciously kept them at some distance from intimacy. Cora had become reluctant to confide in her new girlfriends, whom she expected to prove untrustworthy, and often cited the betrayal that she had experienced in the previous school as evidence that her stance was a wise one. Moreover, Todd was her very best friend. As Cora's analysis unfolded, an Oedipal phase came into the foreground.

It soon emerged that Cora was using her partnership with Todd in the service of both intensifying an experience of Oedipal competition as well as avoiding it—flaunting her sex life with Todd, who frequently came to visit her in her room at home, often when her mother was at home (sometimes both parents) and losing herself in a romantic relationship in a way that avoided a confrontation with her intense feelings of envy and rivalry towards her mother. Cora disclosed that she felt physically inadequate in comparison with her mother and discovered that her trysts with Todd at home had been initiated as a means of enacting this rivalry, both by "showing up" her mother and stimulating her father's erotic feelings. (Both parents, while they disliked Todd's nocturnal visits to their home, had felt uncomfortable setting limits on it, since they prided themselves on being open-minded and modern.) Eventually, Cora and Todd began to visit one another at his home, since his single-parent mother was often travelling and, as an only child, Todd had the house entirely to himself.

However, after this Oedipal manifestation had been analysed, another aspect of Cora's relationship with her mother soon emerged: she had long resented her mother's investment in her demanding career as a physician, and had felt that her mother had abandoned her to the ministrations of one housekeeper after another. Todd also had provided some of the early maternal care that Cora felt had been lacking with her mother: her boyfriend was omnipresent, mirroring and catering to her every need. Although she was in analysis with another career woman—another kind of doctor—Cora took pains to differentiate me from her mother. When I enquired about a negative maternal transference, Cora often vehemently protested this, declaring that I reminded her of her favourite housekeeper, a woman that her mother seemed to have abruptly fired, feeling a rivalry with the woman—an event which Cora continued to experience as evidence of a crushing betrayal by her mother. (Interestingly, at one point in the analysis, Cora's mother had attempted to do the same with me, but her husband intervened.)

While initially, Cora had planned to attend college in Chicago in order to remain with Todd (and Todd had been hoping to attend the same school as his girlfriend when he graduated), as the analysis moved to termination, Cora was able to separate from Todd, as he stayed behind for his senior year, and she chose an academically competitive college on the East Coast that was beyond her boyfriend's more limited intellectual prospects. Cora gently ended the relationship with a tearful Todd, assuring him that they would remain friends. Todd then became quite depressed, necessitating his own treatment.

Thus, in mid- to late adolescence, a sense of betrayal may be more easily covered over by sexualisation or a flight into a particularly tight romantic bond, which may have undertones of a rather primitive selfobject merger, one that interferes with social development. Increased cognitive maturity and emotional modulation may be utilised defensively in the service of enabling older adolescents to keep the experience of betrayal from being felt quite so keenly as do early adolescents. They also can attempt, with greater skill, to bury or channel the intensity of their feelings into all-encompassing relationships that can either distract them or serve as a salve. Thus, in later adolescence, the dynamic tension between a striving for an intimate relationship versus a withdrawal into protective isolation becomes an increasingly salient issue. In contrast, early adolescents, who are in the middle of experiencing puberty and trying to integrate this with all of this phase's accompanying cognitive and affective changes, are more likely to mismanage—and mislabel—a sense of betrayal. Indeed, the onset of puberty itself may be experienced as a kind of betrayal. One of the primary tasks of early adolescence involves a struggle to differentiate from primary family bonds and to establish a relatively autonomous identity. However, as Erikson has demonstrated, the early adolescent must struggle to emerge from being swallowed up in the diffusion of identity engendered by the many somatic and psychological demands of this new phase, as well as confusion among various competing emotional ties, which may seem fraught with the potential for betrayal, of self and others.

Concluding remarks

In this chapter, I have tried to reflect upon the impact and meaning of betrayal in early adolescence as well as in the later period of the teenage years, with particular emphasis upon the lives of adolescent girls. In addition, I have explored the process of betrayal, reparation, and forgiveness, particularly with respect to their facilitation of psychological development, as well as to their contribution to essential tasks of separation-individuation, the formation of a relatively autonomous and stable identity or integrated set of identities, as well as the initiation and deepening of a capacity for a mature love bond. In this chapter, I have striven to illustrate the importance of "essential others" in the creation of a responsive selfobject milieu in which the adolescent may play with different identities and relationships in a move towards maturity. I have noted the ongoing relevance of Erikson's stages of ego development, particularly the challenges posed by adolescent struggles with identity and identity diffusion, as well as intimacy and isolation. In closing, I would like to refer briefly to the work of Jessica Benjamin who has made many important contributions to psychological development and therapeutic action—work that is particularly relevant to the topic of betrayal and its resolution.

Benjamin (2004) has written about the sadomasochistic bond that may trap patient and analyst in a "doer-and-done-to" relation that collapses the potential space of the psychoanalytic process. Writing from a Winnicottian perspective, she has maintained that the spontaneous gesture of the analyst in being the first to make reparations in a stalemate of this kind may allow the patient to first realise that change is possible. The potential space of the analytic third may then be restored as both parties come to understand their own contributions to the stand-off. This extended process of collapse and restoration of the analytic third is what Benjamin believes eventually leads to "mutual recognition" or an awareness of self and other as twin subjectivities, connected but still autonomous with respect to desire and agency.

While Benjamin has largely confined her observations to the analytic encounter and has located the source of this struggle within the crucible of the original dyadic bond between mother and child, it strikes me that the development of mutual recognition is a particularly important developmental achievement for the adolescent. The increased capacity for mentalisation made possible by cognitive development—particularly in formal operations, and the increased capacity for mental state attribution—as well as increasing capacities for affective regulation, are important components of what facilitates the ongoing development of mutual recognition in adolescents, a task begun in toddlerhood. That is, increases in the capacity for empathy and mentalisation, alongside identifications with the affective responsiveness that has been given and received in early relationships, can foster a greater openness to the kinds of spontaneous gestures that promote reparation of injury after a betrayal and hence lead to forgiveness, that is, an open-hearted forgiveness that is grounded in empathy and respect. The late adolescent and young adult, having left home and having had some opportunity to examine their family from a greater distance and an expanded perspective, may then continue a process of recognition of their own parents as centres of their own subjectivity, thus engaging in an internal as well as interpersonal process of forgiveness and reparation: a process that will serve them well as they take on generative roles as adults.

Notes

1. Kernberg (1977) has described adolescence as a time in which border-line psychopathology may come into the foreground of the personality, given the need for firm boundaries and well-delineated structures with which to manage and channel the sexual drives and attain mature love relations.
2. Plaschkes's (2005) discussion of Blum's paper stressed the importance of play in relieving anxiety and promoting mastery. Given that trau-matic play has the qualities of repetition, concreteness, and potential exacerbation (M. Akhtar, 2011), one of the critical functions of psycho-analytic work is to help the patient to re-engage curiosity and interest in introducing new interactional *procedures* that may later gain momen-tum when integrated with language (Stern et al., 1987).
3. Contemporary parents often complain that their children seem "addicted" to video games and the internet, devices that seem designed to disengage the adolescent from family life, and many clinicians have noted that their young patients' adoption of cyberspace often bolsters defences against engagement with others more generally (Dini, 2008; Galatzer-Levy, 2012). When absorbed in these activities, the teen may be physically present and yet psychologically very far away, express-ing in concrete form the adolescent dilemma of needing to explore new relational alliances and identities while still retaining a secure base in the family.
4. This view has received some empirical support from those who study infant development and attachment from a psychoanalytic perspective (Lyons-Ruth, 1999; Stern et al., 1987). Lyons-Ruth has argued for the normative aspects of secure *attachment*—as opposed to separation—in the facilitation of individuation.
5. However, it is important to remember that, while girls must shift their sexual object from the mother to the father, boys do not have to take that additional step. (Boys must make a shift in gender iden-tification instead, which Stoller (1992) maintains explains the greater prevalence of gender identity disorder, e.g., cross-dressing, in men.) This may account for the greater intensity in early female adolescent relations—along with "crushes"—noted by many psychoanalytic theo-rists (Blos, 1962; Kaplan, 1984; Kieffer, 2004; Kulish & Holtzman, 2008). This greater intensity and adhesiveness may then account for the kinds of "blow-ups" that I describe in my vignette. While male adolescent

peer relationships are intense, there seems to be a somewhat greater acceptance of autonomy. Of course, these remarks are confined to the arc of heterosexual development, and it is understood that homosexual development has a somewhat different trajectory (Cohler & Galatzer-Levy, 2000).

6. An alternative to such excessive romantic involvement is the "careerism" that was personified by the character, "Tracie Flick" in the film, *Election* (1999).

CHAPTER FOUR

When the body betrays

Mark Moore

The word betrayal has its roots in the word traitor from the Old French *tradere* meaning to hand over or deliver. To betray is commonly understood to mean "to deliver to an enemy by treachery" but it has several other meanings: (i) to lead astray, (ii) to fail in the time of need, (iii) to reveal unintentionally, to show or to disclose in violation of confidence (*Webster's Dictionary*, 1981). To the psychoanalytically informed reader these meanings suggest dynamic possibilities: repression failing to stem the emergence of repressed impulses, slips of the tongue, and the unconscious wish to live forever rudely undermined by the reality of aging and illness. Such associations, however, lend themselves to subtle and complex questions about the subject and object of the act of betrayal. Who is betraying whom?

For example, if we blush and experience it as an unintentional revelation, then do we betray our self-image or a persona we wish to represent to the world? The superego that acts to deny the forbidden thought that gave rise to the blush? Our ego in its attempt to enforce repression and to defend against the emergence of impulses? And who is the traitor? Is it even correct to ask who rather than what, in the context of claiming that the body is betraying us? After all, there is an implication that in the case of betrayal it is the Other, the Not-Me, who betrays. And yet our body is our own—can it be separated out so objectively from our sense of self? If we blush, is the body truly an autonomous traitor or simply the vehicle for betrayal?

This line of thinking carries the risk of reifying structural concepts such as the superego and ego and of becoming mired in a Cartesian idea of the mind and body as neatly split. Freud wrote of the ego as being "first and foremost a bodily ego" (1923b, p. 26), reflecting how the ego emerges from early bodily sensations and how knowledge of the self is obtained through bodily experience such as use of the mouth and hands. Over time a more elaborate sense of the physical and mental self develops, with a resultant body image, or mental representation of the body, taking shape. With increased wilful mastery over the body as reflected by greater muscle coordination, eye-hand coordination, loco-motion, and bladder and bowel function, the representation of the rela-tionship of mind to body is characterised by a sense of conscious control over the body. It is worth noting the specific way in which, when refer-ring to the ego being first and foremost a bodily ego, Freud spoke of the body. He described it as:

> ... a place from which both external and internal perceptions may spring. It is *seen* like any other object, but to the *touch* it yields two kinds of sensations, one of which may be equivalent to an inter-nal perception ... a person's own body attains its special position among other objects in the world of perception. (1923b, p. 25)

Mind and body

Before proceeding with the topic of bodily betrayal, I believe it will be helpful to clarify the relationship between mind and body, and I have found Meissner's series of papers on the self and the body particularly illuminating in that regard. Meissner (1997) notes that Freud, in discuss-ing the concept of a bodily ego, was emphasising the body as an object (even when internally perceived) but neglects how the body is also an agent. Upon reflection, it is evident that the bodily ego perceives as well as experiences being perceived. In clarifying the issue, Meissner uses the concept of *body image* to refer to the more objective experience of the body, in contrast to the *body self*, which has both subjective and objective elements and is reflective of the experience of being an embodied self. In explaining the first term, Meissner (1997) refers to Schilder's (1935) definition of *body image* as "the picture of our own body which we form in our minds" and he clarifies that it is "an integrated mental representation of the sum of our sensory, motor, and affective (both pleasurable and unpleasurable) body experiences" (p. 428) He notes that it is likely neither a single image nor a complete image, and it responds dynamically to varying representations of inner states across time and circumstance and is influenced by feedback from others. He also describes how *body images* stem from "experienced bodily percepts" that can become part of memory and that, when aggregated, form the core of our psychological experience of our self.

The term *body self* as used by Meissner (1997) refers to a psychic structure at the core of self-experience, comprised of bodily experiences associated with a "sense of agency, affectivity, and embeddedness in time and space ... [that is] alien to the representational self in which the body image participates" (p. 433). Such self-experience is comprised of both subjective and objective elements and reflects the unity of body and self. Linked as it is to bodily experience, such self-experience "cannot be envisioned as a subjectively contained center of awareness simply observing the body to which it is attached" (p. 435).

To further clarify, consider the example given by Meissner (ibid.) of how I may relate to my hand—I do not simply observe it as something at the end of my arm since I can also voluntarily move it and experience sensations such as touch, temperature, and pain that originate from it. Such sensations do not occur to something beyond subjective awareness—it is experienced as part of me. At times, I may become unaware of my hand, as when resting, but once I begin to use it, "... its presence and participation in my subjective sense of self, and particularly self-as-agent, is revitalized" (p. 435). Thus, the self system is "inherently linked to the body, but in differentiated and heterogeneous ways" (p. 435).

How then might we understand the notion of bodily betrayal, when an argument can be made for such close integration of self and bodily experience? Indeed, in a second paper in a series on self and body, Meissner (1998, p. 108) concludes that "[M]ind and body are in some ultimate sense one," citing how fantasies, even without reference to the body, are fundamentally embodied activities of central nervous system functioning "without taking into consideration the further penumbra of motivational and other influences arising in the sphere of the body" (p. 108). I suggest that the answer is twofold and requires a separate focus on each of the dual concepts of *body image* and *body self* and how they impact self-experience. *Body image betrayal* concerns betrayal by having secrets exposed, while *body self betrayal* relates to experiences of the body failing us, which I will elaborate in the following two sections.

Body image betrayal: shameful exposure

Freud's (1905e) well-known quote on reading the secrets of others stresses the role of the body—fingers and pores—in betraying us to the scrutiny of others:

> He that has eyes to see and ears to hear may convince himself that no mortal can keep a secret. If his lips are silent, he chatters with his fingers; betrayal oozes out of him at every pore. And thus the task of making conscious the most hidden recesses of the mind is one which it is quite possible to accomplish. (pp. 77–78)

The individual may wish to keep hidden certain aspects of his inner life, or be unconsciously motivated to repress specific thoughts and feelings, and in doing so enable the preservation of a cherished self-image. This self-image is often composed of valued expectations and emotionally vested internal representations of how individuals believe they should experience their body. However, the body is seldom compliant in such matters.

Clinical vignette 1

Mrs. R., a patient of mine, needed to maintain a sense of absolute control of her body at every moment and lived in fear that she would make an odd grimace or tic while talking to others that would make her look foolish. She was invested in a view of herself as unreadable, unremarkable, and completely controlled. This was connected to obsessional defences that served to contain aggression and intense emotion, but it also had a specific antecedent in childhood experiences of becoming tongue-tied as a child while angry and thus being exposed to ridicule by her family when trying to express her frustration. She had learned from her experience that her body could fail her at crucial moments and so it was to be held firmly in check if she was to feel confident in her interactions with others. Of course, the resultant pressure to maintain absolute control over her facial expression created unbearable anxiety and only served to make her seem awkward and stiff. Her body image and self-image were inextricably linked in such a way as to create painful self-consciousness and a debilitating lack of confidence.

In treatment, her concern about slipping up in front of me was defensively reversed into a keen interest in reading my body language. This took the form of listening to how I shifted in my chair, the sound of my breathing, and signs of restlessness in my leg movements. These bodily signals were taken as expressions of my hidden disinterest, impatience, and criticism directed towards her. Initially I found myself surrendering to the countertransferential pull to maintain rigid control over my body, thus enacting Mrs. R.'s own experience of needing to rein in her body, but it also helped me appreciate the tyrannical and unnatural state in which she lived. I was gradually able to use my insight about this experience to help Mrs. R. recognise how she collapsed her experience of herself and her body into a singular dynamic of mastery and pained suppression that deprived her of a basic sense of comfort and ease in herself. This not only prevented her enjoying a wide and rich range of bodily experience but it also forced her to relate to others in a tensely vigilant and paranoid manner that cost her dearly in her personal life and career.

Despite how deep the motivation may be to retain a view of our body as a compliant confidant in our dealings with the world, our body image is subject to alteration by changes in circumstance or the intrusion of reality, and as noted above attempts to completely control how our body expresses itself to the world are both futile and costly. It can be contradicted by as common an experience as an unexpected belch or flatulence in public; a failure to stifle a yawn when fatigue sets in at the end of a long work day, or when we set a "poker face" to hide our intentions but a blush or twitch gives the game away.

Bodily noise as inadvertent revelation

The sense of a secret betrayed or the intrusion of an unwanted experience likely gives rise to pressure in the patient to pass over such experiences without comment. I suspect that a similar reaction may be common in analysts also. In my work with Mrs. R., I noted my own resistance to commenting on odd movements she made in settling down onto the couch or the stiffness of her posture. This was due in part to my conscious concern to avoid seeming retaliatory in response to her constant attempts to interpret my own body language. I suspect that just as I found her constant surveillance intrusive, I was stifled by an unconscious concern that a focus on her nonverbal behaviour was too aggressive or invasive. Indeed, in support of the idea that both analysts and patients avoid too close an inspection of nonverbal behaviour, there is scant reference in clinical literature to the exploration of bodily movements, belching, flatulence, body noises, blushing, or facial grimaces during sessions. For example, a search using the PEP-web resulted in three references to belches or belching and of those only one mentioned belching during a session and that was with a former analyst (Etchegoyen, 1982). Flatus is more commonly mentioned in the literature, with 232 instances on the PEP-web, but almost all are theoretical instances or feared possibilities, rather than actual occurrences. For example, Ferenczi (1926) noted:

> It sometimes occurs that analysands have to resist the inclination to pass a clearly audible and also noticeable amount of flatus in the course of the hour; this usually happens when they are being refractory with the doctor. This symptom, however, is intended not only to insult the doctor, but to intimate that the patient intends to allow himself things that his father forbade him, but permitted himself. (p. 325)

Note the experience-far tone and absence of a specific clinical example, as if in writing of such matters one needs to keep a disinterested distance.

In the Wolfman case, Freud (1918b), noted that after promising the patient that he would help him recover normal intestinal activity he (Freud) "then had the satisfaction of seeing his doubt dwindle away, as in the course of the work his bowel began, like a hysterically affected organ, to 'join in the conversation', and in a few weeks' time recovered its normal functions after their long impairment" (p. 76). In both cases, however, no mention is made of how this was addressed with the patients and if they were encouraged to associate to the intrusion of bodily sounds into the session. One is left to guess that in Ferenczi's case, if the flatus expressed aggression, it is probable that the patient experienced it as a betrayal of dark intent, while for the Wolfman and Freud, it was an unacknowledged expression of therapeutic gain and a shared sense of satisfaction. Yet finding two cases among 232 instances—and both cases scant on details—suggests that there may be discomfort for both the analyst and the analysand about delving further into what is being expressed by the body.

Da Silva (1990) writes about borborygmi, or gurgling abdominal sounds, and their significance as markers of psychic work in analysis, as they "often signal a convergence of physiological sensations and emotional contact producing 'moments of truth' about the patient–analyst communication" (p. 641). Unlike belching or flatulence, wherein there is a degree of conscious control over the escape of gas, with borborygmi the phenomena are:

> ... felt to be outside conscious control and difficult to localize precisely within a somewhat estranged part of the body ... a system within the primitive maternal transference ... felt to be under the special care of God, fate, nature or doctor ... all images of the primal object representation. (p. 642)

Akin to my findings on flatulence and belching, he notes a remarkable absence in the literature on borborygmi, despite his assumption that they are commonplace in most analyses, and thus he surmises that "[R]eporting them must encroach on a taboo involving the most intimate communication within the most intimate relationship of primal maternal transference with merging components" (p. 643). He notes how he repeatedly finds borborygmi associated with fantasies of devouring the object, hallucinatory sensations of reliving experiences of satisfaction, and of being fed by the analyst. In such instances, it would overstate the case to argue that a patient commonly feels a sense of betrayal, although there may be reluctance to admit to fears of devouring the other or to dependent urges to be fed by the analyst.

However, McLaughlin (1992) provides a somewhat different perspective on the meaning of borborygmi in his report of the analysis of a woman in her twenties, during which the analyst noticed sounds of the patient's gut rumbling and then felt "surprised, and a bit abashed" to hear his own "gut sounds, piping a kind of counterpoint, or obbligato, to hers" (p. 145). On later occasions when discussing her mother's attentiveness to when she was hurting, and her stomach would begin to sound again during the session, the patient seemed to be waiting for the analyst's reply. McLaughlin noted that when his stomach occasionally responded he "silently resigned" and that although:

> ... I may have been acting analytically ... I felt some anxious press to reclaim the right to speak for myself when I acknowledged that we both seemed to find some special meaning in the images of a caring mother being close to her hurting child. (p. 146)

Note his emphasis of feelings of surprise, abashment, and resignation— as if he had been caught out by his own body. Given the scant attention to such matters in our literature I suspect that both analysts and their patients have a reluctance to further reinforce their bodies' attempts to expose intimate or conflicted feelings, yet it seems to be a rich field of potential exploration into how the body is experienced and incorporated into our relationships and our sense of self.

Cryptic motions and manifest signs

Conflict, experienced as a subjective sense of betrayal, may occur between competing perceptions of how one's body actually is, how it is wished to be, and how it ought to be (which can also be conceived as intrapsychic conflict between the ego, ego ideal, and superego). The term "traducement" might best be used to signify the subjective experience of this particular form of bodily betrayal—an exposure to shame or blame by means of misrepresentation. Shame occurs in the presence of another person who is assumed to be critical, but it can also occur when alone due to internal criticism arising from a variety of sources, including the superego, an internalised rejecting object, or an imagined audience. The body in such instances is experienced as the source of the treacherous exposure—the traitor of the humiliated self.

McLaughlin (ibid.) provides several examples of how his patients experienced their body as exposing them to shame or blame. One of his patients would pick at the skin of his thumbs causing them to bleed. The therapist began to attend to this behaviour both out of concern for how the patient was mutilating himself but also because he knew from his own analysis of similar behaviour that it could be expressive of rich dynamic material. He assumed that the patient was aware of the pain he was causing to himself but when he mentioned it to him, the patient:

> … showed shock, anxiety and speechlessness … At that moment of his confusion I intervened actively to reflect upon his apparent state and how what I had done had upset him so. Gradually he regrouped and spoke of being entirely unaware of his skin picking, he felt caught and about to be given a beating or told he was unanalyzable and we were through. (pp. 137–138)

Later in the analysis, the patient relayed how his mother would become enraged at him when he bit his nails as a child and yet despite frequent punishment, it was a habit that she was powerless to force him to relinquish. Clearly, the patient was distressed by the bodily expression of feeling caught and exposed to punishment, but the sense of unexpected exposure gave rise to powerful affect and deepening of the therapeutic process.

In a second example of how patients may unwittingly reveal shameful material through bodily motion, McLaughlin (ibid.) describes his work with a female patient who would become increasingly tense and would draw "… her knees upward and flex them so that both feet were flat on the couch. She brought her hands to her shoes, and hooked both forefingers around the heels" (p. 148). This gave rise to anxiety in the patient that she would seduce her analyst or that he would attempt to penetrate her. Later work revealed that she had suffered chronic urinary problems from the age of six to fourteen that required frequent urological exams. She was made to lie still for many urological exams and procedures, often prolonged and painful, on her back in stirrups. Continued exploration of her memories indicated that she had felt "frequent genital stirrings and erotic interest in some of the doctors. She recalled both feeling ashamed and frightened that her excitement might show, as well as defiant protest that it was not her fault the doctors wanted to do these things to her" (p. 149).

It is worth noting that complex dynamics are not only evident in the disavowal of erotic interest through projection onto her analyst and doctors, but also through the embodied expression of desire so that it is experienced as separate from the patient's conscious experience. In acts of betrayal, the betrayed can locate the greater sin of transgression in the betrayal itself, and in a deft form of compromise avoid feeling the depths of shame or distress associated with the revealed secret. Instead, feelings of shock and horror can be reserved for the form of the betrayal—"I cannot believe how my own body exposes me!" As analysts, we may be prone to focus on the revealed content and to feel a measure of satisfaction over deciphering the meaning of the body's communication, but we can miss the subtle ways in which the patient's shock or disgust may be centred on the form of the exposure rather than newly conscious material. However, a more complicated situation exists when a patient has no means to disguise the source of his shame as this next vignette illustrates.

Clinical vignette 2

Mr. F. was a middle-aged patient whom I had treated over the course of several years for depression and masochistic self-loathing. Mr. F. had undergone surgery to remove a sarcoma of his jaw that had left visible scarring and disfigurement to the right side of his face. His relationship to his own body was marked by bitterness as he had suffered from a prior diagnosis of cancer and childhood diabetes; his scarring was the final cruel sign to the world of his physical vulnerability and alienation from others. Depressive episodes as an adolescent, related to his diabetes, had caused him to withdraw from his family: locking himself in his room and vainly waiting for someone to enter and comfort him.

Since his surgery he would oscillate between a desire for connection with others and a tendency to hide from them by ignoring phone messages or cancelling social plans at the last minute. He felt certain that his physical appearance caused others to find him repellent and he was convinced that their polite indulgence would inevitably change to harsh rejection. Furthermore, his loathing of the body that had betrayed him created difficulty for him in enjoying his own physicality; pleasurable activities such as jogging or walking were approached with great ambivalence.

His continued social isolation caused him to feel depressed and he despaired of resolving his loneliness as he felt repugnant and thus unlovable. If individuals recognised him and engaged in conversation, he would assume that it was only his face that they recalled and that their reintroduction to him was not due to any real wish for connection or interest in him as a person. Over time,

I challenged him to recognise that it was he who reduced himself to his facial appearance and that, by projecting this view onto others, he condemned himself to a lonely life of self-imposed exile.

This insight was brought more fully to life in the transference by working through his concerns that I also found him repellant, and by helping him tolerate my gaze without assuming I was disgusted or as condemning of him as he felt towards himself. Not surprisingly, this led to an understanding of the myriad ways in which he punished his body through masochistic deprivation and clarified how he blamed not others for his misery but, more horrifyingly, his own body and waited in dread anticipation for the day when it would completely betray him by developing a lethal cancer.

When a patient's bodily flaws are unavoidably exposed to the world, as in the case of facial scarring, there is a risk that the patient will maintain a sense of being continually betrayed by his or her body. For the patient, due to the chronic nature of this irresolvable dilemma, there can be a deep and persistent sense of indignation and anger towards one's body, which is felt to be a necessary retaliation against a constant enemy. This requires sensitivity on the therapist's part, as the outward manifestation reinforces the patient's conviction that the body's role in the continuing betrayal is an incontrovertible fact and thus unforgivable. Any suggestion that there might be alternative ways to relate to his body will be met with scepticism, and a first step in opening up that discussion requires acknowledgement of the reality of his disfigurement and empathy for how violated and exposed he feels. Only with tolerant empathy and by an honest reckoning of his or her own reactions to the disfigurement, can the therapist then introduce the notion that others may react with less aversion and disdain than the patient reserves for himself. However, this process is made somewhat easier when the circumstances of the betrayal are a fate shared by us all—the mortal givens of illness, aging, and death—as the next section describes.

Body self betrayal: illness, aging, and infirmity

The second major category of bodily betrayal is related to the experience of the body self when our body fails us in a time of need or delivers us to our mortal end. We all fear the likelihood of illness and the certainty of death, although not all of us are destined to experience illness and death as a profound betrayal by the body. Among those who might are individuals who cling to a naïve idealisation of the body's invulnerability and defensively expect to be immune to disease or the ravages of aging. Those who are unable to contemplate threats to the self without a sense of disorganising anxiety may also react to illness or signs of mortality with a sense of shock and betrayal. For others, buried or accommodated conflicts about security and dependence may be reignited by the threat of debilitating illness.

However, even in more common responses to illness and mortality, although the sense of betrayal may not be so profound, it is often present and voiced in the awareness that one no longer feels quite right in one's own body—organs are not working as they should, muscles are tired or pained, movement is slowed, breathing laboured. Somehow, the compact between body and self seems to have broken down and now our body has delivered us to the ravages of time, that great ceaseless enemy forever assaulting the walls that we have placed around our unconscious fantasies of immortality. Where before in a healthier past, we could calmly claim that we knew we would one day die, our failing body transforms that knowledge from something abstract to something pressing and all too real.

Chronic illness

Chronic illness is a common culprit in forcing us to face our embodied limitations and the inescapability of the physical. Among the more common chronic conditions are pain (including chronic back pain, arthritis, neuropathy, and fibromyalgia), stroke, diabetes, Parkinson's disease, and dementia. Less common yet devastating are Huntington's disease and ALS (motor neurone disease). Space precludes a comprehensive discussion of each of these illnesses, so I will focus instead on multiple sclerosis as it is a complicated disease that affects both mind and body and serves to highlight how an individual can feel forsaken by his own body as the result of illness.

Segal (2007) cites that 400,000 Americans suffer from multiple sclerosis, a disease that affects central motor and sensory nerve pathways. She notes that it can manifest itself in a variety of symptoms including impaired vision, mobility, bladder, and bowel functions; paralysis, and cognitive impairment including memory, learning, and attention deficits, executive dysfunction and visuospatial deficits. It often has an unpredictable course and there is neither cure nor a sure means to prevent deterioration, and Segal notes that it can create a sense of impotence in health professionals. The uncertainty and loss of control faced by patients may cause them to make others feel "controlled, hopeless and useless" (p. 173). Unsurprisingly, it is associated with high rates of depression with one study reporting a lifetime prevalence of 50 percent (Siegert & Abernethy, 2005).

Segal (2007) also makes some incisive observations about the interrelationship between physical, cognitive, and emotional symptoms. The body can suddenly give out, causing a loss of balance or a fall; and simple physical tasks may no longer be doable, leading to a loss of security and confidence in one's own body. The mind may slowly degenerate with shifts in capacity for insight, judgment, and empathy, and emotions become labile or flattened. The sensations of embodiment change as sensory pathways are affected and cognitive and emotional changes impact relationships with others, causing the MS patient to feel alienated from his self, his body and others. As the external body fails, it may be experienced as representative of damaged self, giving rise to feelings of humiliation and shame and to anxieties about goodness and badness, care of the self, and the capacity to be loved and to love.

Clinical vignette 3

Mr. W. was a sixty-three-year-old male patient who had been suffering from multiple sclerosis for close to three decades by the time he came to see me for therapy. His condition was complicated by a recent diagnosis of multiple myeloma that required ongoing chemotherapy to keep his cancer at bay, but that also increased his general weakness and worsened his symptoms of MS. He presented early on with a bruise on his right eye that was a result of a fall due to a lapse in attention while walking down stairs the previous week. While his wife tried to be protective of him, Mr. W. was determined to remain independent. He explained that he trusted his unconscious to protect him, although he expected me to be critical of such a view. Exploration of this concern clarified his wish to be prevented from acting recklessly as he attempted to fight, at times self-destructively, against the imposed limits of his MS.

His life was characterised by constant concern about his legs becoming unpredictably stiff or weak and causing him to lose his balance. With regard to his cancer, he feared its recurrence but often found himself "blanking out" awareness of his prognosis for fear of being overwhelmed by feelings of sadness and loss. He became concerned about his legacy, as he had no children, and he had recently started the process of retirement from work. He slowly came to tolerate his sadness in our sessions, and his increased sense of vulnerability enabled him to consider how his choices in life might become increasingly more constrained and so it was imperative for him to have a more meaningful life while he could still enjoy it.

As he continued to struggle with increased weakness from his chemotherapy and the effects of steroids, he felt more and more at odds with his own body and began to project his sense of alienation onto me. He grew increasingly concerned that I had patients with more pressing needs and that I would suddenly abandon him if he became much sicker. Together, we were able to understand that this reflected his growing sense of loneliness as his illnesses narrowed his life and caused him to fear that the sword hanging over his head would cut into his health and cut him off from others. He came to appreciate his deep sense of anger over his failing body and how he often used a show of independence to push others away in order to avoid expected rejection and humiliation.

A chronic illness that causes debilitation can give rise to an illusion that one is at war with one's body and drive an individual to vindictively destructive behaviour aimed towards the body yet ultimately self annihilating. Working through feelings of vulnerability and mourning for his changed body can help bring cohesion to the patient's experience of the body self.

Midlife changes and unexpected illness

Viederman (1989) wrote of mutative change occurring as a result of aging whereby the "inevitable small hurts garnered in the years of middle life ultimately lead to more subtle and malleable ideal self-representation" (p. 224) that allows an individual to accept his limitations and to prepare to confront greater decline as he grows old. However, this mutative process can be rudely interrupted by premature illness. The individual has not had sufficient experience to adjust to the reality of an aging body or to accept more limitations—instead the illness is felt as an unjust shock that often feels like a deep betrayal. Viederman (ibid.) describes how an individual may experience a dramatic change in self representation, which can lead to depression due to a discrepancy between self and ideal self representations. If a more limited aspect of the self is imposed, then the individual may experience mourning for that aspect thereby changed. The individual can also experience a great sense of anger towards his body for depriving him of this aspect or view of himself, and suicidal ideation is not uncommon as an expression of a wish to punish the treacherous body. A second consequence of premature serious illness is that it creates a disruption in the individual's life trajectory. Viederman notes that the schema for one's life trajectory may vary in the degree to which it is founded on "nonconflictual motivations or defenses against unconscious fears of weakness, inadequacy, lack of masculinity, and so on" (p. 233) but, regardless, there are serious psychic consequences when one's life trajectory is interrupted. The following case illustrates these issues.

Clinical vignette 4

Mr. D. was a fifty-five-year-old man who was referred to see me after being recently treated for early stage colon cancer. He had undergone surgery and chemotherapy and he suffered minimal side effects. However, he had been warned that should his cancer recur there were likely no viable treatment options remaining. He had no prior history of serious illness and so he was left not only to cope with an uncertain prognosis but he was also struggling with the unfamiliar awareness of his own mortality. His parents and grandparents had all lived into their nineties and he had always assumed he would do likewise. Early on in the treatment I clarified how the diagnosis of cancer had shattered that assumption and also challenged his view of himself as someone who had always been lucky enough in life to avoid major misfortune and illness. He experienced this comment as a significant turning point in opening him to the meaning and experience of his relationship to his body.

During treatment, he developed a small cyst on his thigh and his concern that it was a tumour caused him to feel drawn down into a dark place of futility and hopelessness. As we explored what this "swamp-like" place was like for him he came to understand that he could not ignore it or lay it aside, but neither did he need to allow it to spread into all areas of his life (akin to his fear of what a recurrent cancer would do). The feelings stirred up in him by his experience of cancer caused him to reflect on how his diagnosis may have been an unusual opportunity to "really think about dying and facing what it means".

During this time, a visit to an archaeological exhibit caused him to feel unexpected sadness when looking at the flint tools used by Neanderthals. Exploration of his feeling clarified that the flint lithics that were used to form new tools not only connected him to someone long dead but also represented an object that had finite use and that would be gradually chipped away and discarded. I suggested that it was possible that the Neanderthal tool-user would not think of the end of the lithic's usefulness but might instead focus on what was left, and Mr. D. responded to this idea by reflecting on how what mattered was his current life and how he lived the time remaining—the end was beyond contemplation. Later concern about fatigue as a symptom of recurrent cancer was understood to reflect a fear of indulging himself in relaxation as it represented giving up on the fight against cancer. He realised, however, that he needed to shift from the urgent need to "keep on living" to an attitude of "going on living".

Over time, Mr. D. became more reconciled to how he related to somatic anxiety and he noted how in his dreams of poisonous snakes he was able to transform them into harmless creatures: representative of untamed fears yet significantly less threatening. He reported that his anxiety had changed from a feeling that "starts on top and pushes down until it's unbearable" to a feeling that "comes up from below" and dissipates more easily. He framed this as a more natural feeling of somatic anxiety that felt less overwhelming because it was not repressed, but instead experienced as appropriate. His body was no longer felt to be an enemy, even when it was a source or discomfort or worry.

Unexpected illness or sudden physical changes due to aging can be experienced as a surprise attack by the body: a betrayal made all the worse by its "blindsiding" us. The shock can make the wound feel deeper, and early work in therapy often needs to centre on coming to terms with the reality of this narcissistic injury and consequent disappointment.

The body's ultimate betrayal: death

Equanimity and tolerance towards the body is difficult to maintain, however, in the face of pending death. Death, once it makes it entrance upon the final act of our life, is seldom graceful. Its early stages are marked by cognitive impairment in the ability to grasp ideas, disorientation, loss of visual acuity, dulling of some senses and heightening of others (such as sensitivity to bright lights), increased heart rate and breathing, gasping for air, apnoea, gradual loss of the ability to move, urinary incontinence or retention, and an inability to cough or clear secretions resulting in gurgling or congested breathing, also known as the death rattle. Its final stages are typically characterised by loss of consciousness, eyes that are half open and no longer blinking, doubled heart rate and irregular rhythm, cool skin, and mottled extremities (Berry & Griffie, 2010). It may seem that in the face of such an end, there is little to be done by way of psychotherapy.

Hulsey and Frost (1995), however, argue that psychoanalytic psychotherapy with its emphasis on the unconscious and analysis of transference helps to soothe dying patients by providing a level of understanding beyond the obvious and by clarifying core dynamic conflicts that may allow the patient to make more conscious choices about the experience of dying. Further, they argue that the "same pattern of conflict and defense that served to shape the personality in life also shapes the death and the response to death" (p. 147). What is striking in their paper, however, is the scant attention given to the patient's relationship to his or her failing body. Typical case studies describing work with dying patients neglect to elaborate on the patients' fantasies about their bodies, instead focusing on fantasies regarding the illness itself or describing the concrete limits imposed by the progression of the illness. For example, Minerbo (1998), in describing her work with a patient dying of cancer, reflects on how the patient's disease caused her to live in slow motion and the patient laughingly agreed; closer to the end of her life, the patient also mentioned feeling glad that her hair had not fallen out but also being disappointed that she had not lost more weight from the chemotherapy. These two references to the body were unelaborated and the central (and—I must stress—quite impressive) work of the therapy was around reconciliation with the patient's family and the deepening of her capacity to feel genuinely loved. It is odd that the patient had so little to say about her body, although I suspect that was in part due to the disembodied nature of the therapy as it was conducted by phone.

One might imagine that in the final stages of life we become consumed with the body and overcome with a deep sense of anger and resentment over how it has let us down, along with frustration over how it is barely under our conscious control. Yet I have not found that to be a common experience for the dying patients I have worked with. McDougall (2004), in writing of her treatment of a patient dying from cancer, addresses her patient's tendency to experience herself as a disembodied mind. Yet what is striking about this is that the patient's disembodiment preceded her cancer—in fact McDougall points out that it seemed that the patient could only have a body on condition it suffers and threatens her with death. I suspect that death, rather than creating estrangement from the body, may create an unexpected reconciliation and an unavoidable deepening of the experience of embodiment as the life-giving and ultimately delicate link between mind and body becomes ever more apparent.

Clinical vignette 5

I am reminded of a final session of Mrs. D., a fifty-eight-year-old woman who was actively dying of liver cancer. She had come to me initially because she had started to become upset by the onslaught of physical symptoms she was experiencing and by their impact on her functioning. As her condition worsened, she was most afraid about uncertainty and being unprepared for death. She regretted the loss of her physical strength and independence, yet she was not estranged from her body, and instead continued to take pleasure in her limited capacity for independent movement.

However, she declined quickly towards the end, and she was housebound and bedridden when I visited her for what was to be our final session. She was experiencing intense pain in her abdomen and legs and she had difficulty speaking. Yet she had no wish to die any sooner than she must, despite her bodily discomfort, and carefully enunciated to me that she was "not scared to die but simply not ready to die". We discussed many things in that final session, including our awareness that it was possibly our last meeting, but what stood out to me was her response to my question as to what she wanted most in the time before she died.

She grasped my hand tightly and with a determined voice told me that what she most wanted was to enjoy sex with her husband. I confess that this was the last thing I expected to hear coming from the mouth of a woman with a swollen and painful abdomen and barely enough energy to move her head, but human nature never fails to surprise and delight. Her response was a reminder to me that even in the face of death, as the body fades, we need not treat it as an enemy or traitor. In fact, it can still give rise to the most human of desires—the longing for embodied intimacy.

Betrayal, especially as ultimate a betrayal as death, can foster profound despair within us. The enemy is within the gates and all hope now seems lost. Yet dying can also be a final opportunity to reconcile ourselves to the experience of embodiment and, while mourning its ending, to revel in every last moment of what it is to live in the wondrous embrace of this mortal coil.

Concluding remarks

In this contribution, I have considered the nature of the relationship between body and self and suggested how we might meaningfully speak of a betrayal by the body. Our bodies may betray us by revealing hidden aspects of ourselves that run counter to our expectation that we are absolute masters of ourselves, or by subverting our attempts to keep our unconscious muted and imprisoned in the deep recesses of our body self. We may also experience betrayal when our body begins to fail us in its safeguarding of our physical health and in its final submission to the demands of time and mortality. These concerns are an unavoidable aspect of the human condition and thus are worthy of analytic attention, and we must be prepared for the range of intense reactions that patients may have to this experience of bodily betrayal.

Betrayal elicits a variety of responses within us: shock and denial, a wish for retaliation, hopelessness, and a profound confusion over why we were betrayed. The more intimate the relationship to the traitor the greater the shock and denial, and if we believe it is our body that has betrayed us then the denial may run deep: to the point of neglecting our physical well-being. Such neglect may become a form of retaliation against the body, carried to an extreme when death is wished for and sought out. Despair may set in, as there may seem to be no escape from the machinations of the treacherous soma. And when the body seems opposed to the well-being of the self, boundaries become bewildering and the conscious and unconscious assumptions and expectations we once held dear are suddenly bereft of substance. Yet there are other possibilities that can be facilitated by a psychoanalytic process. Intolerance for guilt-ridden secrets and fear of loss of control can be tempered into acceptance and understanding. Indeed, the body can come to be regarded as a welcome messenger from the unconscious, an ally in treatment and in life. Elaboration of the meaning of bodily expressions through exploration of fantasy and interpretation can lead to a profound and enlivening reconciliation with our body. Even in the face of illness and death we need not be estranged from our physical self; indeed, that is often a time when it is crucial to remember how truly the ego is first and foremost a bodily ego.

PART II

LITERARY REALM

CHAPTER FIVE

The theme of betrayal in the works of "William Shakespeare"

Richard M. Waugaman

We have betrayed Shakespeare. We have failed to recognise his true identity. Any discussion of the theme of betrayal in his works must begin here. We psychoanalysts have also betrayed Freud, in "analysing" rather than evaluating objectively Freud's passionately held belief during his final years that "William Shakespeare" was the pseudonym of the Elizabethan courtier poet and playwright Edward de Vere, Earl of Oxford (1550–1604).[1] Freud realised one unconscious motive for our betrayal of Shakespeare[2] is our implacable wish to idealise him. That is, we prefer to accept the traditional author not just *in spite of* how little we know about him, but precisely *because* we know so little about him. Thus, we can more easily imagine that this shadowy ink blot of a figure was as perfect a person as are his literary creations. The real Shakespeare was a highly flawed human being who knew betrayal first-hand since his childhood, from both sides, as the betrayer and as the betrayed.

Betrayal in the works of Shakespeare

Betrayal recurs as a salient theme throughout the works of Shakespeare. Shakespeare was never content with simplistic explanations of any action or emotion, including betrayal. Characteristically, his writings are so alive and true to life because he recognised and depicted the full complexity of the real world, avoiding the oversimplified representations that so often scotomise and limit our understanding of people. So it is with his portrayals of betrayal. He thus helps us reflect on the many levels of meaning of feeling betrayed; of being overly trusting; or of realising one has betrayed another.

Perhaps the best known three words in all of Shakespeare are *"Et tu Brute?"* ("Even you, Brutus?"), spoken by Julius Caesar as he realises Brutus has betrayed him and has joined the treasonous conspirators.[3] Caesar's next words are "Then fall Caesar." Betrayal by someone he so deeply trusted leads the mighty Caesar to crumble and submit to his assassination. Characteristically, Shakespeare gives us such a balanced picture of Caesar and his enemies that we can view both sides with some sympathy. Like a good psychoanalyst, Shakespeare refrains from being judgmental. The conspirators have good reason to fear that Caesar intends to subvert their beloved Roman republic, and revert to a dictatorship.

One way Shakespeare saves Caesar from our complete contempt is through unconscious communication with the audience (Waugaman, 2007). Contrary to past assumptions, it now seems likely that Shakespeare easily read both Latin and ancient Greek. So he knew that Suetonius wrote that Caesar's last words were *"Kai su, teknon?"* or "Even you, my son?" But, in addition, Shakespeare was echoing the form of Jesus's expression of betrayal by his heavenly Father in his dying words in his native Aramaic, *"Eloi, eloi, lama sabachthani?"* ("My God, my God, why hast thou forsaken me?"). This illustrates Shakespeare's unrivalled use of unconscious communication as one of the many ways he moves us. That is, Caesar "code switches" to a foreign tongue to ask a question at the moment of his betrayal and submission to death, just as Jesus does in two of the Gospels. The audience is subliminally encouraged by this parallel to view Caesar as a Christlike martyr, and therefore a more sympathetic figure.

Shirley Garner (1989) writes that betrayal is such a recurrent theme in Shakespeare that we can make some plausible speculations about conflicts with trust and deception in the life of the author. In particular, Garner focuses on the five plays where men feel profoundly betrayed by women (falsely, except in *Troilus and Cressida*). Garner shows that the jealous men in these plays have such deep mistrust of women that they engage in compensatory idealisation, which makes them all the more vulnerable to disillusionment. Garner believes that the sequence of the plays suggests that Shakespeare gradually came to understand that the primary problem was not that women actually betray men, but that some men suffer from a "diseased imagination" that leads to their *false* suspicions of women. She also infers that Shakespeare keeps repeating a core fantasy that women will always forgive the man who wrongs them, including wronging them through men's pathological jealousy of women. So Shakespeare makes it clear that the subjective feeling of betrayal may result from pathological jealousy, rather than from actual duplicity. Simultaneously, there may be "pathological trust" in the wrong person.

Here is a brief summary of the themes of betrayal in the five plays Garner addresses:

- In *Othello*, the title character develops pathological jealousy of his new wife, Desdemona, as a result of his falsely placed trust in Iago. Iago fiendishly plays on Othello's insecurities to manipulate him into misinterpreting Desdemona's innocent behaviour as certain proof that she has been unfaithful. In a pattern found in other plays by Shakespeare, Othello's erroneous belief that he has been betrayed by Desdemona leads *him* to betray *her*—in Othello's case, by murdering her.
- Similarly, in *The Winter's Tale*, Leontes is pathologically jealous of his wife, Hermione. When she is innocently hospitable towards Leontes's visiting friend Polixenes, Leontes convinces himself (without the help of any Iago-like character) that Hermione is in love with Polixenes. Leontes then turns on Hermione so viciously that she dies of grief because of her husband's betrayal. But many years later, a statue of Hermione magically comes to life, and she is reunited with Leontes.
- In *Much Ado about Nothing*, Claudio and other characters falsely believe Hero has been unfaithful to him. It is the treachery of Don John that slanders Hero's virtue. Hero is so horrified by Claudio's false accusation that she faints and is believed to be dead. By the end of the play, Don John's plot is exposed, Hero has revived, and she marries Claudio.
- *Troilus and Cressida*, set during the Trojan War, borrows its plot from the poem of the same name by Chaucer. The Trojans Troilus and

Cressida fall in love with each other. But soon after their love is consummated, Cressida is forced by her father to be turned over to the Greeks, whom he has joined. The incredulous Troilus watches at a distance as Cressida is unfaithful to him with Diomedes, a Greek.

- In *Cymbeline*, Posthumus marries Imogen in Britain, then he leaves for Italy. While he is away, Imogen falsely believes he has been killed. Jachimo, Iago-like, then falsely claims to Posthumus that Imogen has cuckolded him with Jachimo.

To this list, I might add two additional plays where betrayal is also a central theme, but it is a group of people rather than one woman which is the perceived betrayer.

- The title character of *Timon of Athens* is generous to a fault, lavishly (and manically?) entertaining his large circle of ostensible friends, and showering them with expensive gifts. But when he learns from his servant that he is insolvent, not a single "friend" is willing to help him. After this betrayal, Timon says "I am Misanthropos, and hate mankind" (IV. iii. 54).
- *Coriolanus* is a courageous and successful Roman general, who returns from war and is expected to humble himself before the people so that he will be elected consul, a high political office. His pride will not permit him to follow this tradition, and he instead insults the people. Their adulation quickly turns to scorn, and they banish Coriolanus from Rome. Feeling betrayed by them, Coriolanus betrays the Romans by joining with their enemy.

Connections between the life and the works of "Shakespeare"

Shakespeare's sonnets reveal a poet who knows first-hand the deeply deranging power of jealousy: "For if I should despair, I should grow mad,/And in my madness might speak ill of thee" (Sonnet 140). And of betrayal: "For, thou betraying me, I do betray/My nobler part to my gross body's treason" (Sonnet 151). Garner (ibid.) perceptively contrasts the theme of betrayal in Shakespeare's plays with its role in his sonnets. She speculates that the more autobiographical sonnets record Shakespeare's betrayal by the Fair Youth and by his mistress. Garner considers the plays to be a sort of reparative "counterfantasy to the

Sonnets—men banding together, in the plays, to protect themselves from imagined betrayal by women. She writes, "I have wondered whether Shakespeare needed to repeat in reverse the experience of the *Sonnets* [in writing his plays] in order to come to terms with it" (p. 149).

It has become surprisingly controversial in recent years to speculate about connections between the works and the life of Shakespeare. Theories of literary criticism during past decades (including New Criticism, New Historicism, and Postmodernism) have all undermined traditional interest in connecting a work with its author. There is sometimes a dangerously misleading false dichotomy that claims Shakespeare illustrates the creative potential of native genius, so that he did not need relevant life experiences to shape his literary works. Courageously, Norman Holland has continued to assert a legitimate role for psychoanalytic literary criticism, in the face of this growing opposition. As Holland (Holland, Homan & Paris, 1989) puts it, "The psychoanalyst plays by different rules from the literary historian. A historian of Renaissance literature might feel it right, useful, or necessary to think always within the Renaissance concept of the self ... [while] [t]he psychoanalyst tries to interpret individuals ... more fully than they can interpret themselves" (p. 5). Remarkably, given his traditional authorship assumption, Holland admits that one way Shakespeare copes with his core aggressive conflicts is "by making himself invisible" (p. 7). Indeed. This goes to the heart of Freud's theory that "Shakespeare" cloaked his real identity in literary anonymity, through the use of a pen name. Naturally, this is not what Holland meant. He merely implied that Shakespeare hid behind his literary creations.

However, I agree with Freud that a meaningful psychoanalytic investigation of the works of Shakespeare requires us to know who the author actually was. As a result, some of my publications on Shakespeare have had to pursue literary and historical evidence as to his true identity. This chapter includes such details. I hope that readers will bear with me. Such work is needed so we can persuade defenders of the traditional author that they are wrong.

Here, I will focus on the theme of betrayal in Sonnet 121 ("'Tis better to be vile than vile esteem'd"). The sonnets are a rich lode of some of Shakespeare's most brilliant and psychologically complex creative work. But they have suffered from relative neglect ever since 1623, when they were omitted from the *"First Folio"*, the first edition of Shakespeare's collected plays. By contrast, the literary precedent for Shakespeare's 1623 collection, Ben Jonson's "*First Folio*" of 1616 *did* include Jonson's poetry, along with his plays. The sonnet's story includes repeated acts of betrayal, by the poet, by the Fair Youth, and by the Dark Lady.

Many psychoanalysts remain unaware that Freud was keenly interested in the question of Shakespeare's true identity. When he died, half of Freud's books on English literature were devoted to that topic. And he became "all but convinced" by 1920 that Edward de Vere, Earl of Oxford was the author of the Shakespeare canon. Roland Emmerich's 2011 film *Anonymous* has brought increased public attention to this theory. But it remains surprisingly and bitterly controversial, especially among academic Shakespeare specialists.[4] In every field, major intellectual breakthroughs are sometimes made by non-specialists, who are not as wedded to the dogmatic assumptions that dominate specialists in that field, and who do not have as much at stake if their innovative ideas are rejected. For example, it was a non-geologist who discovered continental drift, some fifty years before geologists stopped ridiculing his theory and accepted it as accurate.

Space does not allow me to give a full account here of the fascinating evidence that has accumulated since Freud's day that he was correct about Shakespeare's identity. Two books that originally belonged to de Vere have strongly supported Freud on this score. These two books, bound together, are the *Geneva Bible* (1570), and the Sternhold and Hopkins *Whole Book of Psalms* (1569). Their handwritten annotations show a remarkable overlap with biblical passages that most influenced the works of Shakespeare. Those who support the traditional authorship theory have mostly ignored this evidence, or have tried to dismiss it by speculating that someone other than de Vere made these annotations, after reading Shakespeare's works; or that these were simply the most popular Bible verses of Shakespeare's day (they were not). This resembles efforts to defend the once traditional Ptolemaic geocentric solar system by creating ever more "epicycles" to rationalise apparently contradictory evidence from new observations of the movement of the planets and stars. Further, no one had previously recognised that the primary source for Shakespeare's abundant allusions to the Psalms was that now obscure translation owned by de Vere, until the present author found them, thanks to the twenty-one psalms that are marked by hand in de Vere's copy (see Waugaman 2009a, 2009c, 2010a, 2010c, 2011a).

Betrayal in the life of Edward de Vere

As I hinted earlier, there was no lack of betrayal in the life of Edward de Vere. As we ponder these pivotal betrayals during his early development, it is easy to infer that he was left with multiple narcissistic wounds, and the sort of narcissistic rage that is ever on the lookout for future hurts, real or imaginary, in order to rationalise wishes to take revenge. In addition, his capacity to trust must have been profoundly shaken. His father died when he was twelve. Soon afterwards, his older sister Katherine took de Vere to court, unsuccessfully trying to have the court declare him a bastard. If she had succeeded, she hoped to take away his sizeable inheritance. He was then removed from his mother, who died six years later, when he was eighteen.

Queen Elizabeth had him raised by William Cecil, though de Vere may have suspected Cecil of having had his father killed. The queen proceeded to seize much of de Vere's wealth by the time he turned twenty-one (Nina Green, 2009). Cecil, as de Vere's guardian, had control over whom he married. Cecil had de Vere marry his own daughter (and de Vere's "foster-sister") Anne, thus elevating her to the rank of countess. The queen elevated Cecil to Lord Burghley at the same time. Although the queen kept her word about the mysterious annual pension of 1,000 pounds she began paying de Vere in 1586, de Vere's surviving letters suggest that he felt the queen broke many other promises she made to him of other forms of financial assistance.

Like many victims, de Vere sometimes turned the tables and identified with the aggressor, becoming a ruthless victimiser. For reasons that remain unclear, he killed a servant in Cecil's home when he was seventeen, with his fencing rapier. Some have speculated that de Vere became murderously enraged when he learned this servant was spying on him. Cecil did employ a large network of spies. Eight years later, de Vere seemed to suffer from malignant jealousy of his first wife, Anne. They married when he was twenty-one. When he was twenty-five, he travelled without her on the Continent for fourteen months.[5] When he learned while on this trip that Anne was pregnant, he became convinced it was not his child (thus turning against his child his sister's earlier accusation of illegitimacy). He therefore refused to live with his wife for several years after he returned to England. It has been speculated that he falsely thought he never consummated their marriage. One possibility is that his wife played a "bed trick" on him (as in *All's Well that*

Ends Well and *Measure for Measure*; see Janet Adelman, 1989), and that she got pregnant when he had sex with her, while falsely believing he was having sex with a different woman. Since de Vere was bisexual, it is also possible that conflicted homosexual fantasies contributed to his pathological jealousy of Anne, a dynamic that has been reported by Freud and subsequent analysts.

When he was twenty-nine, de Vere felt insulted by Philip Sidney, a respected poet whose earlier engagement to Anne Cecil was broken by her father so she could marry de Vere. Sidney challenged de Vere to a duel, and de Vere accepted. But the queen forbade the duel, on the traditional grounds of Sidney's lower social status. De Vere later boasted to friends that he could have Sidney killed without getting caught. When he was thirty, he betrayed both his wife and the queen by impregnating one of the queen's ladies-in-waiting, Anne Vavasour. When their illegitimate child (Edward de Vere) was born, de Vere, Vavasour, and their infant son were all imprisoned in the Tower of London.

After his release a few weeks later, de Vere was exiled from court for two years. When de Vere was thirty-three, his wife Anne died a few days after giving birth to their fourth child. During the years following her death, de Vere seemed to feel remorse for how wretchedly he had treated her. His plays suggest he may have developed some insight into his past proclivity to feel groundless jealousy of her. In fact, he may have used some of his plays to make reparation to his deceased wife, as he accused himself of acting like Othello and Leontes.

There is circumstantial evidence that de Vere was involved in at least two pivotal love triangles. As I have mentioned, de Vere was bisexual. When the twenty-five-year-old de Vere returned from Italy, he brought back with him a sixteen-year-old Italian choirboy; de Vere's enemies accused him of using this boy sexually. De Vere seems to have begun an intense love affair with the seventeen-year-old Earl of Southampton in 1590, when de Vere was forty. There were contemporary rumours about the bisexuality of both de Vere and Southampton. The narcissistic aspect of their relationship is underscored by Southampton also being an earl who was raised by William Cecil after his father died. However, Southampton defied Cecil's order to marry de Vere's daughter (that is, Cecil's granddaughter). The first seventeen sonnets seemed to reflect de Vere's efforts to persuade the seventeen-year-old Southampton to accept this marriage. Southampton has long been the leading candidate as the Fair

Youth of the first 126 sonnets (see Waugaman, 2010b). Shakespeare's long poems *Venus and Adonis* and *The Rape of Lucrece* were both dedicated to Southampton, in 1593 and 1594 respectively. A painting of the young Southampton was long misidentified as that of a young woman, because of his feminine beauty, and because he even followed the women's fashion of his day by wearing his long hair in front of his left shoulder; this is perhaps the only early modern English portrait of a male that includes that detail. In that connection, one thinks of Sonnet 20, which begins, "A woman's face, with Nature's own hand painted,/ Hast thou, the master-mistress of my passion."

There is a "rival poet" in some of the sonnets. The allegedly gay Christopher Marlowe has often been proposed as that unnamed rival poet. If so, we might speculate that de Vere's rivalry with Marlowe was both literary and amorous. I believe the ostensible premise of Sonnet 80 ("O how I faint when I of you do write") is that Marlowe, author of *Hero and Leander*, is the better poet (Waugaman, 2011b). Marlowe was murdered in 1593 under bizarre circumstances, ostensibly over a "reckoning", or bar tab. Recalling de Vere's earlier boast that he could have Sidney killed and not get caught, one might wonder if he successfully carried out such a plan against Marlowe. Sonnet 89 ("Say that thou didst forsake me for some fault") may allude to Southampton's rage over de Vere's role in Marlowe's death. De Vere's other love triangle also included Southampton, and the sexual relationship that both de Vere and Southampton had with the still unidentified Dark Lady of Sonnets 127–154 (e.g., Sonnet 134, "So, now I have confessed that he is thine").

One might chart a "developmental line" of the evolution of de Vere's defences against feelings of betrayal. Profound self-awareness helped advance his capacities to contain and master his earlier propensity for retaliating when he felt betrayed. The late plays such as *A Winter's Tale* and *The Tempest* suggest that de Vere was striving to temper his past vindictiveness with forgiveness towards those who wronged him, along with the hope of being forgiven for his own transgressions (Beckwith, 2011).

Betrayal in Sonnet 121

I turn now from de Vere's tempestuous life to one of his literary works—Sonnet 121.

> 'Tis better to be vile than vile esteem'd,
> When not to be, receives reproach of being,
> And the just pleasure lost, which is so deem'd,
> Not by our feeling, but by others' seeing.
> For why should others' false adulterate eyes
> Give salutation to my sportive blood?
> Or on my frailties why are frailer spies,
> Which in their wills count bad what I think good ...?
> No, I am that I am, and they that level
> At my abuses, reckon up their own;
> I may be straight, though they themselves be bevel
> By their rank thoughts, my deeds must not be shown
> Unless this general evil they maintain,
> All men are bad and in their badness reign.[6]

De Vere is unexcelled in his capacity to create seemingly infinite layers of interrelated meanings in his sonnets. He was probably better attuned to words than any other writer has ever been. Close study of any sonnet with the *Oxford English Dictionary* at hand suggests that de Vere was mindful of the multiple meanings of every word he used, and also of their etymologies. Further, we know his (now lost or unidentified) Latin poetry was deemed to be of high quality by one scholarly contemporary (Gabriel Harvey). So he also thought even more broadly of semantic possibilities, given the further Latin meanings of words that other writers have not exploited. For example, I have suggested that "saucy" in Sonnet 80 might derive from the Latin word *saucium*, meaning wounded, alluding to de Vere's permanent lameness after a duel over his affair with Anne Vavasour (Waugaman, 2010c).

In Sonnet 121, Shakespeare reacts to betrayal with profound cynicism. He begins the sonnet by asserting that it is better to go ahead and be "vile" than to be (falsely) considered vile. This is a strategy of desperation. He tries to deflect attention from his morally questionable actions by focusing on the immorality of his critics. Recall that one of the latter was Philip Sidney, whose lower social standing did not permit him to duel with de Vere. This may be an as-yet unexplored meaning of line 12, "By their *rank* thoughts my deeds must not be shown." That is, in addition to the surface meaning of "rank" as "offensive", it may also link up with "level" of line 9 to imply that de Vere's enemies are too much his social inferiors to have the right to condemn him.

One relevant perspective on Sonnet 121 is *Hamlet*. One could easily imagine this sonnet being recited as a soliloquy by Hamlet. For one thing, it immediately suggests an additional meaning of the phrase, "not to be". The Bergmanns (2008), in their study of the sonnets, agree that "not to be" in line 2 is linked with Hamlet's famous soliloquy (and the phrase "to be" occurs in the sonnet's first line). The simplicity of "I am that I am" then connects with the simplicity of "To be or not to be"; they hinge on different forms of the same verb. The former might even suggest a defiant answer to the mortal doubt of the latter. Further, linking this sonnet with *Hamlet* suggests a relevant implication of "spies". Recall that Polonius, like de Vere's father-in-law Lord Burghley, employed spies. The speaker in the sonnet, like Hamlet, is furious over learning that he is being spied upon. Spying is listed by Garner (1989) as one of the ways that men betray. One recalls de Vere killing the servant at seventeen, and one thinks of Hamlet killing Polonius with his sword, when he thinks it is his uncle, King Claudius, behind the arras, spying on him.

What else can we say about that unusual phrase in line 9 of Sonnet 121, "I am that I am"? Some readers will recognise this phrase from *Exodus*.[7] Moses asks God, "Whom should I tell the Israelites has sent me?" God answers, "I am that I am." That is, this is what God names himself, as it were. Among the very few extra-biblical, early modern occurrences of this phrase are Sonnet 121—and a 1584 letter written by de Vere to his father-in-law Lord Burghley. De Vere dictated this letter to his secretary, then added a postscript in his own hand. The context suggests that de Vere is furious because he has discovered that Lord Burghley has induced two of de Vere's servants to spy on him, and report back to Burghley.[8] The letter alludes to de Vere's having been Burghley's ward after his father died when he was twelve. But the proud de Vere is now thirty-four, and his two-year exile from Queen Elizabeth's court had ended a year and a half earlier. In his furiously indignant postscript, de Vere writes, "But I pray, my lord, leave that course. For I mean not to be your ward or your child. I serve Her Majesty, and I am that I am—and by alliance near to Your Lordship, but free. And [I] scorn to be offered that injury to think I am so weak of government to be ruled by servants or not able to govern [control] myself."

So the "others", the "frailer spies" of the sonnet would correspond to the servants and to Burghley, who is directing their actions. "I am that I am" in this sonnet also suggests that something in de Vere's relationship with the Earl of Southampton has revived past betrayals by de

Vere's guardian and father-in-law. In a sense, it suggests a sort of father surrogate negative transference displaced onto Southampton, five sonnets before the Fair Youth subsequence ends in disillusionment (e.g., "Hence, thou suborned informer!" of Sonnet 125).

Still more speculatively, some of the content of this sonnet suggest associations with Marlowe, de Vere's foremost literary rival. As I mentioned earlier, Sonnet 80 alludes to Marlowe's poem *Hero and Leander*, which he left unfinished when he was killed in May of 1593. De Vere's poem *Venus and Adonis* was published within two weeks of Marlowe's death. As noted earlier, it was dedicated to the Earl of Southampton. It is easy to imagine that Marlowe, like de Vere, planned to dedicate his poem to Southampton.

Recall that Marlowe's death was allegedly over a tavern bill, or "reckoning". So "reckon up" in this sonnet may be intended to remind Southampton of Marlowe's death, especially since one of the several meanings of "reckon up" here is to "count" up the sum of some numbers. So, the poet's "frailties" and "abuses" might include his role in Marlowe's death, for which Southampton probably never forgave de Vere. "Spies" also might allude to Southampton's erotic relationship with the Earl of Essex, after Marlowe's death. Essex is known to have employed a network of spies himself. It is possible that these spies had reported to Essex and Southampton about de Vere's love life, and de Vere had learned of this.

Since the Bible is Shakespeare's most influential literary source, several *Sonnets* commentators have understandably speculated about possible biblical echoes in Sonnet 121.[9] Katherine Duncan-Jones (1997) thinks "give salutation" in line 6 might allude ironically to the Annunciation, since three of the eight uses of "salutation" in the Geneva Bible occur in Luke's description of the angel announcing to Mary that she will give birth to the Messiah. Stephen Booth (1977), a brilliant *Sonnets* commentator, hears faint echoes of the last eight chapters of *Acts*[10] in this sonnet. If he is correct, three words in a large font at the top of the page containing Chapter Twenty Six might be relevant to Sonnet 121: "Paul counted [considered] mad." This may contribute to the meanings of "count bad" in line 8.

Helen Vendler (1997) intriguingly speculates about an additional biblical allusion in Sonnet 121: the Gospel story of Jesus defending the woman who was caught "in the very act" of adultery (in *John* 8:1–11). That is, she was watched by "spies". If Vendler is correct, it might suggest that de Vere's motives in writing this sonnet included his attempt to cope with having been caught in *flagrante delicto*. By implication, the "others" with "false adulterate eyes"—the "frailer spies"—are being compared with the scribes and Pharisees of the Gospel story. And de Vere is comparing himself not just with someone committing adultery, but specifically with a woman.

To my knowledge, no *Sonnets* commentator has noticed another possible biblical allusion in Sonnet 121. The phrase "false adulterate eyes" in line 5 makes one think of 2 *Peter* 2:14—"[*False* prophets and *false* teachers,] [h]aving *eyes* full of *adulterie*, and that cannot cease to sin, beguiling unstable souls: they have hearts exercised with covetousness, [those] cursed children." And "evil" of line 13 (itself an anagram of "vile" of line 1) occurs three times in this chapter, referring to these false prophets. The summary of this second epistle of Peter in the Geneva Bible speaks of God "punishing the hypocrites who abuse his Name". These further biblical allusions cloak de Vere in religious righteousness, if not divinity itself, as he replies to his accusers.

Line 8 of the sonnet has the phrase, "Which in their wills *count bad* what I think good." Some dozen times, the Geneva Bible uses the verb "count" to mean making a moral assessment. For example, the dying King David tells his son Solomon (in 1 *Kings* 2:9), "But thou shalt not *count* him [that is, Shimer, who had earlier cursed King David] *innocent*: for thou art a wise man, and knowest what thou oughtest to do unto him: therefore thou shalt cause his hoary head to go down to the grave with blood." We know that de Vere paid special attention to this biblical verse, since he underlined most of it. It may have influenced his similar phrase in Sonnet 121, "count bad", which is equivalent to David's "not count innocent". De Vere underlined the following words in the preceding verse 8—"Shimer, which cursed me with an horrible curse." As I have stated, the Bible was the most influential literary source for Shakespeare. We might wonder if de Vere's reflections in Sonnet 121 about being betrayed by his enemies make use of his identification with King David to justify himself in the face of his critics' accusations. This impression is further strengthened by the one phrase that de Vere underlined in the summary of this book of the Bible: "[F]lourishing kingdoms, except they be preserved by God's protection (who then favoreth them when his word is truly set forth, virtue esteemed, vice punished, and concord maintained) fall to decay and come to naught." "Virtue esteemed" in this underlined passage recalls the contrasting "vile esteemed" in the first line of Sonnet 121.

One might correctly conclude from these biblical allusions that de Vere had high self-esteem, if not a pathological degree of arrogance. Sonnet 62 ("Sin of self-love possesseth all mine eye") openly admits he suffered from the "iniquity" of excessive narcissism. De Vere seems comfortable comparing himself respectively with King David, with Saint Paul, with the unknown pagan god, and even with the Judaeo-Christian God himself. It is not surprising that someone with such extreme narcissism would be vulnerable to feelings of betrayal.

Conclusion

Freud asked his followers to re-examine Shakespeare's works psycho-analytically, based on a new awareness of Shakespeare's true identity. I hope that recent evidence that Freud was correct about Edward de Vere having written these works will encourage many psychoanalysts to take up Freud's challenge. We can thus help restore the crucial connections between the literary works and the life experiences and psychology of their author. Doing so will enrich our psychoanalytic understanding of literature. It should also help to rejuvenate literary studies, which have been led astray by false assumptions about Shakespeare's identity, and about the allegedly minor role his and other authors' life experiences played in their literary creations.

Betrayal in the life of Edward de Vere helps illuminate the theme of betrayal in his works, including his plays and his Sonnet 121. Most pointedly, the phrase "I am that I am" in this sonnet draws attention to de Vere's use of the same phrase in his angry 1584 letter to his father-in-law, Lord Burghley. Both the letter and Sonnet 121 seem to allude to de Vere's profound sense of betrayal when he learned he was being spied upon. We can begin to uncover new levels of meaning in this sonnet—and in Shakespeare's works in general—when we restore the lost connections between the works and their true author.

The profession of psychoanalysis was founded on a willingness to pursue the truth wherever it might lead, despite the patient's reluctance to face the truth about him- or herself. Psychoanalysis is unavoidably controversial when it pursues its highest ideals. James Strachey persuaded Freud to censor the publication of his beliefs about Shakespeare's identity, for fear of offending the English. We can no longer allow a fear of offending the English professors to continue to stifle our pursuit of the truth about who wrote Shakespeare's works.

Notes

1. See Waugaman (2009b).
2. I will continue to use the traditional name of the author, just as we still speak of the works of Mark Twain, although we know his legal name was Samuel Clemens.
3. Both "betrayal" and "treason" come from the same Latin root, "tradere".
4. See Waugaman (2012).
5. The year he spent in Italy explains the detailed knowledge of it in the plays of Shakespeare (Roe, 1011).
6. I have restored much of the punctuation of the first edition, since the changes made by recent editors of the Sonnets may deprive us of some of the poet's meaning. I have added an ellipsis at the end of the eighth line, to highlight the fact that the poet leaves this question unfinished, inviting the reader to imagine what words are suppressed here. The elliptical phrase might be reworded as, "Frailer spies are ... on my frailties. Why?" The missing word might be "spying". Why is this question interrupted before it is completed? De Vere often echoes the content of his poetry in its form. The secrecy of the spying might be enacted, for example, in his leaving the word out. Alternatively, he may be enacting here a particularly sharp volte-face or turn from the octave to the sestet in this sonnet.
7. It is also found in Corinthians. The passage from Exodus is quoted in John Lyly's 1578 novel Euphues. It occurs in a 1578 prayer by Edward Dering, to be recited before reading the Bible ("Flesh and blood cannot reveal the mysteries of thy heavenly kingdom unto me, but by thy blessed will I am that I am, and by the same know I that I know"). It is also in C.K.'s dedication of the 1596 The History of a Florentine Woman, by "C.M.": two more pseudonyms of de Vere's?
8. Another theory is that Burghley had asked the financially reckless de Vere to let a trusted servant manage his financial affairs.
9. Scholars agree it was the Geneva translation of the Bible that most influenced Shakespeare; it is this translation that I quote here.
10. Acts 17:23, in the Latin Vulgate translation, provided one of de Vere's literary pseudonyms: "Ignoto", from "Ignoto deo", referring to the statue to the unknown god in Athens. Acts 17:28 refers to "poets"—apparently the only reference to "poets" in the Geneva Bible.

CHAPTER SIX

Betrayal as the creative force behind Oscar Wilde's "The Ballad of Reading Gaol"

Eugene J. Mahon

*T*he *Ballad of Reading Gaol* is a remarkable document, not only as poem, but as historical record and indictment of a primitive judicial system that betrayed its poets and children and even more its serious offenders by housing them all under the same sadistic penal roof. Oscar Wilde (1854–1900) spent two years of his short life in Reading Gaol for a crime that would not be considered a crime at all by today's standards. The society he had charmed with his plays and outrageous wit turned savagely against him as it deployed its primitive sense of institutional justice to incarcerate him in a penal institution that included manual labour as part of his punishment. He was betrayed by a society he had regaled for years with his brilliant sardonic intelligence: out of his sense of betrayal, he fashioned a poem that breaks the heart even as it enlightens and uplifts it.

In a book about betrayal, this chapter addresses how the anguish of betrayal can be turned into a ballad that not only "sings in its chains like the sea", but frees itself from its bondage through the sheer power of its song. Love and betrayal, it could be argued, have been the stuff of literature since Helen ran off with Paris, or Pinter, a few thousand years later in his play *Betrayal*, took up a similar theme. In literature, whether betrayal is depicted as historical fact or fictive speculation, it is the emotional complexity of the dramatic conflict that will capture the reader's attention. In Aeschylus's *Agamemnon*, Helen can claim to be innocent, blaming the whole affair on Aphrodite. Euripedes can add to the complexity by slyly suggesting that it was an effigy of Helen, not the real woman who was carried off to Troy, the whole war instigated more by fantasy than by reality! A fantasy of betrayal can of course inflame the mind as much as reality can, as Shakespeare has brilliantly illustrated with his creation of Iago and Leontes, and "the green eyed monster that mocks the meat it feeds on" has no more real substance than the internal shadows of doubt and paranoia it relies on for its psychic existence.

The word "betray" coming from the Latin *tradere* shares an etymological bed with tradition, the latter a handing down of culture from one generation to another, the former a handing over of the betrayed to the authorities, suggesting that hands can be honourable or treacherous in the complex transactions of the human condition. All the perfumes of Arabia cannot sweeten human hands, according to Shakespeare, when instinct and guilt are denied rather than acknowledged and analysed. In the case of Oscar Wilde, for example, one could argue that a repressed, unanalysed Victorian tradition betrayed him, and handed him over to the fierce justice of Reading Gaol where he spent two years of imprisonment (1895–1897) with hard labour for sexual acts that today's more civilised traditions would not find punishable at all. Traditions change, but before they change they betray themselves, having institutionalised their prejudices rather than analysing them. A society that is frightened by certain aspects of the polymorphous perversity that all society springs from may condemn what it has repressed in itself and wage war against the return of the repressed in others. The celebrated comment of Terence (Publius Terentius Afer), "I am a man, nothing human is alien to me" does not apply when "human" is defined prejudicially. "The devil can quote scripture for his purpose," as Shakespeare put it in *The Merchant of Venice*, implying that scripture can be used to send a man to the gallows. Is such righteousness not the greatest betrayal of all, human instinct the casualty?

A careful reading of the poem

The gallows of betrayal are at the centre of Oscar Wilde's poem, *The Ballad of Reading Gaol*, and in this essay, I have chosen to write about it since, more than any other work of literature I know, one could argue that a sense of betrayal was the creative engine that launched the poem in the first place. There are two versions of the poem. The revisions seem slight at first glance, but like all changes to a text, they surely have significance. More of that later. First, let me synopsise and review the text and then then attempt to analyse the psychological complexity, especially as it relates to the topic of betrayal.

The poem begins abruptly, not unlike *The Rime of the Ancient Mariner* by Samuel Taylor Coleridge, an influence Wilde does not deny, and in fact embraces.

> He did not wear his scarlet coat
> For blood and wine are red,
> And blood and wine were on his hands
> When they found him with the dead.
> The poor dead woman whom he loved
> And murdered in her bed.

This refers to Charles Thomas Wooldridge (1866–1896), aged thirty, who was hanged in Reading Gaol while Wilde was incarcerated there. A trooper in the Royal Horse Guards, Wooldridge had killed his twenty-three-year-old wife, Laura Ellen Wooldridge: she had aroused his jealousy. He deliberately waited for her on the road near her house and slit her throat three times with a razor borrowed from a friend. Wilde had seen the hangman, Billington, crossing the prison yard with gardener's gloves and a little bag. At eight o'clock in the morning of July 7, 1895, Wooldridge's feet were fastened. Billington adjusted the cap and drew the bolt. Wooldridge plunged to his death. His body, covered with lime, was buried in a grave in the prison yard. Wilde would incorporate much of this imagery into his poem, poetic licence changing some of the details (e.g., "The poor dead woman whom he loved / And murdered in her bed" was actually on the road, as mentioned earlier).

Wilde feared that the propaganda elements in the poem (the indictment of cruel Victorian justice that housed children who stole rabbits, poets with homosexual instincts, and murderers under the same penal roof) would ruin the pure poetic energy and momentum of his artistic creation but there is no doubt that the poem in its entirety packs an incredible aesthetic punch. As Richard Ellman (1988), Wilde's great biographer, put it: "Once read, it is never forgotten."

The rest of the poem in a prose rendition with some excerpts could be summarised as follows: Wilde and the other prisoners see Wooldridge walking about "in a suit of shabby grey" and they wonder if he had done "a great or little thing", when a voice behind Wilde whispered low, "That fellow's got to swing." Hearing this, Wilde cannot feel his own pain any longer, only the predicament of the man who "... had killed the thing he loved/And so he had to die." Then follows the most famous and celebrated refrain of the poem:

> Yet each man kills the thing he loves
> By each let this be heard.
> Some do it with a bitter look,
> Some with a flattering word.
> The coward does it with a kiss.
> The brave man with a sword.

The poet questions this discriminating logic of justice:

> For each man kills the thing he loves.
> Yet each man does not die.

The poet's identification with Christ is echoed in the lines that question this selective justice: if all are guilty why does each and every man not "feel upon his shuddering cheek/The kiss of Caiaphas"—Caiaphas being one of the high priests at the trial of Jesus?[1] Wilde and the other prisoners forget about themselves as they ponder the fate of the man who is destined to be hanged "and dance upon the air" when the trap door opens beneath him and the rope breaks his neck. Wilde's identification with the condemned man breaks out in the following lines:

> Like two doomed ships that pass in storm
> We had crossed each other's way:
> But we made no sign, we said no word,
> We had no word to say;
> For we did not meet in the holy night
> But in the shameful day.

Wilde's sarcasm becomes intense:

> The Governor was strong upon
> The Regulations Act:
> The Doctor said that Death was but
> A scientific fact:

And twice a day the Chaplain called
And left a little tract.

On one occasion, poet and fellow prisoners notice that a fresh grave has been dug. They return to their cells, haunted by what they have seen.

Right in we went, with soul intent
On Death and Dread and Doom:
The hangman with his little bag
Went shuffling through the gloom
And each man trembled as he crept
Into his numbered tomb.

Wilde decided to make these last two lines even more personal in the revised version, where "each man" is rendered "I":

I trembled as I crept
Into my numbered tomb.

In their "numbered tombs" the prisoners begin to hallucinate:

That night the empty corridors
Were full of forms of fear,
And up and down the iron town
Stole feet we could not hear
And through the bars that hide the stars
White faces seemed to peer.

Paradoxically, the condemned man seems to "sleep so sweet a sleep" despite the reality of "a hangman close at hand". There is no sleep for the others however as:

Through each brain on hands of pain
Another's terror crept.

The guilt was also transmitted from the condemned man to his fellow inmates, as Wilde describes in a very astute psychological poetic passage:

Alas it is a fearful thing
To feel another's guilt!

> For, right within, the sword of Sin
> Pierced to its poison hilt,
> And as molten lead were the tears we shed
> For the blood we had not spilt.

The prisoners hallucinate in fear, waiting for the morning of execution to come and for "God's dreadful dawn" to arrive. At eight o'clock Wooldridge would be hanged when "With sudden shock the prison clock smote the shivering air."

> And as one sees most fearful things
> In the crystal of a dream
> We saw the greasy hempen rope
> Hooked to the blackened beam
> And heard the prayer the hangman's snare
> Strangled into a scream.

In the immediate lines that follow, Wilde insists that his own unique reaction was even greater than that of his fellow inmates:

> And all the woe that moved him so
> That he gave that bitter cry,
> And the wild regrets and the bloody sweats,
> None knew so well as I:
> For he who lives more lives than one
> More deaths than one must die.

Once again, the poet seems unable to maintain the objectivity of displacement and the *cri de coeur* of the "I" insists on howling out its own particular sorrow. What does Wilde mean by "he who lives more lives than one/More deaths than one must die"? Is he referring, perhaps, to the intense identifications an artist must employ to get beneath the skin of his characters into their very souls, an example of "Madame Bovary, c'est moi" as Flaubert typifies it? Does a great artist live more lives than one in these intense aesthetic identifications? And does he die a sort of metaphoric death when his creations die? When we place these lines alongside the most famous lines of the poem (where each man kills the thing he loves), we come close perhaps to understanding the unique suffering of a poet who is unable to distance himself from the tragic conflicts of even the most troubled human minds. "Justice may be able to do it," Wilde seems to be saying, "but I can't". He knows he has often killed the thing he loves in his heart and he makes no distinction between the internal affairs of the heart and their external manifestations in human behaviour.

After the execution of Wooldridge, the prisoners mope around the prison yard in their collective state of shock, but once again Wilde singles out those with the most acute psychological pain.

> For there were those amongst us all
> Who walked with downcast head,
> And knew that, had each got his due
> They should have died instead:
> He had but killed a thing that lived
> Whilst they had killed the dead.

> For he who sins a second time
> Wakens a dead soul to pain
> And draws it from its spotted shroud
> And makes it bleed again,
> And makes it bleed great gouts of blood
> And makes it bleed in vain.

What does Wilde mean by "He had but killed a thing that lived/ Whilst they had killed the dead"? Is he suggesting perhaps that Wooldridge killed impulsively but only once in a state of jealous passion, while justice kills with premeditated precision; and after the execution, the body of the victim is covered with lime, which eats away flesh and bone with its savage inanimate teeth, in a kind of second execution and desecration? Or is this much too concrete an explanation for the essentially internal psychological mystery Wilde is posing for all of us? Is he not trying to fathom the complex guilt of the survivor who "Wakens a dead soul to pain" each time memory resurrects the dead in the agony of mourning "And makes it bleed again"?

After the execution of Wooldridge, the prisoners moped around the yard, "Horror stalking before each man/As terror crept behind". They see the warders in their Sunday suits, "But we knew the work they had been at/By the quicklime on their boots". The open grave had been filled in with mud and lime and the executed man "Lies with fetters on each foot/wrapt in a sheet of flame". In its callous wisdom

Justice has decided that no flowers shall be planted on the grave as if "A murderer's heart would taint/Each simple seed they sow". Wilde cannot withhold his censure of such "Justice" any longer:

> It is not true! God's kindly earth
> Is kindlier than men know.
> And the red rose would blow more red
> And the white rose whiter blow.
> Out of his mouth a red, red rose!
> Out of his heart a white!

Wilde continues to lambaste such cruel justice that not only torments the living but dishonours and desecrates the bodies of the dead.

> Yet all is well; he has but passed
> To Life's appointed bourne:
> And alien tears will fill for him
> Pity's long-broken urn,
> For his mourners will be outcast men
> And outcasts always mourn.

Wilde returns to his critique of justice:

> Every prison that men build
> Is built with bricks of shame.

The inhuman treatment of prisoners does severe damage to the body but even worse damage to the heart:

> What chills and kills outright
> Is that every stone one lifts by day
> Becomes one heart by night.

Wilde ends his poem with an indictment of a cruel justice that insists on elevating itself above human nature on its lofty pedestal of hypocrisy rather than acknowledging that "All men kill the thing they love", and that there is no escape from the guilty prison of the human mind where mercy and justice are forever at war as beast and tamer, where id and ego pace interminably in the solitary confinement of their cell.

In Reading gaol by Reading town
There is a pit of shame
And in it lies a wretched man
Eaten by teeth of flame,
In burning winding-sheet he lies
And his grave has got no name.

And there, till Christ call forth the dead,
In silence let him lie:
No need to waste the foolish tear,
Or heave the windy sigh:
The man had killed the thing he loved
And so he had to die.

And all men kill the thing they love
By all let this be heard.
Some do it with a bitter look
Some with a flattering word.
The coward does it with a kiss
The brave man with a sword.

Psychoanalytic reflections

While poetry and betrayal are the central issues under scrutiny in this chapter, the concept of development can instruct us about the genetic elements involved in the complex psychology of betrayal. Betrayal from a developmental point of view could be envisaged as that critical moment when the "facilitating environment" (Winnicott, 1965) fails the child or "seems" to fail the child in the judgment of the internal psychological milieu. The critical moment being conceptualised may be no moment at all but a considerably longer series of complementary moments. The metaphoric "moment" under consideration is that moment when pleasure principle and reality principle first clash, the moment when desire, frustration, and anger first square off against each other. Under ideal developmental circumstances, when desire meets with frustration, the resultant anger is communicated to the caregiver, the anger is acknowledged and validated, and the frustrated infant feels understood. The first oral dialogue is not about calories alone. Emotional synchrony and mutual understanding define the sense of nourishment as much as milk does. The milk of human kindness is affective and calorific all at once. Under less ideal circumstances, when the facilitating environment is out of sync with the infant, a sense of betrayal may define the dyadic communication more than a sense of mutual understanding. A sense of betrayal reflects a dyadic dialogue gone awry. The frustration and anger at the caregiver does not lead to mutual understanding and enhanced communication, it leads instead to passivity and despair. The anger of the infant, instead of being "fielded" and validated by a soothing mother is projected onto her. The nascent ego of the infant becomes passive, disillusioned, and paranoid as it imagines retaliation from its own anger, now re-envisaged in the face of the mother. If the mother becomes wise to the glitch in the communication system the dialogue can be restored to a system of mutual cues and responses. If the offended mother becomes entrenched in her own righteousness (like the Reading Gaol justice system depicted in the poem), childhood development in particular, not to mention the judicial system in general, goes seriously awry.

It is almost impossible to separate the concepts of justice and mercy from the concept of betrayal, at least from a developmental point of view. When the infant bites the breast and the mother retaliates by withdrawing the breast in pain, the stage is set for a dyadic transaction that may lead to further communication and compromise or to a collapse of communication and a sense of betrayal. If "Each man kills the thing he loves" applies to the frustrated infant's assault on the breast, the universality of Wilde's point is irrefutable. In pathology, the infant's rage at the breast is split off from his love; fusion of instincts does not occur. In mental health, fusion does occur. The infant learns frustration tolerance: love is not destroyed by impatience or anger. Love learns to wait. Hatred becomes reasonable. A sense of betrayal is avoided; compromise enhances the give and take of dyadic communication.[2] In judicial terms, Reading Gaol would have entered into a dialogue with Wilde, recognised that his instincts were his own unique business, and set him free. There is no question that a hundred years later English justice, now more enlightened than in its dark Victorian past, would indeed exonerate Wilde and set him free.

Wilde wrote his anguished "love letter" *De Profundis* (1897) to Alfred Douglas in gaol but he wrote *The Ballad of Reading Gaol* after he left prison. If a poem springs from Wordsworthian "emotion recollected in tranquility" it must have been a most turbulent tranquility that the *Ballad* emerged from. Wilde left gaol a broken man from an emotional point of view, and a broke man from a financial one. Whatever tranquility he possessed in the few remaining years of life depended on the kindness of friends who were not only willing to lend him money but a compassionate ear as well. Recollected emotion he certainly had and it poured in to the *Ballad*. If critics had mixed feelings (one comment portrayed it as a mixture of "the good, bad and indifferent"), the public at large embraced it even before C.3.3 (the original anonymous author's identity went only by the number of his cell) was revealed to be none other than Oscar Wilde.

Earlier in this contribution, I suggested that a sense of betrayal was the creative engine that launched the poem, and that the emotional components of that psychological state need to be examined. Anger, helplessness, shame, guilt, yearning, love, are surely some, if not all, of the components of the complex state of betrayal that informed the poem's anguished stanzas. All are certainly represented in the poem. From an aesthetic point of view, displacement was crucial if the poem was to work, not only as the tormented wail of the stricken author but as the plight of Wooldridge, who in a state of jealous passion and premeditated hatred has slain his wife. Displacement gave Wilde a less maudlin, victimised position from which to conceptualise his profound argument. In a nutshell, the argument of the poem suggests that if man by definition is a guilty animal, is civilisation not in a perpetual state of self-deception if its sense of justice makes a mockery out of its sense of mercy? If the quality of mercy is twice blessed, blessing "him that gives and him that takes" why can there not be a similar quality of justice that marries power and sympathy? Wilde assigns this ideal sense of justice to Christ, Victorian justice portrayed instead as a product of the devil. Ironically enough, two years after Wilde's release from Reading Gaol, Victorian justice changed radically, a Christlike modicum of sympathy changing its configuration radically.

The invocation of Christ in the poem needs to be considered as more romantic than religious perhaps. Ellmann (1988) claims as much, when he writes that Christian humility is a slippery term in Wilde writings. According to Ellmann, Wilde:

> ... blends Christianity with aestheticism ... Christ appears as the supreme individualist, uniting personality and perfection, saying beautiful things, making of his life the most wonderful of poems by creating himself out of his own imagination ... It recognizes no

morality but that of sympathy. Christ is a precursor of the Romantic
movement, a supreme artist, a master of paradox, a type of Wilde in
the ancient world. (p. 515)

This sounds like the ancient pre-Christian voice of Protagoras, or
Terence: "I am a man: Nothing human is alien to me", or the modern
voice of Freud, who counsels us to change the irrational shrill sadism of
the superego into the reasoned tones of the sympathetic ego: "*Tous com-
prendre, c'est tous pardonner.*" Man betrays his human nature when he
allows unanalysed fragments of the psyche to define morality through
a twisted, sadistic lens. This is the caricature of justice represented in
Measure for Measure (1603) where Angelo is willing to pardon Claudio
if his sister Isabella is willing to sleep with him, rather than Portia's
authentic justice in *The Merchant of Venice* (1596), which has a quality
of mercy in it. Paradoxically even Portia's mercy seems to end with her
"quality of mercy" speech, since she later turns her savage sophistry
against Shylock as she uses his pound of flesh logic against him. In
any case, what I am stressing is that Wilde's appeal to sympathy as the
greatest of virtues is contrasted dramatically with the glaring lack of it
portrayed so vividly in *The Ballad of Reading Gaol*. If the criminal betrays
his capacity for sympathy by killing his victim, the state betrays its
capacity for sympathy towards its instinctual citizens when it executes
rather than rehabilitates them. If each man kills the thing he loves, it is
unfair for justice to distance itself from universal culpability. Human
nature is instinctual and rational all at once. Blind justice is not as fair
and unprejudiced as its metaphor of a blindfold implies: if man blinds
himself to his own repressed instincts, he betrays himself, claiming only
a portion of his nature, discarding the rest. Justice is not well served by
this kind of judicial absolutism. Capital punishment repeats the crime
of the murderer. Justice cannot claim its hands are clean by assigning
the dirty work to the Billingtons of this world.

Wilde makes this point over and over again as the line "Each man
kills the thing he loves" hammers its incantatory repetitions into the
mind of the reader, the hypocrite reader of Baudelaire who may look
down his nose at Baudelairean or Wildean filth all he wants, but cannot distance himself from it totally without doing violence to his own
nature. If blind justice can push a button in London to kill a mandarin
in China, the self-deception is more difficult to maintain when the mandarin lives next door and the culpability of the finger is impossible to

deny. If the justice which ordered the execution of Wooldridge could not assign the task to the hangman Billington, Wooldridge might never have been executed. Such societal, institutional self-deception reminds me of a child in analysis who would build elaborate Rube Goldberg-like interlocking pulleys connected to blocks of wood, whereby his action at one end of the elaborate gadgetry would cause a reaction so far removed from the initial action that if the blocks tumbled on the analyst's hands, the child could disclaim any guilty responsibility for the deed or any hurt it had caused. Wilde seems to be exposing a similar kind of sophistry or hypocrisy in the "blindness" of justice. None so blind as those that will not see. Ironically, in the poem all the inmates are unable to distance themselves from the sympathetic guilt they all feel for the condemned man "who has to swing". Wilde stresses a tragic irony in this manner: the fellow prisoners embody empathy; justice embodies cruelty and censure. Wilde describes the condemned man Wooldridge being able to sleep well while his fellow inmates are tormented with guilt. This psychological transaction of contrast between the condemned man and his colleagues in chains is haunt-ingly described by Wilde.

> Through each brain on hands of pain
> Another's terror crept ...
> And as molten lead were the tears we shed
> For the blood we had not spilt.

Wilde is highlighting an irony that allows the condemned man and society at large as his executioner to sleep unperturbedly while all the inmates feel the terror of the condemned man and weep molten tears for the "the blood we had not spilt". Towards the end of his short life, Wilde came to believe that morality without sympathy was no moral-ity at all. While poets might agree, the judicial system that believes it has to protect society would surely not, wedded as it is to Hobbes's conviction that morality without a sovereign state to enforce it has no practical meaning. And yet, humanism demands that mercy and justice must coexist even if absolute mercy could lead to lawlessness and mer-ciless justice could lead to a police state. These great ideals (mercy and justice) betray each other, however, when each invokes splitting and disregard for each other's arguments rather than engaging in the neces-sary humanistic act of dialogue and compromise.

From a purely aesthetic point of view, a younger Wilde would have argued that "propaganda" has no place in poetry, *ars gratia artis* the catchphrase of the aesthetes. Earlier in life, Wilde had scoffed at Dickens's attempts to raise the social consciousness about Victorian insensitivity to childhood poverty and penury. For the young Wilde, reality was simply the raw material a poet uses for aesthetic purposes. Realism in art was a bore. But when the reality of Victorian judicial cruelty ensnared him, his aesthetic sensibility could ignore reality no longer. He would have had to betray his own moral voice, his own inner rage to do so. That poetry should be silent or silenced when atrocity goes by the name of Auschwitz or Reading Gaol may be the initial reaction to such traumas, as Adorno (1949) has suggested ("To write poetry after Auschwitz is barbaric"), but surely the more abiding goal of poetry will always be to turn sorrow into song and force atrocity and all forms of hatred to study how it paradoxically kills the thing it loves. A purely "aesthetic" poetry that ignored reality and fiddled while Rome burned would surely betray itself and the complexity of its humanistic mission.

I have suggested elsewhere (Mahon, 1987) that Coleridge nearly "ruined" the *Rime of the Ancient Mariner* by dragging in the Pilot's Boy episode towards the conclusion of his celebrated poem. I argued that the Pilot's Boy episode was a disguised representation of Coleridge's rivalry with his brother Frank and that "neurosis" more than aesthetic judgment alone had guided him or misguided him in the inclusion of this genetic material. When Yeats "cut out all the message" (Ellman, 1988, p. 534) from *The Ballad of Reading Gaol* when he compiled the *Oxford Book of Modern Verse*, he may have been uncomfortable with Wilde's impassioned diatribes against judicial authority. But do we not betray the psychological predicament of the author if we doctor his aesthetic creation in such a manner? Such aesthetic questions can never be answered perhaps.

Concluding remarks

From a psychoanalytic point of view as opposed to a purely aesthetic perspective, one could argue that while it is no doubt the function of sublimation to cover its tracks and reveal no trace of the genetic realities that spawned it, insight is not ashamed of the humble origins its flights of aesthetic fancy were launched from. When the past "instinctualises" the present, it nourishes it, revives it, humanises it. *The Ballad of Reading Gaol*, uncut and unexpurgated, is a profound document of a great writer wailing from *de profundis* and bequeathing the depths of his suffering to his readers. If we are not ennobled by it, we betray ourselves and some endangered aspect of the human condition's capacity to sympathise with the conflicted nature of itself. If each man kills the thing he loves, he also loves the thing he kills in the conflicted world of unconscious reality. If we hold a mirror up to our own nature, it seems to reflect the following wisdom and if it could speak would say: "You are an animal declaring yourself a man. If your unconscious can kill and love and integrate both, you will be coward and brave man all at once and you will betray no aspect of your human complexity." If Wilde's *Ballad* can teach humanity that it will have learnt a lot.

Returning to *The Ballad* again and again and reflecting on Wilde's misery as he put pen to paper, the reader can develop the illusion that Wilde met the fate that Wooldridge suffered and that the reader is a witness to this miscarriage of justice. Wilde's spirit was broken as surely as Wooldridge's neck was snapped. It is not possible to be a witness of such barbarity without feeling the agonies of empathy depicted in the poem. Literature as witness would be a mere frivolous pastime if great poetry did not hurt as it was being read. Not to feel some vicarious version of what the poet felt would be a betrayal of literature, a betrayal of the self. We would be killing the poetry we love by not identifying with the affects that produced it. If the coward does it with a kiss and the brave man with a sword, the hypocrite does it when he reads *The Ballad* as a quirk of judicial history gone awry, rather than as a tendency of human nature and its institutions to betray themselves constantly whenever morality as sympathy is disavowed and blind neurosis masquerades as justice.

Betrayal is surely only one trigger of great art, but like a hunger for unrequited love, or a passion for revenge, it has a restless voice, a thirst that cannot be slaked until language brings a kind of redress of the internal sorrow at the root of it. Shakespeare's Hamlet feels betrayed and if, as I have argued elsewhere (Mahon, 2009), Shakespeare himself may have felt betrayed when his only son Hamlet died in childhood, fictional character and real life playwright reflecting similar affects, transformed of course by the latter into immortal expression. If a sense of betrayal, a sense of tragic misunderstanding, is dyadic by definition (one party is terribly out of sync with another), the affects can only be resolved through dyadic rapprochement, something that Wilde was not able to accomplish, given the deafness of Victorian justice to his plea for a measure of sympathy and understanding. Psychoanalysis is forever addressing such misunderstandings, such imagined betrayals as transference and countertransference present and re-present their conflicted dramas again and again in the theatre of transference neurosis, never at ease until understanding and maturity eventually prevail, as the nets of transference are finally set aside and the great hall of insight has accomplished its mission of individuation and enlightenment. The psychoanalytic and the aesthetic share this search for a momentary stay against confusion as the human heart, betrayed by its own finiteness, cries out *de profundis* for contact, understanding, and recognition.

Notes

1. Dante (1300) placed Caiaphas in the sixth realm of the eighth circle of Inferno, where hypocrites are punished by being eternally crucified.
2. See Klein (1940, 1946) for the developmental vicissitudes of infantile aggression, especially how it gets split off and under what circumstances it gets amalgamated with libido.

PART III

CLINICAL REALM

CHAPTER SEVEN

The compulsion to betray and the need to be betrayed

Salman Akhtar

The English word "betrayal" is derived from the old French *traïr* and the Latin *tradere*, both referring to "traitor". Indeed, the dictionary meaning of "betrayal" includes "to deliver to an enemy by treachery" (Mish, 1998, p. 109). Among other explications are "to lead astray, to fail or desert especially in time of need, to reveal unintentionally, [and] to disclose in violation of confidence" (ibid., p. 109). These phrases indicate that: (a) betrayal involves breaking someone's trust in one's reliability and availability, and (b) betrayal can be deliberate or unintentional. A third feature, though not explicit, can also be discerned. This involves the fact that (c) betrayal causes hurt. The Hindi word for betrayal, *vishwas-ghaat* (literally, wounded-trust) captures the essence of this phenomenon.

Moving from the confines of the dictionary, I propose two other facets of betrayal: (d) the phenomenon comes in active and passive forms (i.e., betraying others and feeling betrayed) and, (e) the affects connected with these forms are conscious or unconscious sadistic glee and sharp "mental pain" (Akhtar, 2000; Freud, 1926d; Weiss, 1934), respectively.[1] Yet another facet is that (f) betraying and being betrayed are not as aetiologically, dynamically, and phenomenologically apart as they initially appear. The drive to betray others and the need to be

117

betrayed invariably coexist. The former is more evident in narcissistic characters and the latter in masochistic characters. However, the opposite wish is also present in each of them. Narcissistic individuals betray others while also arranging unconscious betrayals of themselves and masochistic individuals engineer being betrayed while betraying others themselves. Cooper's (1988) proposal of the "narcissistic-masochistic character", while addressing a somewhat different terrain of psychopathology is, in part, my heuristic ally in making this assertion.

This Janus-faced syndrome of betrayal, which has remained inadequately addressed in psychoanalytic literature,[2] forms the focus of my contribution. With the help of two detailed case reports, I will elucidate the unrelenting need to betray others and the comparably driven, albeit unconscious, need to be betrayed. I will follow these case reports with comments on treating patients in whose lives themes of betrayal figure prominently and whose transferences are accordingly shaped and coloured. I will conclude by pulling this material together and pointing out areas that warrant further attention.

The compulsion to betray

In clinical practice and in life-at-large one often encounters people who are utterly unreliable. They promise to be somewhere, arrive at a certain time, bring something, and do some task but habitually fail to meet such expectations. Their behaviour hurts others who gradually begin to mistrust them and become wary of them. Behaviourally homogenous, such unreliability is actually of three different psychodynamic varieties:

a. *Diffuse ego-impairment*: these are hapless individuals who agree to others' demands because they lack the courage to say "no"; subsequently feeling burdened by what they might genuinely be unable to carry out, they end up disappointing those who are banking on them.

b. *Identification with over-promising parents*: these are adults who, as children, were repeatedly misled by their parents; the latter made all sorts of boastful declarations that never came true. Such dashing of hopes on a repeated basis deeply traumatised the children who, in an "identification with the aggressor" (A. Freud, 1946), unleash similar torment upon unsuspecting others once they grow up. Their actions are often subtle and out of their conscious awareness. Their betrayals of others occur despite their good wishes and, at times, are a source of surprise and disappointment to themselves.

c. *Sadistic triumph over envied others*: individuals who betray others with conscious sadistic glee usually display "malignant narcissism" (Kernberg, 1984), that is, a combination of pathological self-absorption, cruelty, and antisocial behaviour. They have experienced severe betrayal trauma during childhood and often view themselves as the most unfairly treated among the family's children. They envy other siblings and harbour intense envy and hatred for their privileged status. Their betrayals are enactments of their destructive impulses towards their siblings, though, at its base, their hostility is directed at their parents. Superego functioning is often compromised and an element of viciousness lurks underneath their overt seductiveness.

The following case illustrates this sort of compulsion to betray others.

Clinical vignette 1

Tall, big-boned, and bold in his gestures, sixty-year-old Paul Ruby sought psychotherapy reluctantly and pursued it in staccato fashion. He did accept my recommendation of twice-weekly sessions but took frequent and long leaves during the course of work which lasted nearly seven years. Paul had been forced to seek help by his daughter after his divorce when he had begun drinking excessively and missing work-related appointments. A prosecuting attorney of considerable repute, Paul had been a consummate womaniser and his divorce was precipitated by an affair which fizzled out once he was on his own. He could not tolerate his girlfriend's demands for deeper relatedness.

Over the course of time, I learned about two other affairs and a long series of one night stands. Paul seemed embarrassed about some of these, while reporting others with a sense of triumph. Betrayal figured in all of them and curiously, the more conscious it was, the more it seemed to energise him. And, mind you, I am not referring to the betrayal of his wife—that was taken for granted. The betrayals in question were those of the various women he seduced. While the theme appeared again and again in the account of his life, two episodes struck him—and me—as paradigmatic of his driven need to betray, though from different vantage points and with different psychic consequences.

The first of these was "the story of Ellen McGuire" (he named his various escapades like chapters of a novel),[3] a stunningly beautiful woman whom Paul had known since their childhood. She came from a more sophisticated and elite family than Paul's, though they had grown up in the same affluent suburb of Pittsburgh as children. As a child and later as a teenager, Paul had been intimidated by her snobbish manner, her fine looks, and her elegant clothes. Then, decades later when he had become quite successful as a lawyer and had made a lot of money, Paul unexpectedly ran into Ellen who, in his words, "had not amounted to much". She was still beautiful, though. Paul "worked on her" for over one year, befriending her, showering her with gifts, and helping her obtain a decent-enough job. Soon, they became lovers. Paul had no shortage of money by this time. He rented a fine apartment and handed her the keys. A site of their amorous interludes, soon it became Ellen's place. Then after he had "fucked her and fucked her real hard and real good" many, many times, one day Paul arrived at the apartment and announced that he had terminated the lease and she had to vacate the place within a week. To a horrified Ellen, he now recanted with glee how this had been his plan all along and how this was his only way to overcome how intimidating he had found her during their childhood and adolescent years. What is more chilling here is that Paul was hardly regretful in telling me all this. On the contrary, he regarded his victory over Ellen as a sign of courage, determination, and manliness. Her pain at his profound betrayal was peripheral in his version of the story.

In contrast, Paul felt much shame and even a twinge of remorse in recounting "the story of the Yemeni woman". I could see that his betrayal of her had a less calculating and more "accidental" (i.e., more unconsciously driven) quality about it. Paul had much difficulty recounting what happened between them. Haltingly, he gave the following account. He had gone to London, presumably for a business trip but actually to meet a woman whom he had been courting off and on for a while. With characteristic flair, he rented a high-end apartment for a week with tip-top amenities— concierge, chauffeur, cleaning service, and so on. The very first afternoon before his British lover-to-be could arrive at this fancy place, a poor Arab woman rang the doorbell. She was there to clean the apartment but, within twenty to twenty five minutes, Paul had worked his magic and she was in his arms. They were interrupted by a call from the concierge, announcing the arrival of a "guest". The woman from Yemen went back to dusting and cleaning. Paul's British girlfriend entered the apartment and almost immediately he opened a bottle of champagne. As he went to the kitchen to fetch two glasses, he caught the hurt and accusing eyes of the cleaning woman. Paul claimed, and I believed him, that he never forgot that glance and he gets filled with remorse and shame each time he recalls it.

Though Paul's behaviour in the two scenarios differed—the first, deliberate and near sociopathic, the second, unmentalised and compulsive—the core sequence of seduction followed by betrayal was evident in both. (And, there were more "stories" like these in Paul's repertoire; only one was different since it pertained to *his* being betrayed by a young paramour.) But why was Paul acting this way and what connection did such behaviour have with his frequent dropping out from treatment (more marked in the earlier part of our work) and with his childhood background?

As we explored this, it became clear that Paul had himself suffered significant betrayals in his life. A first-born child and an "undisputed darling" (Freud, 1917b, p. 156) of his parents, Paul had been abruptly sent away to live with his aunt in Pittsburgh when he was just two years old. He grew up with his aunt until he finished high school, visiting his parents only once or twice a year; the presumed reason for his exile was the birth of his younger sister who was a sickly baby and demanded a lot of attention from their parents.

In my estimation, Paul had been badly traumatised by this early betrayal. Then, the discovery that his father was having an affair when Paul was ten years old and of his uncle and aunt's enrolling their son into a private school while Paul attended a public school also were experienced as serious betrayals. He grew up determined to make loads of money, never depend upon anyone, and get even. His promiscuity was based upon his attempts to reverse the narcissistic injuries of his childhood, and his frequent withdrawals from me—just when I began to be optimistic about our work—embodied the all-too-familiar seduction-betrayal pattern.

An important aspect of Paul's transference was his sense that I was enjoying his dependence upon me. He suspected that I was gloating over my importance to him. This would anger him greatly: "Why should I be reliably present for you? Come here on fixed times, like a dog? What have you done to deserve such loyalty and obedience from me?" Painstakingly and in a piecemeal fashion, we sorted all this out to indicate that Paul wanted to be a reliable parent to me (in a reversal of his own anaclitic longings) but then would feel envious of my being the recipient of his reliability. I began appearing to him like his younger (and in his eyes, more fortunate) sister and he would have to rupture the treatment; the envy was simply intolerable. Then, after a few missed sessions, Paul would reappear with promises to be regular in attendance.

As these cycles were repeated, we reconstructed the pain he felt at having to separate again and again from his parents when he visited them during childhood. Turning passive into active, Paul had become "addicted" to betraying (instead of being betrayed). Working through the hurt, pain, and profound rage that were intermingled in this relational scenario gradually led to the emergence of genuine sadness about how his life had become messed up and remorse over how he had hurt so many women in his life. Paul's relationship with his sister improved. Though not entirely able to "forgive" her for having displaced him, he did become capable of seeing that it was hardly her fault. The rage at her was a displacement of the fury he felt towards his parents for having sent him away. We were also able to link the seduction-betrayal drama he had played out with Ellen to the amalgam of his feelings towards his sister and his mother. As the treatment approached its end, Paul was able to sustain a loving relationship with a woman. He was not free of impulses to cheat and to betray her but was able to handle them by suppression, by masturbating to fantasied sex with other women, and, at times, by making fun of his greed and potential cruelty. Analysis had not "cured" him but had indeed made his life less driven, less sadomasochistic, and less complicated. For me, this exemplified what Freud (1933a) had meant by his statement that as a result of psychoanalysis, "where id was there ego shall be". (p. 80)

This case poignantly illustrates the deleterious effects of pathological narcissism upon the capacity for object relations. Viewed within a long-term perspective of time, "[T]he grandiose self always has been, and remains, alone and in a strangely atemporal world of repeating cycles of wants, temporary idealizations, greedy incorporation, and disappearing of supplies by spoiling, disappointing, and devaluation" (Kernberg, 1980, p. 138).

Also pertinent here is Rosenfeld's (1964, 1971) observation that narcissistic object relations are characterised by omnipotence and defences against any recognition of separateness between self and the object. The narcissist's omnipotence is manifest in his ruthless use of others (see also Coen, 1992, in this regard) with concomitant denial of any dependence on them, since its recognition implies vulnerability to love, pain of separation, and envy of what others have to offer. A more malignant situation prevails when angry and destructive aspects of the self become idealised. Then the individual attempts to destroy whatever love is offered to him in order to maintain his superiority over others. In becoming totally identified with the omnipotent destructive aspects of himself, he kills off his sane, loving, and dependent self. At times, he remains wistfully aware of his inner imprisonment and feels that there is nothing anybody can do to change the situation. Avoiding the risk of being betrayed by anyone ever again, the narcissist isolates himself and thus ends up betraying his own needy self. Such was the case with Paul Ruby before he came to see me.

The need to be betrayed

In sharp contrast to him are persons who find themselves betrayed over and over again. Their employer fails to recognise their valuable contributions. Their friends do not reciprocate their party invitations. Their spouses rarely acknowledge their love and their offspring never celebrate their sacrifices. In Bergler's (1949) terminology, such individuals are "injustice collectors". Psychically bruised and embittered, they recount their woes with pained disbelief; it is as if they had hoped for better treatment from others but were jilted and rebuffed.

That the central problem in such individuals is that of masochism is clear.[4] Less evident is the reason *how* and *why* being betrayed (as against being beaten, being sexually abused, and so on) becomes the central feature of some masochistic individuals. The answer to *how* it happens is the following: the masochist possesses a remarkable, though latent, gullibility. He believes everything he is told and overlooks facts that contradict his rosy expectations. In other words, he sets himself up for failure, injury, and feeling betrayed. In this aspect, he is like some paranoid personalities who, while contemptuous of others' naïvety, themselves display a peculiar vulnerability to believing in what they hear from gossip-mongers (Stanton, 1978). The next question—*why* being betrayed becomes the phenotypical expression of "moral masochism" (Freud, 1924c)—leads not only to diverse sources of unconscious guilt (Akhtar, 2013; Asch, 1976; Modell, 1965; Niederland, 1968) but also to psychically felt betrayals in the form of *actual* losses during childhood. In the course of later development, these experiences tend to become libidinised and imbued with masochistic pleasure.

Clinical vignette 2

A diminutive and bespectacled middle-aged physicist of Viennese origin, Joel Lobner arrived at my office because he was considering divorce and wanted to be "really sure" about the correctness of his decision. In the first session, he recounted in great detail how unappreciated he felt by his second wife, Erika, who, he acknowledged, was quite beautiful and, at times, "great fun to be with". He said that he had been of help to her in numerous ways, including bailing her out of a serious financial mess during their courtship. With pained disbelief in his voice, Joel repeatedly talked about how hurt he felt at her ingratitude towards him. He had decided to divorce her but was afraid of becoming alone, not finding anyone to love and marry, and regretting his decision. That is why he had come to see me, that is, to sort out his ambivalence over the decision he was about to make.

The subsequent sessions were filled with his providing more "proofs" of Erika's thankless attitude towards him, her imperious stance, and her jealous rages. Joel repeatedly forgave her for such insults, began trusting her, but was betrayed over and over again. Just when he would relax and be spontaneous, she would throw a jealous temper tantrum, destroying his mental peace. Joel had shared some of these details with two of his friends back in Europe and both had called him a "masochist" for staying in such a painful marriage. They urged him to get a divorce.

Further details gradually emerged. It turned out that even before their marriage, Joel had ample evidence of Erika's narcissistic character structure and great sense of entitlement. He recalled that when they were dating and took their first vacation together, not only did he pay for all their travel expenses but the bills for all the ten to fifteen meals they ate together in the lovely West Coast town. Erika never offered to share any costs of the trip and, in fact, never uttered "Thank you" upon his paying all the bills. Joel recalled that he had noted this with mild unease but rationalised it, thinking that she was just wanting to be pampered, was letting him run the show, helping him be a big man, and so on. But now, he considered her behaviour as entitled and, in retrospect, as a betrayal of his trust in her as a mutual and reciprocal adult. Charmed by Erika's fun-loving style, which lifted his inwardly depressive self to new heights, Joel had overlooked other aspects of her character.

Erika was Joel's second wife. Joel had been married before and had felt severely betrayed by his first wife, Johanna, as well. She had misrepresented her social status, lied about her educational background, and misled Joel about her prior romantic and sexual history. Joel was deeply hurt by all this but somehow forgave her and they got married. More and more lies about Johanna's social circumstances gradually emerged later and each time Joel experienced the piercing and sharp pain of betrayal, but each time he forgave her and they carried on with their humdrum domestic life over the subsequent years. During this time, Joel had a few one-night stands and a more sustained extra-marital affair (i.e., he betrayed her), which blew up in his face and resulted in the break-up of his marriage.

Over the subsequent years, Joel's parents passed away and, at the age of forty, he moved to the United States. He then had many short-lasting relationships and one that felt deep and sustainable to him. In the company of this woman, Paula, Joel was ecstatic. What he was ignoring was how narcissistic Paula was. Sheepishly, he acknowledged that the first time he visited her apartment, he noted that the living room walls were adorned with her own photographs. Joel ignored this. He also overlooked her intense ethnocentrism and her prejudice against ethnic and racial minorities. Joel "forgave" her self-willed nature which frequently caused him hurt. Soon after they agreed to any plan, Paula would come up with something else to do or would do something behind his back which derailed the course of action they had agreed upon. Joel felt betrayed and hurt, but smitten by her beauty and intoxicated by their glorious intimacy, overlooked all this. Then one day, he felt greatly betrayed by her concerning a promise that she broke and, in a fit of rage, broke off with her.

All three women in Joel's life (his ex-wife, Johanna, his girlfriend between his two marriages, Paula, and his current wife, Erika) seemed to betray him in one way or the other. All three appeared to be phallic-narcissistic characters: proud, strong-willed, and self-centred. What became evident during the course of our work, though, in that Joel too had betrayed them (e.g., by an affair, by many one-night stands), was that he had repeatedly overlooked the unsuitability of these women for him. Or, to put it correctly, he had overlooked their narcissism and their potential for entitlement, lying, and walking all over him. Joel *was* a masochist.

Joel's childhood background was quite unstable. He was born in Vienna and was a sickly infant. He was hospitalised twice during the first three to four years of his life. His family moved frequently and, by the time he was five, they had lived in three different cities. Around six years of age, he became very ill again and soon afterwards, his parents were divorced. His mother took him with her to live with her parents. Joel's father moved to a neighbouring country and kept promising to take Joel there but this never materialised. Joel's hopes were repeatedly dashed. He was deeply hurt but somehow solaced himself thinking that he "deserved" such pain since his chronic illness in childhood was most likely the cause of the parental discord.

Joel continued to live with his mother and his grandparents. Over time, he grew very attached to an older boy in the neighbourhood who often stole from him, mocked him, and betrayed his trust by telling everyone things Joel would beg him to keep secret. As if this were not enough, Joel was sexually abused by a trusted and admired older cousin; in a household chronically burdened by the maternal grandparents' aging and infirmity, as well as by scarce economic resources, there was no one to protect Joel; his mother had begun dating and was frequently absent from the domestic scene. Matters were made worse by the fact that Joel's grandfather sexually exposed himself to Joel repeatedly before passing away when Joel was eighteen years old.

All in all, Joel had grown up with betrayal as his constant companion. And, in a major disidentification with his unreliable carers, Joel had become a fiercely loyal and reliable friend to many individuals. He took great pride in the fact that some of these friendships went back to as much as nearly fifty years. These friends were all men, however; with women, the scenario was entirely different. Like Limentani's (1989) "vagina man",[5] Joel had a tendency to find phallic-narcissistic women; they brought excitement and thrill to his otherwise depressive lifestyle and his latently effeminate character. Johanna buttressed his narcissism since he could easily project his inferiority-laden self-representations into her. Erika and Paula enhanced his self-esteem by their professional prominence. Parallel to such a narcissistic agenda of his own, Joel had a masochistic aim as well. He would cling to these self-absorbed women under the cloak of forgiveness and generosity while feeling repeatedly stabbed by their betrayals. This, it seemed, was his punishment for "causing" the parental divorce. The clinical picture was further complicated by the fact that he drew certain tangible gratifications (e.g., good food, sex, social prestige, and company) from these relationships while also "loving" these women in his own fundamentally affectionate and "good" way.

In his treatment with me, Joel looked on the one hand for validation from me that he indeed was being betrayed, and that his current wife was (and previous women had been) treacherous and ungrateful to him. On the other hand, he repeatedly defended her, forgave her, and felt that if he left her, she would suffer greatly. He desperately sought my empathy but felt squeamish about receiving it. He seemed accustomed to his masochistic stance and could not bear a challenge to it nor tolerate my attempts to unmask how he used his suffering as a justification for ignoring his wife's needs (betraying her, in a way, by being so absorbed in his work). Fixed in this sadomasochistic equilibrium, Joel decided abruptly to terminate treatment, thanking me profusely, and saying that he would let the passage of time decide whether he should get divorced or not. He seemed to be ignoring the possibility that a few years down the road, he might regret his indecision (actually a "decision" to stay masochistic) and blame time as having betrayed him. Fascinatingly, one of his favourite novels was Louis Begley's (1994) *The Man Who Was Late*, a wry account of a man unable to bear being loved and ending up committing suicide in late middle life. Joel left me sad, worried, and feeling betrayed.

This case—and the failure of treatment in this case—impels us to consider the pleasure and power of masochism. While an exhaustive review of such matters is beyond the scope of this chapter, some attention certainly needs to be paid to them here. In Brenner's (1959) perspective, masochism reflects the acceptance of a painful reality for guilt-ridden, Oedipal sexual impulses. This is often true. More pertinent to the case presented here, however, are the views of Bergler (1949) and Cooper (1988). Bergler posited that the preservation of infantile omnipotence is of prime importance to the reduction of anxiety and as a source of ego satisfaction. When the child faces excessive frustration, this omnipotence is threatened. The child feels humiliated and, as a result, furious. Being helpless to "get even" with his adult offenders, the child discharges the aggression upon himself. But, in order to maintain a semblance of omnipotence, he libidinises it and learns to extract pleasure from displeasure. Some inborn tendency made the occurrence of a pleasure-in-displeasure pattern possible.[6] These events later evolve into adult patterns of psychic masochism. Bergler delineated a three-step process as being paradigmatic in this context: (a) the masochist unconsciously incites disappointment and humiliation by his behaviour and equally unconsciously derives pleasure from it, (b) he replaces the knowledge of his own provocation and reacts to the insult with righteous indignation, and, (c) after such "pseudo-aggression" creates further defeats, he indulges in conscious self-pity. Unconsciously, he enjoys the masochistic pleasures.

In elaborating upon Bergler's ideas, Cooper (1988) noted that the capacity to defensively alter the meaning of painful experiences of childhood is largely for maintaining an illusory self-control. He states that:

> Where the experience of early narcissistic humiliation is excessive for external or internal reasons, these mechanisms of repair miscarry. The object is perceived as excessively cruel and refusing; the self is perceived as incapable of genuine self-assertion in the pursuit of gratification; the gratification obtained from disappointment takes precedence over genuine but unavailable and unfamiliar libidinal, assertive, or ego-functional satisfactions. Being disappointed or refused becomes the *preferred* mode of narcissistic assertion to the extent that narcissistic and masochistic distortions dominate the character. (p. 128, italics in the original)

Cooper emphasised that the pleasure sought in such cases is not genital-sexual; it is pre-Oedipal and pertains to self-esteem and self-coherence. The coexistence of narcissism and masochism is central to Cooper's conceptualising. He declared that:

> In any particular instance, the presenting clinical picture may seem more narcissistic or more masochistic .... However, only a short period of analysis will reveal that both types share the sense of deadened capacity to feel, muted pleasure, a hypersensitive self-esteem alternating between grandiosity and humiliation, an inability to sustain or derive satisfaction from their relationships or their work, a constant sense of envy, an unshakable conviction of being wronged and deprived by those who are supposed to care for them, and an infinite capacity for provocation. (p. 129)

Cooper's eloquence is humbling. It also serves as an exquisitely appropriate starting point for considering the problems in treating such patients.

Treatment considerations

Before elucidating the nuances and strategies of technique, two caveats must be entered. First, the suggestions I am making regarding the treatment of the betraying and betrayed patients are not to replace the customary work of empathic affirmation, transference interpretation, reconstruction, and countertransference vigilance.[7] Nor are these suggestions meant to interfere with the "trio of guideposts" (Pine, 1997, p. 13) of abstinence, neutrality, and anonymity that are a cornerstone of our approach. What follows are not rules to be followed in working with all such patients. Indeed, the more psychologically sophisticated and "analysable" the patient, the less attention needs to be paid to these guidelines. Second, even though I make separate suggestions for treating narcissistic-betraying patients and for treating masochistic-betrayed patients, the fact remains that hybrid forms of such psychopathology are common, and shifting attention to narcissistic and masochistic aspects of the patient's functioning might be essential; this would call for the use of both types of technical interventions in one and the same patient.

Having entered these two caveats, we can move on to a consideration of treating narcissistic-betraying patients. The following sequence of interventions, though appearing overly schematic when put in writing, applies here. After ample psychic space has been provided for the analysand to present his version of events and a therapeutic alliance has evolved, the analyst needs to confront the patient with (a) the driven quality of his seducing and betraying others, (b) the contradiction between his seeking love and security while not providing those very experiences to people he is involved with, (c) the denial of one's hostile and destructive aims towards others who are puppets in an inner theatre of vindictiveness, (d) the active jettisoning of moments when empathy towards one's victim is experienced and of similar affecto-cognitive movements in the transference experience. The analyst also needs to help the patient (e) become aware of the pleasure he derives from betraying others, thus seeking to render that pleasure ego-dystonic, (f) mourn the lost opportunities for love, and (g) bear the newly emergent remorse over his cruelties towards others.

Throughout such work, the twin dangers of a moralising countertransference and of causing injuring to the patient's self-esteem should be avoided. This would necessitate a coupling of interpretative unmasking with empathic-reconstructive remarks (consistently indicating the traumatic origin of the patient's behaviour). The defensive functions of betraying others (e.g., turning passive into active, warding off dependent longings) and the felt need for such defences must also be underscored.

Just as the treatment of narcissistic patients who betray others is difficult, so is working with masochistic patients who keep bringing the same tale of being betrayed in various guises again and again. Such work requires enormous patience. The analyst must not rush the process even though the material might appear eminently "interpretable". Although made in a different context, the following comment by Amati-Mehler and Argentieri (1989) is pertinent here.

> The patient ought to experience for a sufficient length of time and at different levels of the soundness of the therapeutic rapport, the security of being understood, the benefit of a careful and thorough working-through of the transference, and a relational structure that enables him or her to contain the comprehension and the elaboration of the disruption of the transference play. (p. 303)

Such disruption of the patient's masochistic proclivity, though long in coming, is ultimately essential. The analyst must (a) understand that there is a sort of "success" in all the failures reported by the patient;

(b) recognise that "… wreckage may represent more than painful defeat or punishment. For example, it may also represent the triumph of archaic moral aims over infantile libidinal aims" (Schafer, 1988, p. 83), or it may be a way to avoid separateness and aloneness by clinging to a hurtful "inconstant object" (Blum, 1981); (c) "point out to the analysand how, when, and why he or she tries to bring about failure or to experience failure, or dwells on failure in the analytic situation" (Schafer, 1988, p. 89), especially when good things are about to happen and happiness seems to be just around the corner;[8] (d) help the patient see how and how often he dismisses or minimises the presence of reliable people in his life, that is, people (including the analyst) who do not betray him; (e) unmask and interpret the patient's envy of the analyst's reliability (Kernberg, 1992) and, in a paradoxical turn of perspective, of their own reliability in keeping the analytic appointments; and, (f) manage, control, and learn from the countertransference feelings of exasperation and hostility as well as defences against these burdensome affects (Asch, 1988; Maltsberger & Buie, 1974).

A note of caution is needed here.[9] In focusing upon the betrayer's sadism and the betrayed one's masochism, one ought not overlook that the former is continually depriving himself of genuine love and affection (i.e., he is being masochistic) and that the latter in harping on about his suffering is displaying his moral superiority and a condescending attitude towards others (i.e., he's being sadistic). Remembering Freud's (1905a) declaration that sadism and masochism invariably coexist helps the analyst retain a complex and multifaceted perspective on patients' associations and transferences.

Concluding remarks

In this contribution, I have delineated some phenomenological and metapsychological aspects of betrayal. Utilising two case reports, I have attempted to show the lived and transference experience of betraying others and of feeling betrayed by others.[10] I have emphasised that these narcissistic and masochistic scenarios often coexist even if one is more overt and the other covert in a given case. Following the discussion of these cases, I have outlined some guidelines for the treatment of betraying narcissistic and betrayed masochistic patients, while reminding the reader that the suggestions I have made are neither essential nor applicable in all cases. Moreover, they are not intended to replace our usual ways of conducting analytic treatment.

While I have cast a wide net, a few questions remain unanswered. First, since both the betraying and the betrayed types seem to have suffered severe betrayal trauma in their childhood, what accounts for their phenotypical difference? In other words, why do some victims of childhood betrayal become narcissistic betrayers and others masochistic seekers of betrayal? Such "choice of neurosis" (Freud, 1896b, 1913c) is most likely dependent upon some difference in constitutional endowment with the more inherently aggressive child "opting" for the narcissistic route and the inherently less aggressive (or less outwardly aggressive) child succumbing to masochism. Perhaps the age and the degree of ego maturity when the childhood betrayal occurred and the qualitative difference in helplessness it produced (e.g., by broken promises *vs.* actual death of a parent) also play a role here. Putting all these possibilities together gives rise to the following speculations. Betrayed children who were constitutionally less aggressive, traumatised earlier, repeatedly, and had no recourse but to cling to their betrayers while growing up, most likely turn out to be masochists. Betrayed children who were constitutionally more aggressive, traumatised somewhat later, less frequently, and had recourse to carers other than their betrayers, most likely turn out to be narcissists. However, more data and more thought are needed about these issues for one to be certain about these hypotheses.

Another area that needs further exploration is why some narcissistic and some masochistic patients improve with analytic treatment while others do not. While patient-based variables (e.g., honestly, psychological-mindedness, absence of substance abuse, work-related sources of efficacy and pleasure) contribute much to the prognosis, quality of the "fit" between the patient and analyst might also matter; this non-optimally explored realm merits more investigation. And so does the potential impact of gender and culture upon which pole of the betrayer-betrayed scenario will predominate in the final psychopathological picture in those exposed to the trauma of severe betrayal during childhood.

While answers to such questions are awaited, one thing remains clear. Betrayal is both a specific form of trauma and a constituent of all psychic trauma. Sexual abuse, physical maltreatment, profound neglect, mockery, and bullying all include an element of betrayal. All involve breaking someone's trust and putting someone's faith and hope in question. As a result, the dynamic and technical observations contained in this chapter might apply—in small or large measure—to all traumatised individuals while maintaining their specificity for those who have been hurt by their carers' betrayals.

Notes

1. Having unintentionally betrayed others, however, leads to remorse, and realising that one has been unintentionally betrayed diminishes mental pain.
2. The word "betrayal" appears only eighteen times in the entire corpus of Freud's writings (Guttman, Jones & Parrish, 1980, pp. 272–273). Five of these usages are colloquial and carry little scientific significance. Nine pertain to "psychical self-betrayal" via slips of tongue (1906c), clumsy testimony during a court trial (1906c), or bodily fidgetiness in a failed attempt to suppress a secret (1905). The remaining four usages are in the context of compulsive rituals (e.g., keeping scraps of paper) to control a fear of betrayal (1896b), the mass paranoia of a nation defeated in war defensively evolving a collective "delusion of betrayal" (1895b), and the masochistic tendency of certain individuals who find themselves repeatedly betrayed by friends (1920g).
3. Besides his calling these relationships "stories", Paul always referred to various women by both their first and last names. I have encountered this phenomenon in another narcissistic patient and believe that it is an unwitting fetishistic ploy to turn women into caricatures.
4. While the term "masochism" has been used in many ways (see Maleson, 1984, for a comprehensive review), Brenner's (1959) definition remains authoritative. Masochism, for him, is "the seeking of unpleasure, by which is meant physical or mental pain, discomfort or wretchedness, for the sake of sexual pleasure, with the qualification that either the seeking or the pleasure or both may often be unconscious rather than conscious" (p. 197).
5. Limentani coined this term for an individual who harbours a powerful wish to be a woman and has deep envy of everything female. He also has a secret fantasy of possessing a vagina. Intelligent, charming, and friendly, the "vagina man" reads voraciously, looks at things intently, and insatiably seeks the company of others, especially women. He is feminine but his femininity is hidden behind his attentiveness towards women. Owing to this attentiveness, his sexual performance is better than average. According to Limentani, such a person has been raised by a mother who was somewhat masculine, while also treating her child as her phallus. The "vagina man" constellation results from an identification with such a mother. It serves as a defence against homosexuality.

Moreover, the fantasy of belonging to the other sex helps avoid the fear of castration.

6. The binding of the death instinct by the libido lays down the ground for such "primary masochism" (Freud, 1924c). While many psychoanalysts have reservations about such a formulation, poets have subscribed to this view wholeheartedly. A recent illustration (1968) is evident in the line *Ghum ke sehnay mein bhi qudrat ne mazaa rakhha hai* (literally, "Nature has created the potential of deriving pleasure from pain") by the Urdu poet, Nasir Kazmi (1925–1972).

7. Our clinical work is a peculiar amalgam of a warm relationship which we approach with "evenly suspended attention" (Freud, 1912e, p. 111) and "without memory or desire (Bion, 1967, p. 272) and a theory-driven deliberateness, hierarchy of interpretation (Lowenstein, 1951), and 'strategy' (Levy, 1987) of technique. We respond to the analysand's material with an admixture of 'free-floating responsiveness' (Sandler & Sandler, 1998) and selectively paying "attention now to defence, now to what is defended against, depending upon which is apparent in a patient's communications" (Brenner, 2000, p. 548). My proposal of certain guidelines for treating betrayed and betraying patients reflects the spirit of focused attention and strategy pole of psychoanalytic technique.

8. This, of course, is the essence of what Freud (1923b) termed "negative therapeutic reaction". He held that unconscious guilt over the wished-for childhood Oedipal transgressions of incest and murder were responsible for such a reaction. Subsequent analysts have, however, added additional dynamics including anxiety over separation from mother (Asch, 1976; Gruenhert, 1979), envy of the therapist's ability to soothe and help (Kernberg, 1984), and identification with a masochistic parent (Akhtar, 2009).

9. This discussion of betraying and being betrayed has remained patient-focused. It has not addressed betrayals of the patient by the analyst. While their gross forms (e.g., sexual boundary violations) are well-known and written about (Celenza, 2007; Gabbard & Lester, 1995), more subtle betrayals by the analyst often go unrecognised or are subsumed—by the analyst—under the rubric of "technical errors" (see Charles, 1997, for a meaningful discussion of this matter).

10. Although the two cases described here involve men betraying women or feeling betrayed by women, this does not mean that women cannot do and feel the same. Moreover, betrayal can also occur in the "non-erotic" realms of money, academic collaboration, national security, etc.

CHAPTER EIGHT

Sexual abuse of children as the betrayal of a sacred trust

Calvin A. Colarusso

C an you imagine a more hideous betrayal than that inflicted on children by a sexual perpetrator? I cannot. Further, abusing children is not an isolated or infrequent occurrence. One in three girls and one in six boys is abused before the age of eighteen. One in five young people have received a sexual approach or solicitation over the internet in recent years. Of all forcible rapes, 29 per cent occurred when the victim was under eleven years of age, while 15 per cent of sexual assault and rape victims are under the age of twelve. Children with disabilities are four to ten times more vulnerable to sexual abuse than their non-disabled peers. Nearly 30 per cent of child sexual assault victims identified by child protection service agencies were between four and seven years of age. The enormity of the betrayal is underscored by the statistic that 93 per cent of juvenile sexual assault victims know their attacker, 34.2 per cent of attackers were family members and 58.7 per cent were acquaintances, and only 7 per cent of the perpetrators were strangers to the victim. It is estimated that there are 60 million survivors of childhood sexual abuse in America today.[1]

In this contribution, I plan to first present a selective review of the literature on child sexual abuse that clearly demonstrates the enormity of the problem and the horrific developmental and emotional consequences. Then, since the topic of this volume of articles is on betrayal, I will present clinical material that focuses on the methods and behaviours of the adult perpetrators who abuse children and the devastating consequences of their betrayals. I do not plan to present complete histories or discuss treatment or prognosis. For those who are interested in a more intensive study of the long-term consequences of child sexual abuse across the life cycle, *The Long Shadow of Sexual Abuse* (Colarusso, 2010) might be a good place to start.

In the fifty years that I have been practising child and adult psychiatry and child and adult psychoanalysis, and in the thirty-plus years that I have served as an expert witness in over 100 cases of child sexual abuse, I have collected material which describes the emotional consequences of the sexual abuse at the time it was occurring and for up to fifty years afterwards. One conclusion is obvious—the effects of chronic child sexual abuse last a lifetime and profoundly complicate and undermine normal developmental processes at all phases of childhood, adolescent, and adult development. More apposite to our focus here, the case studies provide examples of how perpetrators groom their victims and the lengths to which they go to psychologically and physically dominate them. The identity of those involved has been protected by changing their names and in some instances combining material from more than one case. I have not evaluated or treated any of the perpetrators who will be described. I have evaluated and treated a number of perpetrators who will not be described to ensure confidentiality. Again, my focus in this contribution will be on the perpetrators—their methods and the fact that almost anyone known to the child may be a potential perpetrator, be it a family member, teacher, neighbour, coach, or member of the clergy—and the lifelong, terribly destructive psychopathology which develops in their victims. In each of the cases presented here, the perpetrator was convicted of the sexual abuse in question.

Contemporary literature on the effects of child sexual abuse

Child victims and adult survivors exhibit similar core symptoms of anxiety, depression, dissociation, and sexual problems. "New symptoms and defenses emerge during adolescence and adulthood, such as substance abuse, somatization, eating disorders, and personality disorders. These are maladaptive attempts to cope with the anxiety and depression linked to the childhood sexual trauma, which threaten to erupt when the victims are faced with establishing intimate or sexual relationships in adolescence and adult life. These defenses often coalesce into personality traits, attitudes and identifications that become ego syntonic and lose their connection with the childhood trauma" (Green, 1995, p. 665). Childhood sexual abuse also results in a "selective restructuring of reality" (Summit, 1983, p. 184) that, although adaptive, in some ways, occurs at the expense of good reality testing. Ehrenberg (1987) suggested that survivors of sexual abuse in childhood confuse fantasy and reality as a way of dealing with all relationships— a defensive adaptation that occurs as a means of integrating abusive experiences, and that may continue into adulthood in the absence of continuing abuse. Traumatic stress also has damaging effects on other aspects of ego functioning, such as the capacity for representation and the capacity for self-regulation (Saporta, 2003).

A variety of formal adult psychiatric diagnoses are clinically associated with childhood sexual abuse. These include the DSM-IV diagnoses of major depressive disorder, borderline personality disorder, somatisation disorder, substance abuse disorders, post-traumatic stress disorder, dissociative identity disorder, and bulimia nervosa disorder. Depression in adults and sexualised behaviours in children were the best documented outcomes. As a group, individuals with a history of childhood sexual abuse, irrespective of their psychiatric diagnoses, manifest significant problems with affect regulation, impulse control, somatisation, sense of self, cognitive distortions, and problems with socialisation. A history of childhood sexual abuse has been associated with higher rates of all disorders diagnosed in women. As is evident in the clinical material to follow, childhood sexual abuse victims, male and female, are particularly prone to use dissociative mechanisms, including amnesia, in an attempt to cope with the trauma. The use of dissociative mechanisms, including amnesia, is particularly related to chronic abuse beginning at early ages (Chu, Frey, Ganzel & Matthews, 1999; Kisiel & Lyons, 2001). Dissociation is also an important predictor of which individuals are at risk of developing post-traumatic stress disorder (Putnam & Trickett, 1997). A study by Widom (1999) indicated that slightly more than a third of the childhood victims of sexual abuse (37.5 per cent) in his study met the DSM criteria for lifetime PTSD.

Sexualised behaviours have been closely linked to child sexual abuse (Paolucci, Genuis & Violato, 1995). A history of childhood sexual abuse, but not a history of physical abuse or neglect, is associated with a significantly increased arrest rate for sex crimes and prostitution, irrespective of gender (Widom & Ames, 1994). An array of sexual activities is covered by the term child sexual abuse. These include intercourse, attempted intercourse, oral-genital contact, fondling of genitals directly or through clothing, exhibitionism or exposing children to adult sexual activity or pornography, and the use of the child for prostitution or pornography. This diversity alone ensures that there will be a range of outcomes. In addition, the age and gender of the child, the age and gender of the perpetrator, the nature of the relationship between the child and perpetrator, and the number, frequency, and duration of the abuse experience all appear to influence some outcomes. Thus, sexually abused children constitute a very heterogeneous group with many degrees of abuse about whom few simple generalisations hold (Putnam & Trickett, 1997).

Girls are two and a half to three times more likely to be abused than boys. However, approximately 22 per cent to 29 per cent of all child sexual abuse victims are male (Fergusson, Lynskey & Horwood, 1996; Finkelhor, 1993; U.S. Department of Justice, 1997). Boys are underrepresented in psychiatric samples, especially older boys who are often reluctant to admit to being sexually abused. *Research indicates that mental health professionals rarely ask adult males about childhood sexual abuse* (Lab, Feigenbaum & Desilva, 2000). The risk of being sexually abused rises with age (Finkelhor, 1993; U.S. Department of Health and Human Services, 1998). Data from 1996 indicated that approximately 10 per cent of victims were between the ages of zero and three years. The percentage almost tripled (28.4 per cent) between the ages of four and seven years. Twenty-five percent of cases occurred between the ages of eight and eleven. Children twelve years and older accounted for the remaining third (35.9 per cent) of cases (U.S. Department of Health and Human Services, 1998).

Sexually abused children have an increased suicide risk. Survey data from 83,731 students in the sixth, ninth, and twelfth grades (i.e., aged typically eleven, fourteen, and seventeen) revealed that 4 per cent of the students reported sexual abuse by a non-family member, 1.3 per cent by a family member, and 1.4 per cent by both. Young people with a history of childhood sexual abuse were at increased risk of suicide behaviours compared with others of the same age group but the risk is reduced when protective factors are in place.

> Family connectedness, teacher caring, other adult caring, and
> school safety were associated with lower levels of suicidal idea-
> tion and attempts for both male and female adolescents. Family
> connectedness appeared to have a particularly strong protective
> association with the outcomes. (Eisenberg, Ackard & Resnick,
> 2007, p. 485)

A recent study of thousands of health maintenance organisation
members (Anda et al., 2006) once again confirmed the relationship
between early adverse childhood experiences such as childhood sexual
abuse and a wide variety of psychological disorders and problems. But
more important, the researchers also found a clear relationship between
the number of adverse experiences in childhood and the degree of
psychopathology in adulthood. *Earlier and more intense adversity produced a greater number of maladaptive outcomes.* Thus, from this selective
review of the literature, it is clear that childhood sexual abuse causes
various disorders in childhood including depression, anxiety, behav-
ioural problems, sexualised behavior, and post-traumatic stress disorder (Saywitz, Mannarino, Berliner & Cohen, 2000). But it is also clear
from the case studies in this article and the literature that individuals who have been abused as children are at risk of serious problems
in adulthood such as substance abuse, impaired social relationships,
depression and suicide attempts, and sexual inhibition and acting out
(Brent, Oquenda & Birmaher, 2002; Nelson, Heath & Madden, 2002).
Indeed, research is indicating that abused children with post-traumatic
stress disorder symptoms may have smaller total brain and corpus cal-
losum volumes and lower IQs than carefully matched controls. These
differences were correlated with age of abuse onset and longer duration of PTSD symptoms (DeBellis et al., 1999). "Thus there is strong
evidence that CSA, and in particular CSA-related PTSD, places children
at increased risk for suffering potentially life-long difficulties" (Cohen,
Deblinger, Mannarino & Steer, 2004, p. 393).

Clinical illustration 1: preschool bus driver and child care worker

George and Mr. S.

Mother reported that between the ages of four and six, George attended
a preschool where Mr. S.'s job was maintenance, transportation, and

child-care before and after school. During the summer, he took the children to a nearby swimming pool on a regular basis and on occasional field trips. George was always eager to go to the preschool, particularly during the summer. In the middle of the summer when George was six, he began to resist going to school. When George was taking a bath, he told his mother how Mr. S. would "clean" his penis. He demonstrated the up and down masturbatory movement that Mr. S. used. After mother called the school and a police investigation followed, it was discovered that Mr. S. had been accused of abusing two boys at another school where he had previously worked. Mr. S. was tried and convicted.

The abuse

In the first diagnostic interview after general discussions about school and his interest in sports, I asked George to tell me about his experience with Mr. S. He drove the children on field trips, took them to the pool, and supervised the playground. When asked what Mr. S. did, George answered, "He would have me sit on his lap and stick something up my butt." George was unsure what Mr. S. put in his butt. This occurred in the bathroom after swimming at the pool. Both George and Mr. S. were naked. George wasn't sure how often this happened but he thought about ten times. "It hurt!" Mr. S. would push the thing in and out. "He would just do it." George never talked to the other children about what Mr. S. did to him or the similar things that he saw Mr. S. do to the other children. George volunteered that after the anal penetrations, "My poops would be hard and I would get constipated for a long time."

Mr. S. would also "clean" George's penis. George made a masturbatory motion as he described the cleaning. He thinks his penis got hard when Mr. S. rubbed it. He later learned about masturbation but he didn't know what was happening at the time. "I was too young to understand." The masturbation also occurred "a lot, I think more than ten times". George saw Mr. S.'s penis but didn't remember being asked to touch it.

Six years of symptoms

Mother reported that nightmares began shortly after she removed George from the preschool. They continued for approximately two years after the abuse ended. George said that the content of his nightmares consisted of "him doing it again". George's paediatrician prescribed antidepressants, which seemed to help. George began to become fearful months before the abuse was discovered. He insisted on having a night light on and refused to go to the bathroom alone. "I was afraid of him being in the bathroom and doing something to me again. I stopped being afraid once he was in prison." At the age of twelve, George still wants a night light on. "I got used to it."

George was toilet-trained by the age of two and a half for both bowel and urine. After being dry for about two years, George began to wet the bed. Between the ages of six and twelve, he wet the bed every night. More recently, the bed wetting diminished to once or twice a week. During his last summer at the preschool, George began to smear faeces on the wall. This continued for approximately a year after he left the preschool. Mother thinks that George "plays with himself in his rear". He gets up on his knees and has his hand near his rectum. Mother tries to get him to stop when she sees this behaviour but suspects that it occurs when George is alone. George was seen by a therapist who made reference to George touching another child in an inappropriate manner. George's teacher heard him talk about "humping" another child on repeated occasions. He was encopretic during the course of treatment.

Discussion

Mr. S. made little or no effort to groom George. He did not have to, he was dealing with a very young child who had no understanding of what was happening or ability to physically stop the abuse—the younger the child, the greater the power imbalance between victim and perpetrator. Such severe sexual abuse at such an early age resulted in very significant interference with developmental progression. During and following the abuse, George regressed and lost control of bowel and bladder. Faecal smearing, an extreme symptom, occurred for at least a year after the abuse ended. Occasional bed-wetting was still present six years later. George's latency years were compromised by the above-mentioned symptoms and significant levels of depression, low self-esteem, interference with formal learning, compromised peer relationships, a fear of men, an inability to be comfortably alone, and sexual acting out.

On the verge of entering adolescence, it is highly likely that he will have major difficulty integrating sexual maturation and the pressure for sexual activity which results from the outpouring of sexual hormones. Already prone to inappropriate sexual behaviour, George is at great risk of sexual interactions that could result in involvement with legal authorities. Further, his sense of sexual identity is already confused as he enters adolescence. Developing a comfortable sense of masculinity during adolescence will be extremely difficult, even with intensive therapy. George's fear of being alone and requiring his parents' presence will interfere with the separation-individuation process during adolescence. Difficulty in developing the confidence to achieve academically, participate in peer activities such as much-loved athletics, and relating to male peers and adults should be anticipated.

Clinical illustration 2: latency and adolescence—neighbour

Sally and Mr. Z.

Sally was eighteen when I evaluated her in connection with her lawsuit against a neighbour who began sexually molesting her when she was seven years of age. The abuse continued until Sally was aged approximately twelve. However, the molestation was not discovered until Sally was almost seventeen. The perpetrator was convicted and was in jail at the time of the civil suit.

The abuse

Sally was unable to speak coherently about the details of the sexual abuse. It was told in bits and pieces but detailed descriptions of what happened were obtained from legal documents. Most of the abuse took place in Mr. Z.'s home, which was nearby Sally's. Sally's mother reported that the parents had known each other for years but Sally's parents had never suspected that the florid symptoms that they saw in their daughter were related to the friendly neighbour, Mr. Z., who took the children out for ice cream, to the mall, and babysat on occasion. Further, Sally seemed to like spending time at the Z.s' home. Mr. Z.'s behaviour was classical grooming behaviour. He formed a close relationship with Sally's parents. He was always kind and friendly to Sally and other children in the neighbourhood. If Sally's parents had been aware of the connection between Sally's severe symptoms and the possibility that sexual abuse was the cause of them, they might have been able to connect Mr. Z.'s special, continuous interest in Sally with her symptoms and the possibility that he was abusing her.

Sally was able to tell me that when she was seven or eight, Mr. Z. would take her upstairs to his bedroom. At first they just sat on the bed and talked. As time went on, Mr. Z. asked Sally to undress so he could take pictures of her. "He kissed me a couple of times" (she could not continue). Sally nodded in agreement when, using information obtained from legal documents, I mentioned that he had her masturbate him and perform fellatio. Later she added that sometimes he gave her drugs and alcohol. Mr. Z. admitted to giving Sally drugs and alcohol but did not describe what sexual acts he performed on the girl when she was under the influence of these substances. The abuse was repeated a hundred or more times over a five-year span.

Ten years of symptoms

In my diagnostic interview with her, mother described Sally as being very anxious and depressed, eating irregularly, and lacking confidence. She began to notice a dramatic change in her daughter in third or fourth grade (year three or four of school). Prior to that time, Sally was a very easy-going, loving, happy child who separated easily when attending kindergarten. She was considered to be a rapid learner who had a fine memory. Sally was very successful academically in the early elementary grades and had numerous friends.

Sally began wetting herself at school. An evaluation by a paediatrician failed to discover an organic cause. The wetting, always during the day, continued occasionally throughout middle school and high school (i.e., between the ages of twelve and seventeen) and still occurs. Elementary school teachers began to comment that Sally spent her time daydreaming. She was not paying attention and did not seem able to concentrate. In middle school Sally "… really started to fall apart. She shut down and couldn't cope." Mother was particularly distressed when Sally began neglecting her hygiene. She would not take showers for days on end unless forced to do so. On other occasions, she stayed in the shower forever. Sally has difficulty leaving the house and rarely initiates any activities. "Sally missed out on all the normal things that kids her age do—close friends, dating, having fun. There is no bond with friends."

Mother spoke of Sally's "maddening" disorganisation. She is often anxious and depressed. Sally won't get a job and is only comfortable with family. "It's a nightmare that won't go away." Mother discovered the pervasive nature of the sexual abuse by reading legal documents. She was shocked by the accounts of masturbation, oral sex, and the use of drugs and alcohol to enable Mr. Z. to dominate Sally.

Sally was able to talk about the effects of the sexual abuse on her. "The abuse affected me more than I realized when it started. It also affected my mom. I know it's a big deal but I just want to block it out. It's in the past. I just want to forget it." Recently, Sally and her parents moved away from the neighbourhood they had lived in for years to avoid the Z. family and the memories associated with the abuse. "My family trusted them. It was an abuse of trust. I was very shy in middle school. I was always thinking about the abuse. I was hiding it from everyone. I wanted to tell my mother for a long time but I couldn't find the words."

The Z.s would call and offer to take Sally to the mall or shopping. Although she did not want to go and knew Mr. Z. would abuse her, Sally could not bring herself to say no. "I always got nervous when I was with him. I kinda shut down. I wanted to resist him. I'd get worked up and shut down. When I was with him I'd stand there. He'd do things to me. I just shut down." High school records indicated four years of marginal grades, frequent incompletes, excessive absences, little effort, and failure to meet standards. Special class placements and tutoring allowed Sally to meet the minimal standards for graduation, at the bottom of her class.

Discussion

Mr. Z.'s grooming behaviour was classic. With an outward appearance of friendliness to Sally's family and treating her in a special manner, taking her to places, and buying her treats and small gifts, he gained the confidence of the child and her parents. Then he began asking Sally to spend time with him alone in his home. Approximately seven years of age at the time that the abuse began, Sally was innocent and trusting of her caring neighbour. She did not have the maturity to say no when he asked her to take her clothes off so he could photograph her. The sexual abuse began soon after. Sally's immature mind was clearly overwhelmed by the experiences and fell under Mr. Z.'s spell. Like most abused children, she could neither stop the relationship nor find the words·to tell her parents about it. The profound change in her personality and severe arrest of her adolescent development was overwhelmingly evident near the end of adolescence, six years after the abuse had stopped.

Clinical illustration 3: young adulthood—family member

Ben and Joe

Ben was twenty-seven years old when he came for his evaluation. Casually dressed, hesitant but cooperative as the interview progressed, he seemed relieved to finally be able to tell someone "about my secret". Ben had a good vocabulary and was able to express his thoughts and feelings clearly. Throughout the interview, he experienced intense shame, disgust, anger, and depression as he told his story. A clerk in a large retail store, Ben was single and lived alone. Joe, the perpetrator, was a relative who had known Ben all of his life. He had easy access to the boy and knew when Ben's parents would be away working. In addition, Joe offered to have Ben stay at his house when his parents were away for weekends or on business. The abuse began when Ben was eight. Over the next three years, he was abused approximately 100 times.

The abuse

The first episode took place at Joe's house while the two were watching television. Joe put his arm around Ben and then slid his other hand inside the boy's pants. Ben was confused but did not resist. Joe told Ben that he was going to show him how to be a man. Joe had frequently talked to Ben about growing up and going out with girls prior to the first abuse. Ben had not the slightest interest in girls at the time but he did like listening to Joe's stories about having sex with girls and "jerking off". The second episode occurred soon after. This time, Joe moved his hands up and down on the boy's penis. Ben had not masturbated on his own prior to this experience. Joe explained that "jerking off was fun". With considerable hesitation and shame, Ben admitted getting an erection and enjoying the sensation in his penis. As he talked, Ben volunteered that throughout the years, he had tried not to blame himself for getting an erection and enjoying the feeling but he couldn't. He should have told someone, or told Joe to stop, but he was afraid that he would be blamed for what happened. Anyway, Joe had told him that it was their secret and Ben would know more about sex than the other boys.

Over the next three years, Joe abused Ben nearly every time they were together. In addition to sleepovers, Joe frequently drove Ben to school and to sporting events. Sometimes the abuse occurred in Ben's house while his parents were there. Joe would just laugh if Ben worried that his parents might see them. So what if they did, Joe said, they wouldn't care. The abuse consisted of masturbation and oral sex. Sometimes Joe showed Ben pictures of naked girls or pornography. Joe never asked Ben to touch his penis although the boy did see him masturbate on numerous occasions. Ben never understood why the abuse stopped when he was about twelve. Joe just didn't abuse him any more. It is highly likely that Joe stopped abusing Ben when the first signs of puberty appeared. Some abusers are only interested in sexually immature bodies. The dynamics behind this are multiple but certainly among them are the ability to easily dominate and control a young child and feelings of inadequacy when sexually involved with another physically mature body.

The effect of the abuse

When he became an adolescent, Ben wondered if he was gay. By then, he knew that what had happened with Joe was wrong. He never said anything because his parents were close to Joe and he still worried that they would not believe him. After all, Joe was married and had children of his own. He wasn't interested in boys. Ben had many thoughts about the effects of the sexual abuse. "I don't trust any males, including the men in my family. I worry that one of them might abuse me. I don't want to hug any male. Keeping the secret was hard for me. I couldn't tell my friends, they would laugh at me. When I heard stories about kids being sexually abused, I was sure that people knew I was abused too. I learned to hate the word 'faggot' or 'gay'. I got very upset whenever anyone used those words. I got into a lot of fistfights."

When Ben masturbated during adolescence he became very upset because thoughts about Joe would intrude into his consciousness.

"It was always in the back of my mind. It played all the time. I had a mask on. I played sports. I tried to have a normal life. When I see or hear stuff about abuse, it brings back all the memories, like a movie reel." Ben had his first girlfriend and experience with sexual intercourse during high school. He dated the same girl throughout these years.

Now in his late twenties, Ben dates women but constantly worries that they will find out he was abused and suspect that he is gay. When Ben has sex, he constantly worries that he will not be able to perform and is preoccupied with keeping memories of the abuse by Joe out of consciousness. Ben wants to marry and have children but worries that he might not be a good father or husband and might be afraid to touch his children.

A statement of torment

Ben presented me with the following statement. It summarised better than I possibly could the lasting effects of the childhood sexual abuse.

"The memory remains with me. There is no cure for the pain and humiliation I have suffered through as a child. No matter how hard I try to forget the past, the pain will forever be in my mind and in my soul. I am now tattooed with this emotional pain forever. I will take this horrible memory with me until God decides to take me away from this earth. At times, I question God. I ask him, 'If you love all your children, why did you let this happen to me? Was I a bad son?' Was God trying to teach me a lesson?

"I do not have the answers to any of the questions I have mentioned above, but I do believe that God loves me. I believe that God will always be with me in my time of need. I hope that when God decided to take me, the pain will go away and never come back. It is not easy going through life knowing that you have been violated. I can try to forget, but the pain will forever be a part of my life. At times I feel hollow. It is as if my childhood memories have been erased, and replaced with horrible memories. I feel that someone came into my life and took something from me that I could never get back. I wish I could erase my past. I wish I could have lived a normal childhood with good memories like my friends did. I hate living a life that has been violated. He did not only violate me, he violated my family. He violated my trust. I feel that I can't trust anyone. It is horrible to go through life not trusting anyone. At times, I feel I could not trust my own family. The two adults that raised me, I did not trust. Three years of humiliation and violation will forever be in my life. Only three years, three years that have ruined my childhood as well as my adulthood.

"How come I did not ask for help? I was scared. I was scared that nobody would believe me. I was scared that somebody would try to hurt me if I told. I also did not tell anybody because I was embarrassed. Can you imagine if your friends found out that you have been violated? They would single you out or even make fun of you. I already felt alone on the inside. Why do I want to feel alone on the outside as well? Growing up in a small town is not always easy. People talk and things get around. Even if the rumors are false, people still tend to believe them.

"No matter what I try to fill that emptiness with, the past will always find a way to squeeze through to fill the empty spot. I will take this experience and try to leave it where it belongs in the past. It belongs in the past. I will take this whole experience and try to make something positive come out of it. I'm tired of looking at my life through a kaleidoscope. It is a shattered past that went in circles. I can only wish that what I had experienced didn't happen to anybody else because the memories remain with you until you stop breathing. But in all reality, it will happen because there are monsters and predators feeding on the souls of the weak. These people take advantage of other people's flesh and at the same time destroy their minds. It makes me sick to think that there are human beings on this earth that are willing to take advantage of the weak. It makes me sick that in their minds they can justify this type of violation as being 'ok.' It makes me sick that people like this roam the earth."

Clinical illustration 4: the decade of the thirties: teacher-coach

Louis, Bill, and Mr. D.

In the case study that follows, two young boys were sexually abused, alone and together, by a teacher at the school they attended. The boys never talked about the abuse that took place during and after sixth grade (year six of school). After graduating from elementary school, the boys went to different junior high schools and lost contact with each other. After sexual abuse cases began to appear in the media when he was an adult, Louis decided to try to find Bill. Eventually the two men, now in their thirties, met and agreed to openly acknowledge what had happened to them and initiate lawsuits.

Louis was a small business owner who had recently married. Unlike many sexual abuse victims who were embarrassed and timid, Louis was anxious to talk. A grim-faced man, he described what had been done to him and how it affected his life.

The perpetrator, Mr. D., was a single adult male in his forties. Louis and Bill, who were friends, were both in Mr. D.'s class. They were close to Mr. D., who took a special interest in both of them and served as a coach of their basketball team. Mr. D. had been grooming the boys for some time by giving them special attention, making sexual references, and telling dirty jokes. He began to enquire into the boys' sexual interests. One day Mr. D. asked Louis if Bill jerked off. Louis replied that he didn't know (Louis did not know that Bill was already being abused by Mr. D.). Mr. D. asked if Louis had ever had an orgasm. At the time Louis was not very surprised by the questions, although somewhat embarrassed, because he had heard Mr. D. make sexual references before, but never directly about Louis's sexuality. "I was in awe of him. He seemed to know everything. He was really a life mentor." Mr. D. asked if the two boys ever jerked off together. Did they see which of them could shoot the farthest? Mr. D. became a friend of Louis's family. He praised Louis to his parents and was often invited to dinner. "He got in with my family."

The sexual abuse of Louis

The first sexual abuse involving Louis took place at Mr. D.'s home. He had invited the two boys to stop by after basketball practice. Louis could not remember the details of how the boys' clothing came off but he vividly remembered that Mr. D. encouraged the two boys to orally copulate each other. Louis was totally unprepared and surprised by Bill's willingness to suck on his penis but he went along with the activity because he did not know what else to do. While the fellatio was occurring, Mr. D. asked if Louis had come. Was there any "pre-come"? He asked Bill what Louis's come tasted like. Louis thinks that Mr. D. suggested anal sex but he does not remember if that actually occurred. While the boys were involved with each other, Mr. D. had removed his clothes and lay on the bed next to the boys, masturbating. Louis thought that there were other similar incidents in which he also performed fellatio on Bill but he couldn't be sure. I had the impression that some instances of the sexual abuse that Louis experienced were crystal clear but others had been partially or totally repressed.

A week or so later, the boys were taking showers after basketball practice. Mr. D. came into the shower with an erection. He told the boys that he would show them what "real come" was like and ejaculated in front of them. Louis was certain that a similar incident occurred at least several more times. On some of these occasions, Mr. D. would take Louis's hand and put it on his penis, moving the hand up and down. "I can see it in my mind like I was watching and then I don't remember."

Louis described with embarrassment, disgust, and anger how he began to initiate and suggest sexual activity to Mr. D. One day when they were in Mr. D.'s car, Louis began to rub Mr. D.'s shoulders and asked if the teacher was going to let Bill suck his penis. On another occasion, Louis was eager to masturbate in front of Mr. D. to show him how far he could ejaculate. On another occasion Mr. D. took the boys and a third child on an overnight trip to a nearby city. Louis remembers all of them being naked and had a vague memory of being in a bathtub with Mr. D. On this occasion, the teacher showed the boys pornography and told them that they would all get in trouble if they told anyone what had happened. "I know there is other stuff but I can't pull it out of the memory bank."

The sexual abuse of Bill

Mr. D. began abusing Bill when he was in sixth grade. Verbal and physical abuse preceded the sexual abuse. "If I didn't do my homework, Mr. D. would paddle [beat] me. I was terrorized. He threatened me and got red in the face. He was very angry. It was like looking into the eyes of a lion." "Paddling" took place on a regular basis in the classroom and a supply room nearby. As Bill spoke, it was clear that he did not see that the verbal and physical abuse was Mr. D.'s way of grooming him for the sexual abuse that was to follow.

The first sexual abuse occurred in a room off the classroom. Mr. D. asked Bill to undress. Bill expected to be paddled again. Instead Mr. D. had Bill sit on his lap. Bill asked why but Mr. D. did not answer. Instead, he began masturbating Bill, who got an erection and climaxed. He was not old enough to ejaculate. Mr. D. asked Bill if it felt good and told him that the teacher was his friend and this was their secret. Then Mr. D. pulled his pants down, masturbated, and had Bill touch his penis as he climaxed.

The second incident of sexual abuse took place soon after at Mr. D.'s home. The teacher took Bill to his bedroom and told the boy to sit on the bed and watch TV. As Mr. D. stripped to his shorts his erection was evident. He asked Bill to roll on his back. The teacher stripped Bill and masturbated him to a climax. Then he had Bill masturbate him to a climax. He repeated that this was fun and it was what friends did with each other.

The sexual encounters escalated and began to include simulated anal sex and oral copulation. Mr. D. would perform oral sex on Bill. After Bill was old enough to ejaculate—he had his first ejaculation as a result of stimulation by Mr. D.—the man would swallow his semen. These experiences occurred once or twice a week throughout the spring and summer of Bill's second year in sixth grade. As if the realisation of what he had just revealed was too much to bear, Bill confessed, "I knew that guys and girls were supposed to be together. I knew that what Mr. D. was doing to me was wrong." The sexual abuse was most frequent and intensive during the summer after Bill's second year in sixth grade. By then, Mr. D. made Bill fellate him. He was not sure if Mr. D. ever ejaculated in his mouth. Mr. D. would also have Bill put one or two fingers in Mr. D.'s anus while masturbating him.

Mr. D. gradually involved Louis in the sexual activity that had been occurring for some time with Bill. Mr. D. "had us do things to each other. We never talked about it. When Mr. D. would do things to Louis, I would go into a *black hole*. I'd close my eyes, go into the darkness and hear nothing." This happened many times. Bill remembered "drifting right into the scene" when Mr. D. would come into the shower with the boys and tell Louis to touch his penis. He often had a memory gap of minutes or hours after such an experience. The same thing happened when Mr. D. abused Bill, particularly with simulated anal sex or fellatio. "I have a lot of blanks. I can't remember a lot of what happened."

The abuse ended when Bill called Mr. D. after his second year in sixth grade. "I told him I didn't want to do that anymore. I was shaking on the phone. He pleaded with me. It never happened again."

The perpetrator's methods

Once again, we see classical grooming techniques. Mr. D. paid special attention to these two boys who grew to admire and idolise him. He also sought out and built a relationship with Louis's family. The fact that he was the boys' teacher and coach gave him nearly continuous access to them while in a position of authority that allowed him to dominate and control them. Mr. D. also used verbal intimidation and physical abuse to dominate Bill before sexually abusing him the first time, a not infrequent technique in perpetrators.

The symptoms of Louis and Bill

After high school, Louis was having sex with a girl when he had a flashback of Mr. D., Bill, and he having sex. He vomited on the girl. After that, every time Louis had sex he thought about Mr. D. and lost his erection. During his twenties, Louis would think about the "gay stuff" to prevent premature ejaculation. He began using illegal drugs in an attempt to blot out the memories. The use of marijuana for this purpose continues to the present. "If I don't take drugs I'm afraid I'll lose my mind. I don't trust anybody, only my family. I never let people get too close".

His grades "went to hell" in senior high school. Louis was involved in vandalism. "I drive my car way over the speed limit and take chances." He has always been preoccupied with the sexual abuse, more so since going public. "I think I could have done more with my life. I could have gone to college. I had disciplinary problems. I didn't use my potential. My parents never knew what happened. I used to battle with them all the time. I never told them because I thought it would break my mother's heart."

Bill began drinking at the age of fourteen. He drank heavily in high school. "Today on weekends, I get drunk ninety-five percent of the time. I haven't had any DUIs but I've driven drunk." Bill also used numerous illegal drugs throughout his teen years and twenties. He stopped using drugs five years ago when he became a Christian. "I'm thirty-five years old and I barely make enough to live on. I've never been able to save any money. My fiancée pushes me every day. She makes four times as much as I do. I've never had any drive to do more." Bill is depressed and has suicidal thoughts but has not acted on them. He is struggling sexually and avoids sex with his fiancée. Bill tries hard not to think about the abuse while having sex. If he does he tries to finish as soon as possible. Bill watched heterosexual pornography compulsively during adolescence and in his twenties. "I feel bad that I never told anyone. I didn't help the boys who were molested after I was."

Clinical illustration 5: midlife: cose family friend,

Andrew and David

In his forty-eight years of life, Andrew had never told anyone other than his lawyer that he had been molested and had never described the details of the molestation to anyone. Casually dressed and small in stature, Andrew frowned constantly and cried frequently during the interview. Married and the father of a child, he worked in a warehouse.

The abuse

With great reluctance and intense shame, Andrew slowly told the story of the nearly ten years of molestation by a close friend of his family. David was Andrew's father's best friend. He was always at Andrew's home and sometimes served as family chauffeur to relieve Andrew's mother of the burden. She had other children to care for and welcomed David's offer to help. David always offered to take Andrew to the park, to his Little League game or to spend a few hours at his apartment. He had access to Andrew almost any time he wanted it. When Andrew was four years of age, David would grab his buttocks and fondle his penis. Eventually, the touching became prolonged masturbation that "became routine". David told Andrew that if he told anyone, his family would become homeless.

When Andrew was five years old, the abuser began to have Andrew masturbate him. As the molestation progressed, David wanted the relationship to become more personal and began to kiss the boy. Andrew tried, unsuccessfully, to resist. The abuser began to fellate Andrew when he was about eight years of age. Soon after David taught Andrew to perform fellatio on him. When the boy began to ejaculate a few years later, David's interest in oral sex increased. At about the same time, the abuser began to anally penetrate his victim. As he approached puberty, Andrew began to resist David's advances, but despite his efforts the abuse continued until he was in junior high school (aged about sixteen) and able to physically resist his oppressor. Andrew estimated that the total number of sexual molestations was well over 100.

The perpetrator's methods

Once again, we see the same themes. A close family friend, who was trusted by Andrew's parents and had access to the child almost any time he wished, used the trust and access to repeatedly abuse a very young child. He had no reason to give four-year-old Andrew an explanation of what he was doing. He began the abuse before the child had any ability to understand what was happening or to defend himself. He was totally under David's control for years. As he approached puberty, Andrew understood what was happening. Once Andrew was in junior high school, he was big enough and strong enough to physically resist David and stop the abuse.

Andrew's symptoms

Nearly thirty years after the chronic sexual abuse ended, Andrew's mental and emotional life continued to be dominated by its effects. Intrusive thoughts about the molestation haunt Andrew on a daily basis. He continues to have nightmares about David pursuing and anally penetrating him. Other nightmares focus on the perpetrator's attempts to pursue Andrew's child. In addition, he frequently wakes up at night expecting David to be in the room ready to rape him. Premature ejaculation began during adolescence and continues, unabated, to the present. Andrew has problems maintaining an erection and frequently becomes flaccid during sex. When he was involved with David, his erections were firm. In his early twenties, Andrew had two homosexual experiences in which he allowed men to perform oral sex on him. In ninth grade (when aged about fourteen), Andrew began to use drugs and alcohol. Within a year, he was using cocaine, marijuana, and acid. Extensive drug use, which Andrew related to his attempts to control intense feelings of depression and blot out memories of the abuse, continued into his thirties. Andrew had a DUI in his twenties. He has been sober for the past several years. When the abuse became known to his family within the past ten years, it caused a serious disruption in family relationships which continues to the present. "We're strangers to each other. I haven't been talking to my family at all. I get angry being around them. They act like this is all my problem." Soon after the revelation to his family, Andrew made a serious suicide attempt.

Clinical illustration 6: late adulthood: a priest

Monica, Noreen, and Paulette, and Father T.

I have chosen three case examples from among six of women who were abused by the same priest, Father T. In each instance, the devastation began in childhood and continued, decade by decade, culminating in their forties and fifties in fuller realisations by the victims of how the abuse that took place so long ago continues to dominate their lives. These women had never discussed the childhood sexual abuse that occurred more than five decades ago until recently. The intense affects and suffering that accompany their attempts to begin to deal with what happened to them so long ago graphically demonstrate the undiminished, lifelong power of childhood sexual abuse to destroy lives. The three women were abused between the ages of eight and twelve, all members of a church choir, who were among others repeatedly abused by a priest from the parish they and their families attended. At the time of my evaluations, they were in their early sixties. None had come forward over half a century since the abuse occurred until the widespread abuse within the Catholic Church was reported in the press and on television. All pursued legal action at the time and were part of the settlement that resulted from the legal process against a large diocese.

The sexual abuse of Monica

Monica was sixty-two when I evaluated her. She had clear memories of two occasions of abuse and near-rape at her home, and was almost certain that there were more than two. In addition, she has memories of abuse in a car and at choir practice. The first abuse occurred at Monica's home when she was ten years old. Both parents were working and since it was summer, Monica was at home alone. Father T. knew that because he was a friend of the family. He came by one morning when Monica was in her pajamas. "He put his arms around me. He was hot and sweaty and his genitals were throbbing. He moved back and forth when I was on his lap. He French kissed me. I did nothing. I thought I would be sick when his tongue was in my mouth. I was really naïve. He was one mass of sweat. I knew nothing about sex. My parents never talked about it. I had no knowledge of what was going on." Monica was upset about not doing anything to stop the priest. "I'm trying to look at it from an adult perspective."

The second time occurred soon after, during the same summer. "He came to the door and said he wanted to talk to me. I refused to sit near him but he pulled me to him. He was standing, rubbing around me, sweating and kissing me. I couldn't get away. His hands were all over my back and buttocks. After he left I took a bath. I'm not really sure what happened. I can't remember." Monica's memory stops at the point where he is holding her and rubbing his erection against her. "Such a complete blank, it upsets me."

A similar incident occurred shortly after: during choir practice, Father T. sat next to Monica. "I thought he was holding my hand. I can't remember anything else. He was in his cassock." As an adult, she came to believe that he was moving her hand on his penis. "I have such a clear memory of other things. Why didn't I say anything? Why didn't I tell my parents? I hated choir. I have memories of being in the choir and then of leaving and not knowing what happened in-between. I know he sat next to other girls. I remember him comforting one girl who was crying. The nun director would look at him. She knew he was there. He sat wherever he wanted. He was there all the time. It was like he was part of the choir."

Monica went to confession with Father T. She had to. She remembers the nuns telling her to go to Father T. "I was a very compliant child." She did as she was told. Now, she believes that Father T. told the nuns which children he wanted to hear in confession. This occurred several times. "He would say, 'Hi Monica' and laugh. He wanted me to know he knew who I was."

The perpetrator's methods

Father T. was a friend of the family. As a priest, he was revered and considered to be a guardian and protector of the young. His knowledge of Monica's parents' work schedules allowed him to abuse her in her home. Once he was on church grounds, he was totally in control of the environment and brazenly conducted the sexual abuse of Monica and the others in front of the nuns who were present and on occasion observed the abuse while it was occurring. Access, trust, power, and supposed holiness—Father T. used them all in order to violently abuse his victims.

Monica's symptoms

"I've been uncomfortable all of my life with men. I drank a lot and then I could date." Monica did very little dating in high school and college. She was a virgin when she married. "I don't like sex. The only time I could have sex was after I drank a lot. After divorcing, "I had a lot of one-nighters after drinking. When I would drink when I was younger everything was a blur. I don't like French kissing. I never had a good handle on my sex life. I don't like sex with my current husband who is a great guy. We are loving to each other but no sex. I feel guilty all the time about my single days, having sex, using birth control. I've separated my faith from the church. I'm angry at the people who say we should let bygones be bygones. I believe in God but I don't believe in organized religion and I don't go to church."

The sexual abuse of Noreen

Noreen was a sixty-two-year-old married woman when we met. She was more direct than the other women and was extremely angry about what happened to her. Like the others, she was a member of the girls' choir and in sixth grade when the sexual abuse by Father T. began. One day at choir practice, Father T. sat next to Noreen and put his hand under her dress. He then put her on his lap and placed her hand on his penis. When Noreen tried to get him to stop, Father T. said that he would abuse her younger sister if she didn't obey him. He placed his fingers in her vagina and forced her to rub his penis until he ejaculated.

After choir practice, Father T. took Noreen into the church and put his penis in her mouth, forcing her to suck on it until he ejaculated. Noreen gagged, cried and begged but it made no difference because Father T. held her down. Her sister waited on the front steps of the church, crying because Noreen was not there. Mother was angry at Noreen because she left her sister alone. This same pattern took place every Saturday and Sunday. "It was never ending." There were times during the school week when Father T. would ask the nuns if Noreen could help him with something. He always abused her on these occasions.

The children went to confession on a regular basis. Noreen told another priest that she had committed adultery. The priest laughed. When Noreen told him what Father T. had done to her, the confessor called her a liar and said that her sins would not be forgiven until she recanted her lies. Sobbing, Noreen said that the story was true and ran out of the confessional. There were times when Noreen would have to confess to Father T. There was no confessional booth, only a kneeler and a screen on the altar. "Those experiences were torture."

Noreen told her mother that she didn't want to go to choir practice but mother, who was very religious, insisted. When Noreen told her mother what Father T. was doing to her, her mother hit her and punished her for lying. Noreen estimated that she was sexually abused more than 100 times during the sixth and seventh grades (when she was aged eleven to twelve). She was raped on a number of those occasions. Noreen remembered being forced to go to places with Father T. despite screaming to her mother that she didn't want to go. In the car, Noreen was forced to rub the priest's penis. Then he drove to a secluded place and raped her. Noreen remembered screaming from the pain. "I never, ever forgot that," she said. After that, Father T. raped Noreen on several more occasions in church buildings. All of the sexual abuse occurred before Noreen went through puberty at about the age of fourteen. During choir practice Noreen saw Father T. sit next to other girls but she never looked at him. She always kept her eyes closed, hoping that he would not sit next to her. The abuse ended abruptly when Father T. was transferred.

Noreen's symptoms

She began having nightmares shortly after Father T. left. They continue to the present on a two- to three-times-per-week basis. In the nightmares, Noreen is in a pit, trying to get out. Something big is holding her down. "There are penises everywhere." Other dreams are about rape or being pushed into choir lofts in churches. "There is always a power struggle."

"I can't go into churches with choir lofts. I can't go to the places where he raped me. I hate to speak to adults and for the most part I'm withdrawn. I have dreams and nightmares which are terrible. I sleep with something in my right hand all the time because if I don't, to this day, I can feel his penis in my hand. I hold a teddy bear most of the time." She continued, "Sexually life with my husband is hell. He describes me as a dead body." Noreen rarely climaxes. She has to work up her courage to perform oral sex on her husband and gags when she does. "My husband has been very supportive. I told him I was abused when we dated but I didn't tell him about the rapes until five or six years ago."

"I have to control everything. I'm extremely careful of my grandchildren. I don't want to let them out of my sight. My daughter thinks I'm crazy because I'm always telling her to watch her children. She doesn't know what happened to me."

"My weight got up to over 300 pounds. Then, I forced myself to lose some, but I'm on the way back up. I dig at my arms. I bite my nails all the time. I always had a very low opinion of myself. I feel fat and unattractive. To this day, I wonder what my husband sees in me. I think I've been depressed for years. I would go someplace in my mind to avoid painful thoughts." Noreen had and has many suicidal thoughts but has never made an actual attempt.

Mother died without ever believing her daughter. After mother's death, Noreen tried to help herself. She saw a psychologist and wrote letters to her priest, the district attorney, and the bishop. The district attorney never replied. The pastor told her to call the bishop's office. The office offered counselling if they could receive reports. Noreen refused. She contacted an attorney when the newspapers and TV began to describe abuse in other parts of the country. "Every decision I made in my life was a response to being abused, even for something as simple as asking directions."

Like most of the girls, Noreen grew up in an intact family. She was physically healthy. Mother was a full-time at-home carer. There were no significant separations from either parent. Noreen was well behaved during elementary school, the years in which the sexual abuse occurred. Puberty occurred at the age of thirteen to fourteen. Noreen did some dating during high school. She graduated in the upper third of her class and did not have problems with drugs, alcohol, or the police during adolescence. Noreen married in her early twenties to the first man that she dated seriously and spent her young adult years raising children and working. Noreen never let her children out of her sight. At the time of the evaluation, she continued to work. The marriage was intact despite the near-total absence of sexual relations.

The sexual abuse of Paulette

Paulette was fifty-nine at the time of the evaluation. Like the others, she was ashamed and embarrassed during the interview, crying and sobbing frequently. Paulette said that she was abused approximately seven or eight times, possibly more, when she was aged seven. The first abuse occurred in the church when Father T. accused Paulette of stealing. She was unsure of what happened but knows the priest gave her a gift to take home with her at the end of the interaction.

Father T. frequently came to choir practice and sat next to Paulette. He put his arm around Paulette's shoulder and said nice things. Father T. took Paulette's hand and put it in his cassock, on his penis, flesh to flesh. "He moved my hand around on his penis." When he ejaculated, Father T. held Paulette's hand on his penis so that her hand became wet. Paulette did not know what a penis was or what Father T. was doing. She was confused and embarrassed when her hand got wet. The priest had a white cloth that he used to wipe his ejaculate off Paulette's hand. After practice, Paulette washed her hands and went home. She did not tell anyone. She did not know what to say.

The second episode during choir practice was similar to the first. As Father T. approached Paulette, she thought, "He will do it again and make my hand all sticky." This time she resisted but he was too strong. The masturbation was more forceful and faster paced. Paulette looked intently at the nun who was leading the choir. The nun definitely saw Paulette's wet hand and did nothing. The third through sixth episodes during choir practice were all about the same.

Paulette had a vivid memory of being raped. After paying attention to several girls on the church school playground, Father T. asked Paulette to go for a walk with him. She had on a school uniform and a special sweater that she had begged her mother to let her wear to school that day. In a secluded area, Father T. took off Paulette's sweater and had her lie on her back. Paulette has a memory of looking up at the sweater and "being poked with a stick". She has no memory of the priest being naked or penetrating her with his penis. Paulette remembers looking frantically for her sweater. "I never found it. I got into trouble with my mom because I lost it." Paulette does not remember how she got home. She discovered blood on her underwear and legs and a cut on her labia. Urination was painful for some time afterwards. Paulette showed her underwear to her father and said that her privates hurt. Father told mother, who said she was becoming a woman. Mother gave her a vaginal pad and told her to go to bed. Paulette thinks there was a second rape but she has no clear memory of it.

Paulette's symptoms

"It took my soul. It took my trust in God, my self-worth, and my ability to love and be loved. I can't feel loved and I don't trust anybody, no one at all." Paulette described a strong dislike of anything sexual. "I don't have sex. I didn't like sex. I didn't want anyone, including my husband, to touch me. I don't like to be hugged. I never even hugged my children when they were growing up."

Paulette does not have friends. "I want friends but I'm afraid to trust anyone. I don't feel anyone wants to be my friend. This was a priest who did this to me. He was from God. I never thought God would do anything like this to me. My life is to go to work, make dinner, and go to bed. I don't talk to anyone and I don't do anything else." With pressure of speech and associations, she described the loss of her faith. Paulette does not go to church and feels alone and isolated from God. "I struggle with alcohol. I've been battling it all of my adult life. I'm on Antabuse and I've tried everything but I can't seem to stop." Since becoming aware of how widespread the sexual abuse was across the country and beginning to become involved in a lawsuit herself, Paulette has gained nearly fifty pounds. Although she was slightly overweight prior to that time, her weight had been stable for many years.

Concluding remarks

There is very little that I can or need to add to the clinical material just presented. It speaks for itself. In each instance, the perpetrator used his position, power, knowledge, and grooming techniques with the children and their parents in order to create an atmosphere in which the sexual abuse could take place, over and over again. As mentioned in the first sentence in this article, I can think of no greater betrayal than the repeated sexual abuse of a defenceless child by a determined adult. The betrayal destroys the sacred trust a child puts in his parent and is horrific because the effects continue throughout life, destroying developmental processes, relationships, and lives and rendering the adult survivors incredibly troubled and pained.

Note

1. See references to the National Resource Center on Child Sexual Abuse, 1994; the U.S. Department of Health and Human Services, Statistics, 2000; the U.S. Department of Health and Human Services Administration for Children and Families, Child Maltreatment Statistics, 1995; the U.S. Department of Justice Sex Offense and Offenders Study, 1997; and the Reported Maltreatment Types of Victim, 2010 (PDF-4140 KB), Children's Bureau, U.S. Department of Health and Human Services (2011).

CHAPTER NINE

The extramarital affair and the betrayal of a spouse

Elizabeth H. Thomas

Betrayal is a familiar theme in myth, legend, poetry, film, and in classical as well as contemporary literature. It enters our consulting rooms in various guises: the young writer striving to reconcile the incest she suffered as a child, or the middle-aged employee who was let go in the face of an outstanding job review. We are presented with institutional betrayals, as when the army specialist promises reparation to civilians suffering collateral losses and then there is no budget to realise the promise, or the college administrator who is undercut by the university board. It is there in the reading of the will, in the idea stolen from a colleague. And of course there are the betrayals that haunt our own profession, as when a clinician crosses the professional boundary to have a sexual relationship with a patient. We know the phenomenon all too well, because we encounter it regularly in our work and because we live it—as the one who has been betrayed, or the betrayer—every day.[1]

Preamble

Betrayal is powerful, and it is so due in large part to its close association to and repudiation of "basic trust" (Erikson, 1950), that building block of relationships, the foundation of all that follows developmentally in the human being. As we know from research in attachment and infant observation (Bowlby, 1980; Miller, Rustin, Rustin & Shuttleworth, 1989; Stern, 1985), a child's trust in his or her carers is the bedrock of psychic structure. It is present and tested from the beginning. In a good enough situation between infant and mother, trust gradually accrues in the newborn, as does management of inevitable disappointments, so that self and other, at first merged, begin gradually to separate into unique entities (Mahler, Pine & Bergman, 1975). Because when there is trust, the developing human being is allowed to grow and individuate and proceed on the path of becoming.

In healthy development, a preview of the universality of betrayal comes with the realisation that mother is a separate being. She is not me. She is not there for me all the time. Thus, normal omnipotence is challenged for the first time and, under good enough circumstances, is survived, and internal psychic structure is enhanced. Because we understand this development to take place internally, prompted by the reality of relationship, it is not a true betrayal. Rather we understand it as disillusionment, which must be experienced and mastered in order for development to proceed. This is the first of a lifetime of relational disappointments.

Betrayal is an attack on trust in the relational realm, right at that juncture of self and other. When it occurs, it throws us completely off our stride. What we thought we could count on is no longer true, and the universe changes. A sixty-year-old woman sat across from me trying to explain this. She was in the process of divorcing her husband of twenty-five years after discovering as many years of his philandering. "It changes everything," she said. "I look back at the life we had together and it was all a lie. I don't know how to square what I knew then with what I know now. I don't really know who I am anymore. I thought I did, but now I don't know, I don't know."

Betrayal shoves our faces into the absolute terror of aloneness. A comfortable partnership—between husband and wife, business partners, siblings, priest and penitent—is devastated. The one betrayed is suddenly without the partner. In this way, it is like the loss suffered through death, only less final and therefore more confusing. With death, the loss is irrevocable. There is no possibility of reconciliation except as that offered by belief. Eventually, the bereaved finds that he or she can return to life and engage once again in human relationships. In betrayal, however, the return to human interaction is achieved through a different process, one of regaining trust, claiming once again a belief in humanity.

Loss through betrayal is unique because of antecedents. While the one betrayed is naïve to the clues that precede an overt act of betrayal, upon reflection—upon viewing the past through a different lens, if you will—there is evidence that something untoward was in progress. While there can certainly be forewarnings of death, the trail is not characteristically patterned after the final blow. The body can be overwhelmed by disease, lifestyle, age, or accident, and cannot continue. Because the body of one partner fails, the human link is broken. In betrayal, the human link is broken not by the absence of a human being but by the destruction of the link. Physical death results in the loss of a relationship. In betrayal, relationship is not consequential: it is the target.

It is the laceration to the core intrapsychic structure and the resulting "mental pain" (Akhtar, 2000; Freud, 1926d; Joffe & Sandler, 1965; Weiss, 1934) that drives the desperation we see playing out in work with adulterous couples. It is betrayal that fuels the regressions that partners experience when a fundamental relationship is threatened. It is betrayal that renders healthy individuals to feel crazy and not-so-healthy individuals to fear existential annihilation. The partners jockey around betrayals constantly, either as the betrayed or the betrayer.

With this as a backdrop, I will now examine in some detail the therapeutic work with a married couple, focusing on the couple's dynamics from a psychoanalytic perspective as well as through the lens of betrayal. I believe that alongside whatever psychic fissures the couple displays, there flows the spectre of betrayal. While the couple is the focus of attention, the therapist is not beyond betrayal's reach. Thus, I will show, too, how the therapist is both informed of the spectre of betrayal and brought into the domain of ruptured trust. But, before going further, allow me to lay some groundwork for considering betrayal in marriage.

Betrayal in marriage

In marriage, perhaps the most familiar and frequent incidence of betrayal is the extramarital affair. In his 1977 play, titled simply *Betrayal*, Harold Pinter moves from a meeting of two adulterous lovers whose affair ended two years before, backwards through time allowing the audience to witness the stages of their affair, finally arriving at the first seduction, just as the play ends. The play, deemed a success at its opening and having enjoyed regular revivals since, stirs the audience on many levels. Its simplicity belies its complexity, as not one but multiple betrayals gradually emerge during the course of the play. One reviewer observed that the play shows man "trapped in an orbit of betrayal" (Kroll, 1978), capturing the persistence of betrayal's path so that just when it seems it is out of sight, gone, it comes round again. It is a similar process with the couple arriving for therapy in the wake of an extramarital affair. Like Pinter's play, as the circumstances are explored and the history revealed, there emerges not one but a plethora of betrayals, great and small.

When an affair rends the couple relationship, the impact is usually so profound that it can be hard to see any other factors. The picture, we think, is pretty apparent. As the work proceeds, the picture becomes more complex. We begin to hypothesise about developmental and perhaps psychiatric factors and do our best to hold the couple in the treatment while edging towards resolution of the couple's difficulties. In certain cases, therapeutic work with adult couples can present as a tug of war, straining a straight taut line, their prototype for relationship. Through projective identification, partners often take up positions that are polar opposites, while they lob invective across an invisible but purposeful boundary. It is an understandable but misguided effort to fill in their own character lacunae.

These situations alert us to unresolved Oedipal dilemmas residing at various levels of development that have emerged from the personal, intrapsychic realm now to be taken up interpersonally in the couple relationship. What would have been viewed as conflict in individual analysis now unfolds as a drama on the stage of a marriage. In some ways this makes things easier for the therapist because the difficulties are more evident, though often more volatile. When couples offer such a presentation, there is an adhesive quality to their fighting, such that a part of us wonders, why in the world are they together? Why don't they just end the torment and go their separate ways? This vague irritation may be accompanied by an impulse to flee that, if we can make use of this as countertransference information, may help head off an enactment of actual flight dressed up as a schedule suddenly too full. But note, even this split-second internal activity on the part of the therapist provides important data. We have been interpersonally forewarned.

Meanwhile, concurrent with our personal alarm, the couple invariably put forth their arsenal of counter-arguments: we've been together so many years; we have the children to consider; we want to go back to the way it was; etc. And we are drawn back in. Underlying all the rationales is an unconscious search for resolution within the couple of intrapsychic conflicts. Balfour (2005) states it nicely: "Couples are drawn together, at an unconscious level, because of shared or complementary unconscious phantasies. How they represent one another's fears, or project their anxieties into one another, is important in understanding how they act on one another to sustain and perpetuate their shared difficulties" (p. 70). He goes on to explain, in the example of a particular couple, that what can be at stake is one's very being, founded in a shared underlying phantasy: "In this case, their shared fear was of 'psychic take-over', so that between them, they confirm each other's worst anxieties" (p. 70). It is this volatility and tenacity that gets enlivened when the couple is together as Balfour describes. The two are caught up in a life and death battle, so it is no wonder that they each go at it with voraciousness.

The case of Dr. and Mrs. K.

Dr. and Mrs. K. were referred to me by colleagues, who were seeing each of the partners in individual treatment. The precipitating factor was the discovery of Dr. K.'s extramarital affair, now ended. Dr. and Mrs. K. immigrated to the United States separately but from the same country, as a consequence of political revolution. Dr. K.'s situation was relatively straightforward. The parents had brought him and his two younger siblings to the U.S. when Dr. K. was thirteen years old. The family settled in Arizona, where Dr. K. did well in school and got along well with his peers. He related that the stark contrast between his native culture and American customs was "no problem", and he spoke confidently of being "fully assimilated" into American culture. Dr. K. also reported, in a matter-of-fact way, that as a boy, he had been sexually molested by a cousin.

His wife, Mrs. K., was from a prominent and wealthy family that enjoyed a comfortable, probably privileged, life. When she was seven years old, Mrs. K.'s father took her and her two siblings on a trip to France. While in Paris, a violent revolution took place in her native country, making it impossible for them to return. Thus, Mrs. K. was forced to remain with her father, in France and then the United States, and be separated from her mother for six years. This traumatic experience was further complicated by the father's second marriage to a cruel, sadistic woman who refused to accept Mrs. K. into her home. At the age of nine, Mrs. K. was enrolled in a boarding school and, unable to spend holidays with her father because of the stepmother's admonition, she was abandoned to the care of the school or to extract what invitations she could from classmates.

Dr. and Mrs. K. had been married for fifteen years and had twin boys, aged twelve. Interestingly, the boys had been given the names of heroes from the parents' original culture—one was named for a poet, the other for a warrior. Both Dr. and Mrs. K. were respected and successful in their chosen professions. While Dr. K.'s work required regular and sometimes long hours, Mrs. K. had more flexibility in her work schedule, allowing her to tend to home and family obligations.

The event that propelled them into couple treatment was the discovery of Dr. K.'s extramarital affair, which had ended but, I was assured, the damage was great. Mrs. K. spoke passionately about her husband's betrayal and the resulting lack of trust that threatened their marriage. This particular episode of infidelity was not the first. Dr. K. had had an affair several years previously, and the couple had entered therapy at that time, though it was of brief duration. That Mrs. K. was profoundly hurt and shaken by this revelation there could be no doubt, but what made it even more excruciating, she told me, was that her father had also been unfaithful, and this had led to the parents' divorce. Mrs. K. said she didn't know if she could bear this breakdown in trust, compounding that which she already had to bear from her father's infidelities.

Dr. K. harboured a sense of betrayal, too, but his was enigmatic and furtive, like the affairs that threaded throughout his marriage. Whereas Dr. K. displayed apprehension in our early meetings, Mrs. K. exhibited a sense of confidence, as though she had the advantage of an overt betrayal to support the correctness of her position as the aggrieved party. And she had an object against which to align her aggression and to cultivate the sympathy of others. She was pleased to be in couple therapy, as though this were the requisite consequence for a husband who cheated. Both Dr. and Mrs. K. identified lack of trust and lack of intimacy as the key issues needing attention. They both said they wanted the marriage to survive and to grow stronger.

Dr. and Mrs. K. walked into my consulting room for their second appointment, Dr. K. commenting, "Oh, your glasses are missing a lens." Resting on the table next to my chair, my glasses seemed fine. No, I said, they are intact. He insisted, "No, look, one lens is missing." Confused, I picked up the glasses and took a closer look. Everything was in order.

I held the glasses up to show Dr. K. "Oh," he said with a laugh, "it must have been the light. They looked like there was only one lens." They sat down and we got to work.

Dr. K.'s comment struck me as both strange and meaningful. I was not sure how exactly, but the strangeness alerted me to think about the incident as one of contextual transference, with other possible unconscious motivators. This encounter presaged the kind of holding environment (Winnicott, 1960) the therapy would require. There were two aspects to this, one that seemed clear from the start, and another that would only gain significance as the treatment unfolded. The first meaning I gave to Dr. K.'s comments had to do with fairness and objectivity, and the capacity of the therapist to maintain equilibrium while engaged with the two parties of the couple. Dr. K. was alerting me that there was more than one view of their marital difficulties. Mrs. K. had been betrayed by her husband, and she was both hurt and furious. It was possible that Dr. K.'s transgression, so blatant and so indefensible, could define the whole agenda. Would I be able to see beyond the obvious? Would I be able to see both sides of the situation? On a personal level, would I invite Dr. K. into couple work, with the cruel intent of placing all the blame on him? In other words, as a therapist, would I betray him?

Dr. K. wondered if I would have both eyes open to see all the facts, to attend to both partners, so that the truth would ultimately emerge. If he could count on such a stance on my part, then that would give him hope. If not, then betrayal would be the legacy. As I have thought further about Dr. K.'s comments, I can now attach a related meaning to this fortuitous event. It is about how many eyes will be participating in the work. How many eyes and how many "I"s.

A digression into theory

In couple therapy, there are three people, three "I"s, three subjectivities. For patients operating on a narcissistic developmental level, separate subjectivities are unrecognisable and, in instances of extremely disturbed patients, separate subjectivities are threatening. This involves powerful unconscious processes of projective identification on the part of the patient to the extent that the therapist can feel imprisoned and unable to think or have any personal mental space in which to reside. This problem is addressed by Britton (1998), who conceptualises a "third position" or "triangular space" as a solution.

Ruszczynski (2005) elaborates Britton's ideas as they might apply to work with couples. This offers a natural extension "given that the nature of the intimate couple relationship is unconsciously determined by the nature of the two partners' relationships to their parents: imbued with projections, internalized, and enacted in their internal and external object relationships" (p. 32). Ruszczynski ultimately proposes a couple equivalent to Britton's triangular space. He locates each member of the couple, plus the symbolic couple itself as the three points of a "marital triangle", which when operational is indicative of health and maturity in adult couple relationships. Some of the characteristics of healthy couples include, in addition to dependence, "toleration of the loss of narcissism and omnipotence, the capacity to be included and to tolerate being excluded, knowing about one's loving and hating feelings, bearing guilt, and experiencing gratitude" (p. 33). These are all aspects of Klein's (1940) depressive position and are representative of successful negotiation of Oedipal conflicts.

Benjamin (2004) offers a concept of "thirdness" distinct from that articulated by others, drawing more from attunement and differentiation, maternal functions that introduce the third into the mother-infant dyad, and less with functions drawn from Oedipal arrangements. For Benjamin, the function of "thirdness" involves perspectives beyond an independent self. Relationship is built upon and nurtured by mutual recognition. Engagement is that of two subjectivities, just as in the earliest moments and days of the newborn, in communion with mother, both seeking recognition by the other through mutual give and take, approached and gained with some satisfaction. Mother's confidence that the infant's experience of upset will pass and steadiness will once again reign is communicated to the infant in such a way that both gain capability.

Benjamin is interested in the two-person engagement, not only for the benefit of the individual coming for treatment, but also and especially for the interaction that takes place and the essential place of human relationship in the origin and operation of human growth and development. Thus, she speaks of the two-way street that is traversed intersubjectively by the analyst and the patient, versus the more traditional idea of a one-way street, which was supposedly travelled by the patient, with the analyst's guidance or direction, as if a traffic cop. The "third" that accompanies and grows out of the two is a function, not a thing. Thus, patient and analyst are envisaged as operating on a two-way street that allows back and forth. The conceptual framework allows two drivers who must accommodate each other in order to avoid collision or gridlock, or in clinical language, impasse.

In work with couples, this idea of a two-way street might be apt for the two partners' journey, with the therapist as observer. This is in fact the process for much work with couples, when the observations can be processed and made use of by the couple. However, with some couples, the observer is useless at best, and at times even detrimental. I would suggest adjusting Benjamin's metaphor of a two-way street in work with couples. Two-way streets involve intersections, and the risk for the therapist is in becoming a traffic cop, directing who is to go and who is to stop. Perhaps a better analogy for "thirdness" in work with couples is the traffic circle, or roundabout. Here, more than one vehicle operates in cooperation with others. Things keep moving, even in heavy traffic, so that necessary adjustments can be absorbed more readily without causing tie-ups. And if the desired exit zooms by, the driver can just go around again and catch it next time!

These conceptual contributions for healthy functioning recognise narcissism as a developmental liability, wherein the capacity for mutual recognition of subjectivities is lacking. A key indicator of healthy relating is mutual recognition. That is, there is a developmental achievement in one's capacity to recognise the other as a separate subjectivity, with unique thoughts, experiences, feelings that are different from one's own. There really is no couple until this function is achieved.

Holding onto my "objectivity", I was not at first convinced of developmental deficits in the couple I was working with. But soon enough, I came to recognise deep deficits and to wonder if there was the potential for development into a viable couple. Would the therapy have a containing function for the potential of a couple? Would the treatment be able to nurture the requisite capacities so that this couple might develop a "marital triangle" (Ruszczynski, 2005), or so that this marriage might function as a psychological container (Colman, 1993), or so that a dimension of "thirdness" (Benjamin, 2004) might be attained for ongoing couple well-being?

Back to the clinical situation

Both Dr. K. and Mrs. K. were operating from narcissistic structures, with traumatic histories. As individuals, Dr. and Mrs. K. operated from a narcissistic vantage point wherein the world revolved about *them*. Consequently, friction moved quickly to confrontation and alienation, with resentment building on both sides of the marital equation. Because their intrapsychic structures were underdeveloped, and thus internal unconscious conflict was so disturbing and painful, they operated by transferring to the interpersonal realm what they could not resolve intrapsychically.

In one session, Dr. and Mrs. K. related having gone to a local restaurant for lunch, a place that Dr. K. had recommended.

DR. K.:   She can never be positive about the food. It's always just "okay". She's such a princess.

MRS. K.:   Well, I know he'll just spoil any compliment, turn it back so that it's about himself.

DR. K.:   I am hoping for a compliment, some acknowledgement that something I've chosen is a good thing. So I try to set it up, "What do you think of the salad?" I'm trying to connect, to bring about something good for us.

MRS. K.:   I say, "It's okay". I say what I think! This is a set-up and I'm not going to be manipulated into this.

MRS. K.,
(LATER):   He never compliments me, but if he does, it's only partial because he finds a way to compliment himself. He'll say, "Pretty jacket, good thing I told you about the sale at Saks" or "That was a good video, good thing I helped pick it out." You see!?

DR. K.:   I'm just playing, just joking …

It is clear in this segment, against the backdrop of the lunch, that both Dr. and Mrs. K. are object-hungry. They both want acknowledgement from the other; each is afraid of the other's rejection; each tries to get the upper hand competitively so as to avoid damage to the self. Dr. K. complains that Mrs. K. is never satisfied with his offerings, in this case the food he has arranged. He feels not "good-enough", despite his efforts. He expresses his anger with sarcasm—"She's such a princess"—but when he realises he is outmatched, he retreats into jokes, diminishing his needs, seeking shelter from Mrs. K.'s attacks. His assertiveness at the beginning, in bringing up an issue to be discussed, has just been turned against him and he seeks cover. Mrs. K. is suspicious from the start. She is convinced that Dr. K. has nothing good to offer. Fearing capture in repressed need for love, caring, and acceptance, she quickly crouches down for battle and strikes out. She is operating from Klein's (1940) paranoid schizoid position. She is not a partner in a couple. Rather, at this point, she is alone, fearful of the other, closed to any perspective other than the invincible one she has created. And she digs in.

Through the lens of betrayal, we might say that Mrs. K. feels that she is being coaxed by Dr. K. to express enjoyment, with the suspicion that it is all a ruse to take something of great value away from her. Ergo, she is not going along with it. In addition to Mrs. K.'s not wanting to take what Dr. K. has to offer, neither does she want to offer him what he wants. She does not want to gratify him. She is not going to enjoy that salad no matter what. In this hostile way, she distances herself, declaring with sharp, declarative assertions that trust is absent and therefore nothing can be advanced. Dr. K., on the other hand, seems to be operating in innocent good faith, declaring his interest in marital connection, annoyed that trust once undermined is so difficult to restore. He takes responsibility for his part—"I am hoping for a compliment … I try to set it up"—to close the gap, but the chasm is too broad, his adversary too dedicated to the gap. He falls away, his words ineffectual.

Mrs. K. fears betrayal by Dr. K., but in the process of carrying out that objective with such determination, she may actually be betraying herself. She says the salad is "okay" and "he spoils". Her determination to oppose Dr. K. is so all-encompassing that it is impossible to know what she actually thinks of the food, a metaphor for love. Mrs. K. does not accept Dr. K.'s love; she does not trust it. In her strong opposition, she positions herself 180 degrees from Dr. K., thus betraying her own true self with regard to both the food and, more importantly, love. It does not matter what she really thinks about the salad; it is important only that she oppose, as strongly as possible, the position and efforts of Dr. K. For his part, Dr. K. seems a bit naïve. He repeatedly makes offerings to Mrs. K. to express his love. Because of his own insecurities, the offerings contain something for himself. Mrs. K. is right: he does set up the compliments so that they are about himself. So he betrays his dedication to Mrs. K. by making loving gestures conditional on acceptance of himself. We can understand the motive in this, but it is not out of a spirit of generosity that Dr. K. asks about the salad. It is about trying to get a compliment for himself, to shore up his own ego and self-regard.

In this brief exchange, we can see that betrayal is about not being true to oneself. For Mrs. K., her self is distorted and lost due to the power of resentment and hostility, fed by the loss of trust. For Dr. K., professions of generosity belie the neediness so long denied. Here the levels and implications of betrayal multiply, drawn down both by the subject and by the objects of one's affections.

The session continues:

MRS. K.:   This is why I'm not available to you, not kind. I'm mad, mad because he [now addressing the therapist] gives me no attention in the bedroom! So I pull away, to protect myself, so I won't be disappointed. I'm not willing to let down this wall. I feel like he won't, can't do things for me, and it feels like an affront! I won't allow it!

Here, Mrs. K. is speaking to all the people who have disappointed her, who have let her down. She is taking out her vengeance on Dr. K. She has also decided to draw her ultimate weapon, Dr. K.'s inadequacy as a sexual partner. Unconsciously, Mrs. K. applies talion law to her situation. In this, the principle is "an eye for an eye", wherein the punishment must be equal to the crime. Mrs. K. thinks that because Dr. K. was unfaithful in their marriage, then he must have to suffer the punishment of attending "marital therapy". Mrs. K. thinks in concrete terms, so because Dr. K.'s betrayal involved, literally, a specific body part, the penis, then he will have to suffer castration, at least psychologically.

Dr. K. complains of "performance anxiety", that inhibits sexual intercourse. A visit to the urologist showed no physical explanation for Dr. K.'s sexual impotence. Meanwhile, Mrs. K. seems to embody the control and furious power of the phallic woman. This point was powerfully conveyed in one session during the couple's extensive renovation of their kitchen. Dr. K. was upset because Mrs. K. had called the contractor to change the kitchen water taps after they had agreed upon the style. She argued that the original choice, which Dr. K. had favoured, was not good enough, so she thought she'd just go ahead and order what would be best. I remember being stunned at the casualness with which she offered her explanation, having no appreciation for her belittling of Dr. K.'s waterworks!

They continue:

MRS. K.:   He says he wants a hug, well, he comes to me sometimes for a hug. Fine.
DR. K.:   But she won't do that. She never asks for a hug.
MRS. K.:   Yes, I do! I did, last night!

DR. K.:   But it's so hard to get to you. You said, "So, are you going to not give me a hug again tonight?" How can I respond to that?

It is now Mrs. K. who set out her needs—he gives me no attention in the bedroom—and then reveals the impossibility of having them met through her own retreat, while lobbing verbal attacks from behind her bunker. She projects her neediness into Dr. K., and then attacks him for being needy, all the while staying behind her fortress.

Again, the partners are poles apart and are kept apart. Gestures by Dr. K. to reach across the gap are spurned or cut off. Mrs. K.'s seeming gestures to reach across the gap were not intended to make contact, but to enhance her position of power. In preserving the gap, Mrs. K. was preserving her self, her own subjectivity. She uses linguistic gymnastics to keep the arrangement intact.

In this vignette, Mrs. K. is solidly ensconced in Klein's (1940) paranoid schizoid position, from which her unconscious belief draws life. There is no one who can care for her and being weak is dangerous. This is consistent with her transference to me and my countertransference. Mrs. K. would insist that I be more active in the therapy and take up her cause. Thus, very early in the work, Mrs. K. declared that she had an issue with me, "You're too easy on Dr. K., always letting him off the hook. What is wrong with you? Obviously, he's wrong and did a terrible thing. We need to get on with it!" I was pulled into her fact, with pressure to agree with her and to follow through by passing judgment and handing down a sentence. Another time she jauntily declared, "I need you to be a judge. I need you to listen and say who's right or wrong." When I demurred, she insisted, "No, I need a judge!" We then agreed to talk about what was on her mind and see how it might go.

A change occurs

Diametric opposition and binary thinking—what Benjamin (2004) refers to as "complementarity"—characterised most of the couple's interactions through the first two years of our work together. Because there was so little change, I often questioned myself and my skills as a therapist. Like Dr. K., I felt impotent. I sought consultation with a senior therapist, seasoned in work with couples.

Gradually I began to notice change. Things opened up, there was more give and take. Despite evidence to the contrary, the couple insisted that they worked together on things. I was at first disbelieving, thinking they were operating in some form of joint denial, a shared unconscious fantasy, possibly merger. But I began to experience a different tone in the work. There were still strong disagreements between the two and sessions filled with acrimony. But there emerged a sense of the two together, held by their marriage. For example, Dr. and Mrs. K. spoke of the pleasure they each felt working in the garden together. Or their mutual respect for Dr. K.'s computer skills whenever someone encountered snags in software applications. I began to listen more carefully and to see more clearly.

Then something dramatic happened. In the midst of the kitchen renovation, mentioned above, Mrs. K. became ill. All of a sudden, it was as if these two, travelling in separate vehicles, took the same exit. They focused on mutual concerns—the children, their families, schedules for doctors, and tests. They were in sync in a way that had eluded them until now, at least in the treatment. Mrs. K.'s diagnosis was confirmed and surgery scheduled. Mrs. K. was selective as to which friends and family members she confided in about her situation. Dr. K., too, had spoken to only a few trusted colleagues. In this session, Mrs. K. demonstrates an observing ego and shares her own self-states—of fear, of mood swings, of anger—related to her illness and the upcoming surgery. She is uncertain about her own ability to cope emotionally and hopes that others, including Dr. K., will bring understanding to her plight. With some hesitation, Mrs. K. turns to what she understands of Dr. K.'s experience.

MRS. K.: (looking at the therapist): On this question of who to tell, I know I don't want to tell many people, almost no one really, but my in-laws are here now, and I want to tell [Dr. K.]'s mother. I think it would help him, give him someone to talk to when he needs to talk. I know they are close, so it would be a good idea to tell her so she can be there, be a support for him. [pause]

DR. K.: No. That wouldn't be helpful. [They are looking at each other now] I don't have that kind of relationship with my mother. I mean, I love her, but whenever I've talked to her about something difficult, she just goes off on a thing about letting God handle it. She just gets so obsessed with God these days. So it's not helpful. So I don't really talk to her about things that much.

MRS. K.:   What? You talk to her several times a week. For a while it was like every day.

DR. K.:   Not every day. It's probably once a week now. I talk to her to be a support for her. With my father's illness [Dr. K.'s father has multiple sclerosis] a lot falls to her, so I want to be there to help in any way that I can. They're all the way across the country, so that's the least I can do from here.

MRS. K.:   But she could listen to you. I won't be able to handle it. I'll probably have enough to worry about just keeping my own self together! [little laugh]

DR. K.:   If I need to talk to someone, I want it to be someone of my own choosing. And not my mother. I don't want to have it all set up that I talk to my mother. I don't know what I'll feel like. Maybe I'll be fine and won't need to talk to anyone … But if I do, I want to think about who it should be. … Actually, I might be most comfortable talking to one of my colleagues. [Turns to the therapist] Only two of them know—the one who read the first scan, and one other. I could talk to them. [Turns back to Mrs. K.] That would be more comfortable than talking to my mother.

MRS. K.:   Well, why didn't you say that earlier? We talked about it in the car and you didn't say any of this, certainly not this clearly.

DR. K.:   (mildly exasperated): I'm saying it now. I've thought about it and am taking seriously your needs, too. I know there is a lot you're worried about and just managing your own worries. We both have worries and are trying to manage.

MRS. K.:   But why should I have to go through all this? Look what I had to go through … I understand now, though. It's okay.

Amid high anxiety, Dr. and Mrs. K. are having a conversation. And they are finding a solution to what has been raised by Mrs. K. as a problem she foresees for Dr. K. She is concerned that her own capacity to cope had reached a limit and that she would not be able also to carry worries and stress felt by Dr. K. She wants reinforcements. She sees that she has limits and that containing her own anxiety is as much as she can do. She worries that Dr. K. may not have considered this reality, that he may be overburdened, that she may overburden him. She puts forth her solution to a dilemma she perceives. But she is not rigidly endorsing her idea, only posing it as one solution. Dr. K. actually reflects on this idea and realises that, for him, it is not workable. But he recognises that Mrs. K.'s concern is legitimate both for himself and for her peace of mind. So he thinks about the possibility of coming to his own limits and how he might address them.

Mrs. K. introduced an important topic, with some confusion as to where responsibility lay. But this allowed the two of them to solve the problem together. They went back and forth, respecting each other's ideas by listening and weighing the possibilities and allowing emotional resonance—"How would this be for me?" "How would this be for you?" They expressed mutual caring. They were able to think together. They arrived at a solution that was for the moment satisfactory to them both, while holding out the possibility that circumstances might change, new information forthcoming.

Dr. and Mrs. K. have found a third by way of having similar concerns and, at the same time, having separate minds. They recognise the same event impacts each one differently, and stirs different responses. They know that relationally, they bring different needs and can respect those different from their own. The dilemma identified by Mrs. K. can be noted and processed. Complementarity gives way, psychic space enlarges, tensions relax. They negotiate their differences and connect. They swing around the roundabout and come out on the same street, heading in the same direction with intention.

Concluding remarks

In this chapter, I have presented ideas that apply to work with adult couples. Most helpful in this kind of work are concepts drawn from psychoanalysis and that centre on interpersonal relations and intersubjectivity. I chose to illustrate these ideas through the case of Dr. and Mrs. K., a couple who sought treatment because of the betrayal of one spouse through an extramarital affair. This kind of presenting problem—calling into question the role and function of trust—is relevant to the concepts on which I wished to elaborate.

From the intrapsychic world of the individual, we are privileged to enter into the interpersonal world of the married couple, this most relational of covenants, and therefore the most human of dimensions. Work with primitively organised couples presents a special challenge, as their psychic structures operate in such a way as to deepen and preserve opposition. Their marital problems are particularly intractable. Refinement of the interpersonal perspective to thinking intersubjectively provides a key to understanding the dynamics and special challenges with these vulnerable couples. Dr. and Mrs. K. provided a case wherein an extramarital affair was the impetus for the couple seeking therapy. This couple entered treatment citing betrayal as the major cause of difficulty in their marriage. Thus, the focus was directed immediately onto issues of trust and distrust.

Amid the seemingly impossible task of finding mutual recognition and appreciation for another's experience, Dr. and Mrs. K. began to operate differently. They, who had been so invested in the rightness of one perspective, began to see situations through different eyes and thereby, to enlarge the range of possibility. Problems remained and were significant, but the couple had developed a capacity for thinking and imagining mutually satisfying solutions. An intersubjective appreciation for this turn of events would recognise co-creation as an achievement, and that is so in our thinking about individuals. In thinking about couples, the achievement is trust, and in that there is endless possibility for creative solutions, creative journeys.

For the adult human, marriage represents the reach of dyadic basic trust across what separates into another potentiality, what we understand as "thirdness". This idea is what was taking place between Dr. and Mrs. K. in their treatment. The work unfolded in a safe, reliable context. The therapist maintained—with failures and repair—the frame and space in which to think, fight, and survive. For Dr. and Mrs. K., their marriage relationship became a symbol of a mutual mindset wherein trust could be both "invented and discovered" (Benjamin, 2004, p. 18). For Dr. and Mrs. K., trust is what was initially lost, and trust provided the "third" of co-creation in their newly arrived-at mutuality and cooperation.

Note

1. The deleterious effects of an analyst's boundary violation extend far beyond the patient who is the subject of such transgression to include many bystanders, especially his or her other patients. For details on this matter, see Chapter Ten by Adelman in this book.

The injured bystander in analytic betrayal

Anne J. Adelman

When an analyst[1] betrays a patient, it has far-reaching implications, not just for those directly involved in the transgression, but for other patients, colleagues, peers, and the profession as a whole. Yet we find it difficult to talk about analytic betrayal. Experts in ethics teach about the complexity of boundary violations, and in our training institutes we strive to do due diligence in teaching about potential ethical dilemmas. In spite of this, we struggle to understand and deal effectively with the issue.

It is different to think about something in the abstract than to encounter it in our real lives. Then, we see the complexity up close and discover perhaps that things are not exactly as they seem. The emotional resonance of such a personal encounter brings the situation to life in a more meaningful way, casting doubt on long-held beliefs and challenging us to think beyond previously held assumptions.

If we hear of an analyst who is reprimanded by an institute or loses the licence to practise, we are shocked and dismayed. While we may know that we all are vulnerable to boundary violations, whether large or small, we still feel disbelief when a well-known analyst punctures the analytic boundary. We may try to rework everything we thought we knew about that person—indeed, the person we knew no longer exists in our minds in the same way. It is as if our minds refuse to accept it. Instead, we are left with a powerful image of a damaged character, an image that evokes incredulity, despondency, and wistfulness, but also, at times, curiosity, titillation, even giddiness. We are all, in varying degrees, traumatised.

In the following pages, I will try to describe the effects of boundary violations on those touched indirectly by such transgressions, those described by Wallace and Amzallag (2010) as "collateral damage". There has been much written about the potent and destructive consequences of boundary violations for the patient directly affected by a transgressing analyst (Celenza, 2007; Gabbard, 1994), but there has been less focus on those who suffer the ripple effects—other patients, supervisees, colleagues, and the analytic community at large—those whose inner lives are indelibly altered, yet who seem to have no direct claim to harm. For them, the damage can be subtle and often hidden. Wallace (Wallace & Amzallag, 2010) describes it as a kind of "contagion effect":

> I learned from other candidates who had lost an analyst for ethical violations that all of us worried whether another analyst would want to treat us. We felt like damaged goods in the eyes of the analytic community. Are such fears realistic, or is this another example of "contagion fears," or perhaps both? My experience, along with similar experiences of other candidates, would support the latter; we indeed left the ruptured analysis feeling "tainted" to some degree, and the task for our next analysts was also realistically quite daunting. (p. 44)

The effects of boundary violations on those who are indirectly affected can be misunderstood or can surface gradually or only years later, or else in ways that are disguised enough to be nearly invisible. Yet they do leave their imprint, and often the effects are deep, long-lasting, and profoundly disquieting.

How a patient begins analysis

In Truffaut's 1976 movie, *L'argent de poche* (*Small Change*), there is a striking scene that has always stayed with me. We see an apartment door opening, and in bursts Gregory, a mischievous boy of about four, followed by his mother. When the distracted woman realises that she has misplaced her keys, she admonishes Gregory to stay out of trouble, wipes her hands on her apron, and runs down the stairs. Meanwhile, we watch Gregory at play with his cat. When he notices the cat climbing on a chair to gaze out of the window, his curiosity is aroused. First gently, then more firmly and determinedly, Gregory encourages the cat to climb onto the window ledge until it falls finally right out of the window. Gregory's eyes widen in surprise and wonder as he peers over the ledge, looking for his cat. The audience holds its breath, dreading to know what Gregory has seen. The cat, startled and dazed, has landed on a wall and is preparing to leap away. Watching the animal take off for safety, Gregory says in a voice filled with awe, *"Le chat a fait boum!"* ("The cat went kaboom"). Then, as the audience looks on, hearts in our mouths, Gregory climbs onto the chair himself. Painstakingly, yet smiling all the while, he clambers over the ledge, grabbing hold of the safety bar as if it were monkey bars at the playground. The camera moves back and forth between the crowd that has gathered, aghast, tens of feet below, and the little boy far above, swinging his legs casually over the top of the bar.

Suddenly, the boy grins with the pleasure of a new idea that has presented itself to him. We see him squeeze his body all the way through the bars. And in a terrifying instant, he deliberately lets go, freefalling to the ground. Horrified adults run towards him. We want to look away, but we cannot, we are riveted by Gregory's fate. And then, just as suddenly, we let out a simultaneous breath of relief and delight. Truffaut's magical hand has intervened, reminding us of the power of the child's imaginary scope. Gregory lands on the ground and bounces back up, as if buoyed by his own exuberance. He throws his head back in joyful laughter, exclaiming, *"Gregory a fait boum!"* While his stunned mother falls over in a faint, and neighbours gather around her, Gregory brushes himself off and skips happily down the road in pursuit of a rusty tin can, completely unaware of his near-fatal brush with a terrible end.

In this delightful, poignant and, at the same time, deeply perturbing scene, Truffaut captures exquisitely the core of childhood resilience and the true meaning of child's play. Children can play because their imagination bends and swoops past the bounds of reality. The freedom in their play swathes them in a sheath of safety that we think of as childhood innocence or simplicity. Gregory is learning about the boundlessness of his inquisitiveness and about his effect on the world, his ability to make things happen, and his capacity to survive what happens to him. In the movie, Truffaut invites the audience to recapture the exquisite freedom that allows the child to explore the world, test out his or her emerging theories of how things work, be curious, powerful, brilliant, and omnipotent.

Beginning an analysis for the first time is like entering Truffaut's world, where the parameters of reality are suspended. Patients enter analysis in the same way that Gregory climbs over the ledge. Whether or not they sense that danger might be lurking, they proceed because they must, because curiosity compels them, because nothing else will do. They have suffered and, perhaps, have come to understand, or hope, that life need not be lived in pain. They come to analysis to alleviate their suffering. Often, patients do not know exactly what to expect at the beginning of their treatment. Although they may have an idea about psychoanalysis or may know someone who has been in it, still they cannot necessarily conceive of where this interior journey will take them. They may wish to be transformed, to emerge anew and reinvented, or re-created into a version of themselves that is refined and redefined. Beginning analysis requires a kind of letting go, of releasing the reins and running free, guided by an intuitive sense of speed and space. Unlike young children, however, we adults cannot fully relinquish our irrefutable knowledge that imagination in fact provides us no better protection against real-life threats than the illusion of security—another magical belief we also must slowly relinquish.

Do all patients enter analysis with an illusion of safety, even when mingled with profound mistrust? I suspect that on some level, such an *illusion* is a necessary condition for starting treatment—that, while one may fear what lies ahead, what discoveries await, there is still some sense of trust, some understanding that the analyst generally intends no harm. If risk is on the horizon, perhaps they can momentarily look past it, hope winning out over dread.

When things go well in analysis, the journey across the childhood landscape of omnipotence and magical thinking progresses in relative safety. When the analyst can re-create for the patient what Truffaut so brilliantly captures for Gregory—a world that wraps its arms around fantasy and in which a free fall ends in a softly cushioned landing—then the analysis can proceed. It is not necessarily without emotional risk, for the patient is bound to experience painful as well as pleasurable emotions, encounter terrifying ghosts of the past, and revisit long-ago places that still contain the power to unseat the mind. Yet, in the presence of a carefully attentive and attuned analyst, such exploration is in fact a most exquisite form of play—in which the representational world both contains and reveals its meanings over time in the space shared between patient and analyst.

So, what happens when things do not go well? How does the stage get set for a scene in which fantasy and reality collide in a traumatic and devastating way?

Clash between real and imaginary

When I was a graduate student, I climbed over that ledge. I could not foresee that I would have the kind of painful experience I am trying to describe here, the experience of a collapsed analysis. When I began, I was convinced that analysis with a certain analyst, Dr. P., who was also my close friend's analyst, would offer me the transformative experience I was seeking. He accepted me into treatment. I quickly found myself in the thrall of analysis, and developed a strong attachment to Dr. P. I believed that somehow, I was special to him.[2]

The analysis was interrupted when I learned that Dr. P. was, in fact, having an affair with my friend, who had been his patient. Throughout the week that followed my discovery, I felt anxious, disoriented, and frightened. Even as I confronted Dr. P. with what I knew, I still held out the shred of hope that he would tell me I was mistaken. Then all would return to the way it had been. But it was true. And I could not un-know what I knew. There was nothing he could say that could help. Even his efforts to explain, his expressed desire to continue the work, felt suddenly flat, a *Wizard of Oz* movie in reverse, the vibrant colour drained from the analysis. Everything was unfolding in black and white.

I left the analysis. I knew I had to get help, because I was hurt, angry, and lost. Over the next year and a half or so, I had consultations with numerous analysts. I was trying to find a replacement, to pick up where I had left off before the interruption, but I could not. My search for a new analyst had become a Sisyphean task. It seemed that each analyst I met had some flaw. I would go once, twice, but could not seem to stay. The analytic breach had shattered the magic of that kind of transference. I felt deadened.

What I could not appreciate at the time was that, in seeking out consultation after consultation, and in turning down analyst after analyst, I was caught up in a supreme enactment. It was akin to the criminal's need to return to the scene of the crime, or the child's repetitious re-enacting of a traumatic event that has overwhelmed the child's defences and shattered the ability to symbolise. The breach that had occurred had effectively severed my own symbolic capacity. The space for symbolic representation had collapsed and I was left with a compulsion to repeat. I had no avenue to resolve the intense feelings I had allowed myself to feel in analysis. In fact, what I had felt for Dr. P. was yearning, a wish to recapture something lost in childhood and maybe found again in the guise of a young woman in love.

Transference love, in some ways, can be understood as an enactment in which the patient, with the analyst, brings analytic hope to life in the context of the relationship, pressing up against its boundaries. As Chused (1991) writes:

> Enactments are symbolic interactions between analyst and patient which have unconscious meaning to both … throughout an analysis, patients engage in symbolic action (both verbal and non-verbal) which generates a corresponding impulse for action in the analyst. *In the best of all possible worlds, an analyst is sensitive to his patient's transference, as expressed in either words or action, but does not act.* (pp. 615–616, emphasis added)

An enactment becomes risky to a patient when the analyst fails in the task of mediating between inner and outer, between imagined and represented, between felt and lived. When the patient is deeply involved in the analysis in a way that blurs inner and outer, it is imperative, then, for the analyst to intrepidly guard those blurred lines, moving gently and cautiously between adherence to the borders of reality, on the one hand, and an openness to joining the patient's inner world, on the other. Gabbard (1994) writes:

> … in the throes of an erotized transference, the patient cannot maintain this dual state of awareness and sees an action involving gratification of the repressed longings as the only solution. The "as-if" nature of the psychoanalytic enterprise is lost for the moment, and the analyst's burden is to restore the sense that feelings are both real, i.e., new feelings associated with the analytic relationship, and not real, i.e., displaced feelings from an old object relationship, a zone of experience described by Ogden (1986) as "analytic space". (p. 400)

This duality between "real" and "not-real" is at the heart of the psychoanalytic endeavour, and is what makes analysis possible in the first place. Looking back now, I wonder whether what I felt in analysis before the breach was "transference love" or just plain old love. How can we know the difference? The answer lies in the essential analytic commitment to allow the treatment to unfold in the context of a secure, clear, and well-bounded frame. I believe that at times, the difference exists primarily in the mind of the analyst, whose job it is to listen alongside the patient, attending simultaneously to the "real" and the "as-if"—in other words, to create enough space to notice and wonder about such feelings, even as they are being felt. The analyst must preserve the space for analytic curiosity and meaning-making to unfold by considering the patient's experience as important on multiple levels—within the transference, in the patient's relationships to the actual people in her life, and in her relationships to those figures who populate her inner world.

Thus, the expression of a patient's love signifies a potential array of emotions that can be understood in different terms than any existing outside analysis. Such feelings are understood as utterly real but, at the same time, absolutely and purely representational. Here, I am referring to the true meaning of play, where the metaphor is engaged in action, in time and in space. It carries the embedded meaning forth and thus becomes the vehicle for working through.

What is in the mind of the analyst and the patient is not and cannot be the same. The patient trusts the analyst to know more than she does, or to know what she knows in a different way, so while analyst and patient can "play" together, the analyst will not let the play get out of hand. In this way, the analyst, like Truffaut, gently cushions the fall, securing a world in which it is safe to pursue one's curiosity all the way to the edge and beyond. Without security of this sort there can be no play.

Returning to the notion of collateral damage, I think that what is compelling in such cases is that the traumatic breach caused by the *knowledge* of the analyst's misconduct *with another patient* is what leads to the potential enactment and rupture. For the patient with whom the transgression occurred, it happens "in real time", as it were, and the boundary between fantasy and reality is eliminated. The traumatic *sequelae* that may ensue are a direct result of actual events that fundamentally alter the landscape of the patient's lived experience. But for the bystander patient, what is disturbing is that psychic reality and reality become so approximate—fantasy comes so close to reality— that there is no longer any room for play. In other words, a patient (or supervisee, or student, or even close colleague) of an analyst who has been involved in misconduct with another patient is in fact subject to an equally terrifying clash between the "real" and the "not-real". On the one hand, the patient not directly involved in the boundary violation, whom I am calling the "bystander patient", is distraught and horrified. She is left with the devastating and traumatic fracture of a transference that cannot be resolved and is thus at risk to be endlessly and painfully re-enacted. On the other hand, *nothing really happened between the bystander patient and the analyst*—the breach occurred, as it were, behind closed doors, beyond the view of the patient, and outside the realm of what can be analysed or understood.

There is no redress for the bystander patient, because there is no direct link between her own analysis, and what the analyst did outside her treatment. This dichotomy itself contributes to the sense of collapsed analytic space. The bystander patient may be aware of feeling angry, hurt, betrayed, jealous, and so forth, but may still not fully grasp how complex her distress may be. "Why can't I just get out and move on?" she may ask herself. "After all, thank goodness, nothing *really happened to me.*"

The seduction of analysis

I once had a patient who remarked shortly after her treatment began, "I feel like there are lights going on in rooms I didn't even know were there." She was a lovely and highly intelligent young woman whose mother neglected her and whose father controlled her. No one had ever truly listened to her before. Quickly, she became deeply invested in her analysis. In the act of speaking her thoughts aloud to me, they took on new and intriguing meanings. Her treatment got underway in a manner that made me feel like a passenger in a car pulling out before I had even shut my door or buckled my seatbelt. It was heady and exhilarating, but I also understood that, in spite of her enthusiasm, there was risk, here, too.

Meadow (1990) reflects on the significant role that countertransference plays in the process of psychoanalysis. She suggests that for the analyst, it is inevitable to feel stirred by our patients. She remarks,

> We have learned that what the patient feels, even the feelings hidden from his awareness, influences the analyst. These feelings

arouse the analyst's memories and desires, they stir her roots, and they influence the analyst to merge with and repeat the patient's past, either in the identification with the patient or with the objects in the patient's history. The analyst's feelings are problematic only when the process takes place outside the awareness of the analyst and if it results in loving too much or hating too much and in communications that act on these feelings. (pp. 8–9)

In other words, she reminds us that when we are not alert to the feelings the patient awakens within us, we are at far greater risk of enactments. There are many kinds of seductions that can take place in analysis, and many kinds of risks and potential dangers for both patient and analyst. Most of us would agree that the most egregious are those that break the ground rules of treatment, those that assault the frame of the treatment. Sexual misconduct, or indeed physical misconduct of any kind, financial or other kinds of exploitation, breaches of confidentiality, all are unambiguously hazardous and cannot go unaddressed.

However, as others (Celenza, 2007; Chused, 1991; Gabbard, 1994) have shown, many boundary violations are subtle, and may go unnoticed for a long time by both patient and analyst. What I will address here is a kind of heightened allure that may be intrinsic to every analysis, and that requires special care to be taken by the analyst. Bienvenu (2003) writes:

> At the outset, a paradox attracts attention: the analytic situation is an artificial locus that produces an illusion; this illusion, in turn, leads analyst and analysand to an experience of truth, a cure through truth. An external observer from Mars could too rapidly conclude that the analytic site fosters lies, yet the illusion created in the analytic space leads one to an intimate experience of the truth. (p. 400)

In other words, while the conditions for successful analysis require that both patient and analyst enter a shared and mutually created arena of suspended disbelief, the analyst must also keep an eye focused on the horizon beyond, where the illusions created within the transference and countertransference are used ultimately in the service of greater self-awareness. The analytic "illusion" that Bienvenu (2003) is referring to is spun from the threads that form the fabric of the analytic process.

These include: the development of a shared language that is intimate and close, the sometimes prone position of the patient, the frequency of time spent together, and even the very nature of each session, in that two people are in a room together, engaged in an intense and private exchange. The premise of analysis rests on this illusion that makes it possible to create a potential space for the playing out of early childhood neuroses, pre-Oedipal and Oedipal fantasies, and the deepening capacity to experience and tolerate intense emotions—love, hate, greed, envy, despair, and longing—and to survive them. In other words, one significant aim of analysis is to create the potential for pre-Oedipal and Oedipal neuroses to be present in the room. Analysis works *because* it opens up such potential space. Without the frame that holds it together, the work of analysis becomes impossible.

Patients can fall under the sway of the intensity of being listened to with great care. They relish the feeling of being at the centre of the world, at least the one that unfolds in the consulting room. In a sense, in treatment, it is true that the patient is the protagonist of the universe spun into being in our offices. It is their perspective, their experience, their emotional temperature we are most interested in. For many patients, this feels particularly enticing. It creates a feeling of specialness, of a kind of self-importance that may have been lacking or, on the contrary, may have been over-abundant in their early years. As O'Reilly (1998) suggests, however, "The power or 'specialness' of the analyst can become dangerous if the analyst makes use of the position by exploiting the seduction potential" (p. 340).

The intensity of the analytic process can be intoxicating for the analyst as well. The analyst, for instance, may find himself in a position of authority vis-à-vis the patient that stirs feelings of narcissism or grandiosity—whether it is working with a patient who hangs on his every word, or one for whom no prior therapist was ever good enough, or even one who perceives life to be dramatically improved by the treatment. In other words, certain kinds of experiences with patients may contribute to the potential seduction of analysis *for the analyst. All* these reasons strengthen the imperative that the analyst must attend carefully to the frame binding the treatment together.

Our ability to work depends on how carefully we hold simultaneously our interest in our patients' inner lives and our more detached, evenly hovering stance. We wish to convey to our patients that their thoughts and feelings are important to us, but we avoid seducing our patients into feelings of specialness. If we are disinterested or disaffected, the work would be hollow and empty, but, at the other end of the spectrum, if we are too interested, we put the analytic process at risk. To feel special to the analyst can become a burden for the patient in a myriad ways. For example, the patient may now worry about the risk of overexciting the analyst—whether intellectually, sexually, or through some other emotional avenue, such as envy or loathing.

In the case of an analytic transgression, the bystander patient is at risk on multiple fronts. It is as though the background shifts to the foreground. The patient is presented with an entirely different view of the analyst. On the one hand, there may be relief that she did not fall prey to an overstimulated analyst. No taboos were violated. The patient is safe. On the other hand, she is now confronted with the knowledge that someone else has, in fact, "successfully enticed" the analyst into a transgression. The envy and jealousy that arise have no safe avenue for expression. The excluded bystander "becomes locked in an actualized Oedipal situation … [the analyst] can no longer help her relinquish and mourn the Oedipal fantasy and the transference love" (Malawista, Adelman & Anderson, 2011, p. 177). In some ways, the analysis dies an obscured death that has no burial, no funeral ritual, and no way to grieve the loss.

When the boundaries blur, one thing that inevitably gets lost is the patient's capacity to freely explore her impact on others and on the world. In Truffaut's film, we may wonder whether Gregory's act of shoving the cat out of the window was an act of sadism, or an exploration of the cause-and-effect of the cat-out-of-the-window phenomenon. We have no way to know for certain, but we can imagine that either activity may have been sharply curtailed had the scene taken a turn for the real, ending in the bloody outcome we may have expected.

Unlike Gregory's persistent curiosity about the cat's flight from the window, there is no one to cushion the fall when the analyst transgresses with another patient. One's own actions as a patient become heavily burdened. It is no longer possible to yearn to be special or to wish to incite the warmth of the analyst's interested gaze. Because the analyst has chosen someone else, the bystander patient is no longer safe to play out the Oedipal seduction scene. The scene has played out, the victor declared. For all involved, there is no good outcome. As Malawista, Adelman, and Anderson (2011) write, "What is the legacy when hopes of Oedipal love are actualized? … fantasy is inhibited by the intrusion of painful reality. ... When the therapy is derailed by a violation, successful resolution of the transference is also derailed" (p. 179).

For the bystander patient, then, a critical aspect of the "ripple effect" has to do with the distorted replaying of an Oedipal scene gone profoundly awry. The patient has seen too much and now cannot rid her mind of the images seared there. She has lost the potential to work through successfully her own omnipotent wishes to have the analyst/father all to herself, in what became an all-too-real competitive arena. With it, inevitably, she has lost the ability to mourn the loss of the analyst, because no resolution can be attained.

Shock of disillusionment—the fallen hero

A patient of mine named Emily, on the threshold of puberty, exposed her father's infidelity after reading his emails. She then watched, horrified, as her discovery led to the collapse of the marriage, her mother sinking into a bitter depression, her father threatening to abandon the family. She wept in my office, "I don't understand why he left me. I wasn't good enough for him." While both her parents joined together to offer her the reassurance that her father still loved her and that the problems were adult problems only between them, she persisted in feeling that she had been jilted.

After that, she refused to see him or to be alone with him. She felt powerless to hurt him except by withholding her love from him—indeed, that seemed to be her only power, but it hurt her too. For a long time, she remained stuck in this embattled place, neither being able to give in to his pleadings nor to turn away entirely. She demanded to know all the details of the affair, but then became flooded when he answered her questions directly. Meanwhile, she threw herself headlong into her social world, pretending nonchalantly to her friends that her father was away on extended travel. In sessions, however, she allowed herself to weep, wondering over and over again what she could have possibly done wrong. She began to imagine cutting herself. "At least then", she said, "there would be a place to put my pain." This young girl had suffered a trauma, which was the effect of the dramatic disillusionment that accompanied her discovery. While she had idealised her father, she had also loved him. Not yet a full-blown adolescent, she had not begun to systematically unravel herself from this idealisation and bring her father into human-size dimensions—he was still larger than life in her mind when she discovered that he was not the person she thought he was.

Such traumatic disillusionment can have profound consequences for the development of the adolescent. It also provides a model we can draw on to understand the damaging and destructive effects of the analyst's transgressions on those indirectly affected. Drawing on the developmental changes in adolescence provides a scaffold on which to base an understanding of the experience of the bystander patient. A crucial aspect of development involves the gradual process of disillusionment and "dis-identification" with our parents and families. Paz and Olmos de Paz (1992) describe this process in the following way:

> The adolescent is particularly vulnerable because he is in a state of transition in which he loses his security and has to confront the insecurity of the unknown. The passage from latency to puberty involves intense disillusionment with the parents, who, for the child knew everything, but now, for the adolescent, no longer know so much. This disillusionment causes pain and uncertainty, which the adolescent finds it hard to tolerate, while at the same time allowing the child to free himself from submission to the parents who know everything. (p. 744)

In order for the adolescent to successfully achieve a sense of his own identity and autonomy, this process of disillusionment must take place. Without it, the adolescent is at risk of remaining bound up in a hostile dependency with his parents. It is a form of object loss that takes place unconsciously, evolves micro-bit by micro-bit, and is developmentally expectable. While mourning for the lost "idealised" parents of one's childhood—the omnipotent, gratifying parents who could be summoned at any moment to provide a self-monitoring function necessary for soothing and self-regulation—it ultimately leads to greater self-cohesion.

Like the young adolescent, the patient in analysis is also caught in a process of gradually reworking and reintegrating bits of prior idealisations, as well as omnipotent wishes and fantasies, into a core sense of self—a self now sturdy and whole enough to be able to engage in mature, mutual, enduring love, satisfying and gratifying work, and the inner freedom with which to play. The analysis is intended to be a transitional space where the patient can feel held and understood by what

Bienvenu (2003) refers to as the "well-tempered" analyst—one who can accept the patient's amplified feelings of love, hate, desire, destruction, and rage in an even-handed way, and who can tolerate as well the slow progression towards a more tempered patient, in whom excesses of passion directed at the analyst become contained and tamed as internal structure builds.

In analysis, one can say that the analyst functions to some degree as a transference parent, with the potential to guide the patient in a gradual process of relinquishing omnipotent fantasies and replacing them with more mature representations of self and other. However, as Bienvenu (2003) tells us:

> Only if the presence of the analyst is felt can a disillusionment be constructive; consequently, when the disillusionment is brought about by the real (emotional) absence of the object, it remains traumatic. There is obviously a world of difference between an object that is emotionally absent (a real absence) and one whose presence is intense but kept in a state of abstinence (abstentia). (p. 419)

When object loss becomes traumatic, it gives rise to difficulties in mourning. Instead of working through the internalisation and consolidation of a new psychic structure, there is a risk of psychic fragmentation, denial, and splitting. As Blum (2003) puts it, "In traumatic bereavement the object relationship before the trauma no longer exists. The world in which the patient finds him- or herself, and helps to shape after the traumatic loss, is significantly different" (p. 418).

In Emily's case, she can come up with no good explanation for why the breach occurred or why she feels so utterly devastated. She thus generates her own explanation, a faulty one, which is her false assumption that if something has gone wrong, then it must be her fault. When she discovered the infidelity, she became the victor in the family triad by succeeding at separating her parents, and at the same time the loser, because her father could no longer be her idealised love object or fulfil her Oedipal strivings. Such an experience can carry particular potency for adolescents in the throes of separation, whose superego development is unfolding and whose sense of guilt—for the very angry and often hateful feelings they have that underlie adolescent rebellion in the first place—can be acute.

Likewise for the bystander patient, who can generate no good framework for understanding the breach, and thus is at risk of turning helplessness, envy, and rage inward, against the self. Indeed, in such cases, it is often the very sense of utter helplessness to do anything in response to what has happened that forms the basis for psychological damage.

Additionally, in such complex situations involving the fallen hero, there is the problem, that Emily so poignantly identifies, of where to locate the pain. For adolescents, where the sense of self is very porous and boundaries often fragile and easily ruptured, psychic pain can be both translated into and represented by physical pain. In Emily's case, the desire to cut herself in order to be able to localise the pain underscores the fragility of her nascent capacity to order and integrate experience. This is what makes the adolescent so susceptible to the trauma of shattered illusions. The desire to cut is the physical manifestation of the adolescent's breakdown of symbolic functioning, akin to the fragmentation that can occur after trauma. In this case, cutting is a representation of boundary breach but also concretises the breach, by seeking somatic sensation at the boundary of the skin, that is, at the border between inner and outer (Billie Pivnick, personal communication, August, 2012). For the bystander patient, the injury itself—the injury of traumatic disillusionment—is invisible as well, and may lead the patient to seek relief through somatisation or another form of enactment. For some, this is silence, for others, flight, for still others, the search for public retribution, but it remains nonetheless an amorphous, yet insidious, wound.

When the patient loses the analyst to a boundary violation outside her treatment, all play stops, as does the developmental progression described above. This highlights the difference between the developmentally necessary and growth-promoting process of gradual de-idealisation, and the more traumatic and overwhelming experience of a traumatic fall from grace. For the patient trapped in a shattered disillusionment, the expectable phases of mourning the idealised analyst cannot evolve. The fallen hero cannot be remade into a benign, "ordinary" object, but remains a shattered figure, too splintered to make whole again, too damaged to be internalised. There is, then, a corresponding internal splintering that speaks to damage to the internal idealised object. In this way, a boundary violation constitutes a developmental betrayal that reawakens earlier, more childlike feelings of pain and betrayal in the adult, and helps to explain why the bystander patient is not necessarily able to simply pick herself up, brush herself off, and walk away.

Institutional quandary

This brings me to the crux of the matter: since we tend to agree that such extra-analytic lapses exert a profound effect on all patients touched by the transgression, as well as candidates, supervisees, colleagues, and indeed all those connected to psychoanalysis, why then are we not more mindful of taking care of our community when such events occur? What accounts, in our institutes, our societies, and even our intimate professional circles, for the widespread denial and disavowal, the difficulty in addressing these issues head-on, and the general confusion about what to do in the face of a boundary violation? In general, we know how and when to seek legal counsel, when to check with our ethical boards and review technical procedures. But we do not have a systematic method to address the dramatic ripple effects of such egregious and highly dangerous situations.

The examples of such complicated situations are too numerous to mention. But surely, at some point, most of us have been confronted with some unexpected misconduct on the part of a colleague, peer, or analyst. One colleague told me about a patient whose daughter, diagnosed with Asperger's syndrome, had completed treatment with a senior analyst. When he lost his licence after a sexual affair with a patient, the mother was distraught. She wondered how she would broach the topic with her now college-age daughter, for whom much of life revolved around her computer. All the information about her former analyst would soon be available on the internet. "If I tell her, she'll be so devastated," the mother said. "She's worked with him since she was a child. But if I don't tell her, she will surely see it on-line at some point, and then what will I be able to say?"

Part of the problem is that many of us feel helpless and confused in the face of a colleague's misconduct. Most often, the concrete measures that need to be taken—whether legal repercussions, professional reprimands, or licence revocation—are already underway. Many of us are unsettled and at loose ends, but wonder what is there for us to do. There are various factors, conscious and unconscious, which inhibit us and keep us silent. Within our institutes, there is often systematic pressure to protect an offending colleague's reputation or practice, or a trend in the direction of disavowing the true impact that the breach may have had. We may feel reluctant to diminish the idealisation of our heroes and of our field in general. There can be a general collusion to not make waves that can be unconscious and perilous.

Describing the institute's community response to the impaired analyst, Galatzer-Levy (2004) states that:

> The potentially complex interaction of impaired analyst commit-tees and ethics committees has not been fully worked out [in part due to ...] divergent and ill-worked-through attitudes toward eth-ics violations, especially sexual boundaries violations, within the analytic community. (p. 1014)

He goes on to suggest,

> Denial is commonly used to protect the community and its members from primitive anxieties. Information inconsistent with a positive view of idealized figures is put aside, sometimes rational-ized away, or its implications ignored through magical thinking in order to maintain the idealization. (p. 1015)

At times, we may feel besmirched by the exposure to analytic transgressions, especially when it involves a highly respected mem-ber of our field—an ego ideal. Uncomfortably curious, anxious, and agitated, we want to know more. Like the crowd gathered beneath Gregory's window, the details horrify us yet we are unable to look away. We feel compelled to learn about what happened. At the same time, however, we want to protect ourselves from the recognition that wrapped inside our curiosity is some degree of excitement. Like Emily, the patient described earlier, we are overstimulated by what we learn. We want to know more, yet, we also want to distance ourselves. We yearn to feel separate and safe, to remain on the other side of the line that divides us from those who have fallen into the abyss.

We are afraid to face our own risk, too, afraid of our own rage, as well as our potential for enactment. As bystanders ourselves, we may become actively engaged in the thrill of our colleague's destructive course. In fantasy, we may linger too long in the realm of our own pro-hibited wishes, for instance to engage in an affair with a patient, just like the colleague who did it in reality. The bystander is engaged in an active psychic process, by imagining and fantasising boundary breaches in a wishful way, not just an avoidant one. Thus, as onlooking analysts we may need to distance ourselves from the perpetrator because, in our psychic reality, we may still be an active agent. We, too, have fantasised boundary breaches, and both desired and dreaded them. The slim difference, then, between having transgressed *in reality* and *in our fantasy* can collapse to an uncomfortably tight space, one that requires that we intensify our own adherence to the rules of abstinence—a stance that can move us from open engagement to rigid disavowal.

In some ways, this aspect of the bystander's experience is parallel to what others have written on the topic of bullying, violence, and aggression. Twemlow and Ramzy (2004), for example, describe the bystander role in this way:

> The bystander distances himself from the internal world of the victim and/or bully while using them as a receptacle for the projective identification of unwanted parts of his or her own self. Through projective identification into the bully or victim, the bystander experiences himself as more coherent and complete. The affect inconsistent with a coherent sense of self is experienced as belonging to the victim or victimizer, not the bystander. The bystander avoids suffering and guiltily retains only the voyeuristic excitement. (pp. 288–289)

In distancing oneself from the perpetrating analyst, there is a tendency not to recognise the subtle gradations that draw one closer to, or begin to approximate, action. An analyst might feel fairly confident in the notion that he would not transgress with an active patient, but in his private life, might he fantasise, for example, about an alternate relationship from his spouse? Or, might he make an interpretation tinged with an eroticised transference, even without actual transgression, that goes (barely) unnoticed? In other words, there is a series of gradations that may bring one to the edge of transgressions without actually acting them out, yet we maintain sufficient psychic distance that we can fail to perceive such subtle and nuanced enactments.

Szasz (1963) states, "No one, psycho-analysts included, has as yet discovered a method to make people behave with integrity when no one is watching. Yet this is the kind of integrity that analytic work requires of the analyst" (p. 442). We hope to be buoyed by our convictions and our belief in the process to proceed as best we can, but still we know that we are human. Under pressure, we may break. What is important is to know what constitutes that level of pressure for us, and how to get help when we are facing it.

By not addressing such incidents openly, we are at risk of re-enacting the peripheral trauma of analytic transgressions. The healing of trauma requires that we restore symbolic meanings through narrative. What cannot be spoken of risks being relegated to the shadows of hidden shame and guilt, and thus recruits the force of a full-on assault. Are we inadvertently re-enacting trauma by teaching ourselves it is better to put it away, not to ask too much, just to consider each transgression a warning to keep awake and alert? Duly warned, we bend our heads, with the urge to move away and not look back.

Conclusion

Analytic breaches unsettle other patients and analysts alike. Within the analytic community, the bystanders' feelings of anger, hurt, or betrayal may interfere with the ability to examine these issues head-on. Yet we can see that there is much peripheral damage done. As individuals and within our professional communities, it is essential that we deeply consider these issues, and work towards some consensus of what our procedures should be in the face of analytic misconduct.

Would it be possible, for instance, to draw on the medical model of the Morbidity and Mortality Conference, where doctors review together what went wrong? In his book, *Complications*, Atul Gawande (2002) describes the "M&M" Conference as "one place … where doctors can talk candidly about their mistakes, if not with patients, then at least with one another" (p. 57). The confidentiality of this conference is protected from legal discovery or challenge, so that physicians may speak more freely and learn from their errors. According to Gawande, the chief resident often presents the clinical case, and the attending physician assumes primary responsibility for the error, regardless of who was actually at fault. This is intended to diffuse the feelings of shame and blame sufficiently to allow for open discussion and review of errors, with an emphasis on understanding and learning rather than finger-pointing or punishment. That is not to say that there is no individual responsibility. Rather, the general perspective is that mistakes will be made because humans are fallible, and patients will be harmed or even die. It is incumbent upon every physician and surgeon to carefully examine such instances, so that they may be understood and, hopefully, avoided in the future. As Gawande writes:

> How could anyone who makes a mistake of that magnitude be allowed to practice medicine? We call such doctors "incompetent," "unethical" and "negligent." We want to see them punished … There is, however, a central truth in medicine that complicates this tidy vision of misdeeds and misdoers: all doctors make terrible mistakes. (pp. 55–56)

In the emergency department and on the operating table, any number of errors are possible. In the analyst's consulting room, it is no different. True, we have no scalpels that slip, no defibrillators that misfire, no mechanical instruments that fail or that are subject to the operator's error. Instead, we have only ourselves. But it is imperative that, just like a surgeon or an anaesthesiologist, we remain watchful, sharply aware of our own fantasies, fears, and desires. These are the instruments we must learn how to calibrate. Like a scalpel, they are exquisitely powerful. Like the surgeon's knife, they can be used to heal or to harm. For the surgeon, a simple error can result in lifelong damage or death; in our consulting rooms, too, mistakes can lead to deep and multifarious psychic harm for our patients. Yet, in the analytic setting, unlike the medical setting, a patient's injury often does not become apparent until after the breach is brought to light, whether by legal challenge, or a covering therapist, or a patient seeking alternative treatment. Indeed, sometimes it never comes to light.

Gawande points out that, in medicine, the M&M Conference is a socially sanctioned, "cultural ritual", one which discourages self-doubt or denial and insists on the question, "What would you have done differently?" In such a conference, where the underlying assumption is that the work itself carries multiple risks, whether hidden or in plain view, perhaps sharing the collective burden of blame may transform shame, and foster empathy or compassion. As Gawande tells us,

> The M&M is an impressively sophisticated and human institution. Unlike the courts or the media, it recognizes that human error is generally not something that can be deterred by punishment. The

> M&M sees avoiding error as largely a matter of will—of staying
> sufficiently informed and alert to anticipate the myriad ways that
> things can go wrong and then trying to head off each potential
> problem before it happens. (p. 62)

If institutes conducted such conferences—conferences in which the
material is confidential, where all members and candidates were invited
to attend, and the chair of the ethics committee served a similar role to
that of the attending physician in the M&M—might we then, perhaps,
be better equipped to learn from such mistakes? Might we truly perceive
our own fallibility if, instead of hushed, anxious conversations behind
closed doors, such a conference—regularly scheduled and specifically
geared to discussing bad outcomes, boundary violations, patient harm,
even harm to the therapist—could provide a safe forum for discussing
all kinds of "mistakes"? By guarding against the projection of blame,
for instance, the ethics committee chair might facilitate discussion and
provide a forum in which delicate and sensitive material can be discussed. If senior members of the community were invited to share their
own ethical dilemmas, boundary breaches, and difficult decisions, this
too would have a deep and powerful impact in furthering such open
dialogue. It would be necessary for candidates, supervisees, and other
colleagues to participate as well. As bystanders, they might also be
deeply affected by the transgression in ways that may go unobserved,
or may be minimised by the community or by themselves. Indeed, the
exclusion of those indirectly affected by the breach, even in the guise
of preserving confidentiality, may inadvertently heighten the propensity to engage in projected blame, outrage, and distancing oneself from
one's own susceptibility,

    In a traditional clinical conference, the analyst who conducted the
treatment presents the case. For the analyst who committed the breach,
however, presenting at an "M&M" model conference may be difficult or
impossible, on at least two accounts. First, in cases where there is a legal
challenge, they may have been instructed by their legal team to not speak
with anyone, even close colleagues or mentors. Second, the intensity of
the shame and fears of recrimination, alienation, or ostracism may dis-
courage the analyst from attending. And what of the patient involved
in the breach, who may herself be a member of the analytic community?
How can we safeguard that patient's confidentiality?

    Without the presence of the analyst or the detailed history of the
patient, it may be impossible to fully explore the analytic process and

how it went awry. In the case of a boundary violation, who would actually be able to present the case in a conference, and what would be presented? We are left with a dilemma: we must confer frankly and openly, yet we cannot know precisely the course of treatment and the series of derailments that may have led to the breach. Perhaps, the corresponding "M&M" model for the analytic community might be a meeting open to the entire community, subject to the same confidentiality as other conferences, in which what is presented is only what is already in the public record. In some ways, this may not be so different from any other case presentation—can we ever capture exactly and with precision what was said, by whom, with what intent?

There may be no one answer, no uniform standard or guideline, that can allow us to preserve the fine line between protection of privacy and shared clinical insight. Yet, as Gawande suggests, while the system may be imperfect, we must strive nonetheless to develop the optimal conditions for deepening our understanding. It is up to the analytic community, then, to grapple with what can be known, what eludes knowing, what important information can be gained to further our insight and raise our awareness of our vulnerability. Without such recognition, we miss or look beyond the enduring damage that such breaches leave in their wake. Unrecognised, it becomes a form of unacknowledged, disenfranchised grief, and goes underground.

Gawande writes, "Whatever the limits of the M&M, its fierce ethic of personal responsibility for errors is a formidable virtue … it isn't reasonable to ask that we achieve perfection. What is reasonable is to ask that we never cease to aim for it" (p. 74). What, then, does a "perfect" analytic "M&M" aspire to achieve? By providing an opportunity to process the information together, to share reactions and responses, to understand and articulate the potential for enactment, each of us may become increasingly aware, in an immediate way, of individual culpability and vulnerability. Rather than reinforcing the split through blaming and distancing it may allow us to begin to close the gap, diminishing the risks that Gawande describes of denial or self-deprecation. It would provide a forum in which each individual can consider his own clinical work and closely examine the difficult situations we can each find ourselves in.

What sets this apart from voyeurism or idle gossip, I believe, is the shared and earnest endeavour to work communally towards a deepened appreciation of the responsibility placed in our hands by our patients. In this way, as a community, perhaps we could begin to react, respond, mourn the loss of a colleague, or express disappointment or anger, and ultimately, to heal the wounds of the bystanders.

Returning to the situation I found myself in after my own analysis was interrupted, I am once again struck by how immobilised I was, and for how long. The following is an excerpt from a discussion I had with Judy Kantrowitz in July 2009, several years after the analysis ended, that will be published in her book on termination of analysis. I include it here because it strikes me, in rereading my own words, that I was experiencing the effects of being a bystander of an analytic breach before I had even become aware of it:

> … felt I needed more treatment desperately. I saw multiple people and couldn't connect. I finally worked with a woman once a week until I moved [away]. After three years, I went into analytic training. I thought I'd put [the interrupted analysis] behind me. I don't think I realized how much it affected me until I left and moved again. I finished my training in a different city.
>
> I didn't realize how much analysis had been spoiled for me until then. I didn't allow myself to feel deeply immersed in treatment again. The next two analysts [I saw were] women I felt deep respect and gratitude for, but not [intense engagement]. The first woman was very savvy. I was much freer. I took everything with a grain of salt. In [my final] analysis, the [analyst] was smart and very plain spoken. I trusted her, but she felt like a friendly mentor. … I didn't feel special to her or her to me. (cited in Kantrowitz, in press)

I went on to say:

> I feel I understand in a deeper way the importance of the breach. I understand the vulnerability patients feel, but I almost envy my patients. I lost something of the freshness of this work. It's bittersweet … I think I underestimated the attachment I made to my first analyst. I was in shock and denial. … (cited in Kantrowitz, in press)

The process of putting words to this betrayal has deepened my understanding of its effects on me, so early on in my work, as well as others who have gone through similar situations. However, while I may have lost some of the vitality of my earlier treatment that I now observe with my own patients, it has allowed me to reach a deepened sensitivity, an awareness of my own commitment to preserving analytic integrity. Having such personal knowledge of this issue has only served to strengthen my conviction about the profound and enduring value that psychoanalysis can have. I have experienced this with my own patients, where I have witnessed first-hand the power of psychoanalysis to work through unhappiness and change lives.

With hard work, maturation, and time, I have been able to resolve my own interrupted mourning. It is my hope that, by inviting a dialogue, in our institutes, amongst our colleagues in our analytic communities, that is honest and courageous, we will move through the fear, anxiety, and shame and learn to approach this topic with openness and a determination to not overlook the experience of the bystanders.

Notes

1. In this chapter, I refer to the analyst primarily as male, and the patient as female. This is for the sake of clarity, but it is understood that an analytic breach may occur within any type of gender pairing.
2. For a fuller discussion of this incident, see Chapter Nineteen in *Wearing My Tutu to Analysis and Other Stories: Learning Psychodynamic Concepts from Life* (2011), by K. Malawista, A. Adelman and C. Anderson.

REFERENCES

Abelin, E. (1971). The role of the father in the separation-individuation process. In: J. B. McDevitt & C. F. Settlage (Eds.), *Separation-Individuation* (pp. 229–252). New York: International Universities Press.

Abend, S. M. (1988). Intrapsychic versus interpersonal: the wrong dilemma. *Psychoanalytic Inquiry, 8*: 497–504.

Adelman, J. (1989). Bed tricks: on marriage as the end of comedy in "All's Well That Ends Well" and "Measure for Measure". In: N. Holland, S. Homan & B. Paris (Eds.), *Shakespeare's Personality* (pp. 151–174). Berkeley, CA: University of California Press.

Adorno, T. (1949). An essay on cultural criticism and society. In: S. Weber & S. Weber (Trans.), *Prisms*. Cambridge, MA: MIT Press, 1967.

Akhtar, M. (2011). Remembering, replaying and working through: the transformation of trauma in children's play. In: M. Akhtar (Ed.), *Play and Playfulness: Developmental, Cultural and Clinical Aspects* (pp. 85–104). Lanham, MD: Jason Aronson.

Akhtar, M. (Ed.) (2011). *Play and Playfulness: Developmental, Cultural and Clinical Aspects*. Lanham, MD: Jason Aronson.

Akhtar, S. (1994). Object constancy and adult psychopathology. *International Journal of Psychoanalysis, 75*: 441–455.

Akhtar, S. (2000). Mental pain and the cultural ointment of poetry. *International Journal of Psychoanalysis, 81*: 229–243.

Akhtar, S. (2002). Forgiveness: origins, dynamics, psychopathology, and technical relevance. *Psychoanalytic Quarterly*, 71: 175–212.

Akhtar, S. (2009). *Comprehensive Dictionary of Psychoanalysis*. London: Karnac.

Akhtar, S. (Ed.) (2013). Guilt: An introductory overview. In: *Guilt: Origins, Manifestations, and Management* (pp. 1–13). Lanham, MD: Jason Aronson.

Akhtar, S. & Blum, H. (Eds.) (2005). *The Language of Emotions: Development, Pathology, and Technique*. Lanham, MD: Jason Aronson.

Akhtar, S. & Parens, H. (Eds.) (2004). *Real and Imaginary Fathers*. Lanham, MD: Jason Aronson.

Akhtar, S. & Powell, A. (2004). Celluloid fathers: the depiction of parental function in some recent movies. In: S. Akhtar & H. Parens (Eds.), *Real and Imaginary Fathers* (pp. 73–94). Lanham, MD: Jason Aronson.

Amati-Mehler, J. & Argentieri, S. (1989). Hope and hopelessness: a technical problem? *International Journal of Psychoanalysis*, 70: 295–304.

Anda, R. F., Felitti, V. J., Bremner, J. D., Walker, J. D., Whitfield, C. & Perry, B. D. (2006). The enduring effects of abuse and related adverse experiences in childhood: a convergence of evidence from neurobiology and epidemiology. *European Archives of Psychiatry and Clinical Neuroscience, 256*: 174–186.

Anthony, E. J. & Benedek, T. (Eds.) (1970). *Parenthood: Its Psychology and Psychopathology*. Boston, MA: Little, Brown.

Asch, S. (1976). Varieties of negative therapeutic reactions and problems of technique. *Journal of the American Psychoanalytic Association*, 24: 383–407.

Asch, S. (1988). The analytic concepts of masochism: a re-evaluation. In: R. A. Glick & D. I. Meyers (Eds.), *Masochism: Current Psychoanalytic Perspectives* (pp. 93–116). Hillsdale, NJ: The Analytic Press.

Auchincloss, E. L. & Samberg, E. (Eds.) (2012). *Psychoanalytic Terms and Concepts*. New Haven, CT: Yale University Press.

Balfour, A. (2005). The couple, their marriage, and Oedipus: Or, problems come in twos and threes. In: F. Grier (Ed.), *Oedipus and the Couple* (pp. 49–71). London: Karnac.

Barnett, M. C. (1966). Vaginal awareness in the infancy and childhood of girls. *Journal of the American Psychoanalytic Association*, 14: 129–140.

Barron, J. & Wolitzky, D. (Eds.) (1992). *The Interface of Psychoanalysis and Psychology*. Washington, DC: American Psychological Association Press.

Beckwith, S. (2011). *Shakespeare and the Grammar of Forgiveness*. Ithaca, NY: Cornell University Press.

Beebe, B. (1986). Mother-infant mutual influence of self and object representations. In: J. Masling (Ed.), *Empirical Studies of Psychoanalytic Theories* (*Vol. 2*) (pp. 27–48). Hillsdale, NJ: The Analytic Press.

Begley, L. (1994). *The Man Who Was Late*. New York: Ballantine.

Benedek, T. (1970). Fatherhood and parenthood. In: E. J. Anthony & T. Benedek (Eds.), *Parenthood: Its Psychology and Psychopathology* (pp. 169–183). Boston, MA: Little, Brown.

Benjamin, J. (1991). Fathers and daughters: identification with difference. *Psychoanalytic Dialogues*, 1: 277–300.

Benjamin, J. (2004). Beyond doer and done-to: an intersubjective view of thirdness. *Psychoanalytic Quarterly*, 78: 5–46.

Bergler, E. (1949). *The Basic Neurosis: Oral Regression and Psychic Masochism*. New York: Grune and Stratton.

Bergmann, M. S. & Bergmann, M. (2008). *What Silent Love Hath Writ: A Psychoanalytic Exploration of Shakespeare's Sonnets*. New York: Gotschna Ventures.

Berry, P. H. & Griffie, J. (2010). Planning for actual death. In: B. R. Ferrell & N. Coyle (Eds.), *Oxford Textbook of Palliative Nursing* (3rd edition) (pp. 629–645). New York: Oxford University Press.

Bienvenu, J. (2003). Healing through the search for truth: the well-tempered analytic situation. *Canadian Journal of Psychoanalysis*, 11: 399–420.

Billow, R. (2004). The adolescent play: averting the tragedy of Hamlet. *Contemporary Psychoanalysis*, 40: 253–277.

Bion, W. (1967). Notes on memory and desire. *The Psychoanalytic Forum*, 2: 272–273.

Blakemore, S. J. (2008). The social brain in adolescence. *Nature Views/ Neuroscience*, 9: 267–277.

Blos, P. (1962). *On Adolescence: A Psychoanalytic Interpretation*. New York: The Free Press.

Blos, P. (1967). The second individuation process of adolescence. *Psychoanalytic Study of the Child*, 23: 245–263.

Blos, P. (1976). The split parental imago in adolescent social relations: an inquiry into group psychology. *Psychoanalytic Study of the Child*, 31: 7–33.

Blum, H. P. (1973). The concept of erotized transference. *Journal of the American Psychoanalytic Association*, 21: 61–76.

Blum, H. P. (1981). Object inconstancy and paranoid reconstruction. *Journal of the American Psychoanalytic Association*, 29: 789–813.

Blum, H. P. (2003). Psychic trauma and traumatic object loss. *Journal of the American Psychoanalytic Association*, 51: 415–431.

Blum, H. P. (2005). The language of affect. In: S. Akhtar & H. Blum (Eds.), *The Language of Emotions: Development, Pathology, and Technique* (pp. 1–18). Lanham, MD: Jason Aronson.

Blum, H. P. (2008). A further excavation of seduction, seduction trauma, and the seduction theory. *Psychoanalytic Study of the Child*, 63: 254–269.

Booth, S. (1977). *Shakespeare's Sonnets.* New Haven, CT: Yale University Press.

Bowlby, J. (1980). *Attachment and Loss I: Attachment.* New York: Basic.

Bowlby, J. (1988). *A Secure Base.* New York: Basic.

Brenner, C. (1959). The masochistic character. *Journal of the American Psychoanalytic Association, 7:* 197–226.

Brenner, C. (2000). Evenly hovering attention. *Psychoanalytic Quarterly, 69:* 545–549.

Brent, D. A., Oquenda, M. & Birmaher, B. (2002). Familial pathways to early-onset suicide attempt. *Archives of General Psychiatry, 59:* 801–807.

Britton, R. (1998). *Belief and Imagination.* London: Routledge.

Cavell, M. (2003). Forgiveness and freedom. *International Journal of Psychoanalysis, 84:* 515–531.

Celenza, A. (2007). *Sexual Boundary Violations: Therapeutic, Supervisory, and Academic Contexts.* Lanham, MD: Jason Aronson.

Charles, M. (1997). Betrayal. *Contemporary Psychoanalysis, 33:* 109–122.

Chasseguet-Smirgel, J. (1970). Feminine guilt and the Oedipus complex. In: J. Chasseguet-Smirgel (Ed.), *Female Sexuality: New Psychoanalytic Views* (pp. 94–133). Ann Arbor, MI: University of Michigan Press.

Chasseguet-Smirgel, J. (Ed.) (1970). *Female Sexuality: New Psychoanalytic Views.* Ann Arbor, MI: University of Michigan Press.

Chasseguet-Smirgel, J. (1984). *Creativity and Perversion.* New York: W. W. Norton.

Chodorow, N. (1978). *The Reproduction of Mothering.* Berkeley, CA: University of California Press.

Chu, J. A., Frey, L. M., Ganzel, B. L. & Matthews, J. A. (1999). Memories of childhood abuse: dissociation, amnesia and corroboration. *American Journal of Psychiatry, 156:* 749–755.

Chused, J. F. (1991). The evocative power of enactments. *Journal of the American Psychoanalytic Association, 39:* 615–639.

Cline, F. W. & Fay, J. (1990). *Parenting with Love and Logic: Teaching Children Responsibility.* Colorado Springs, CO: Purion Press.

Clyman, R. B. (1991). The procedural organization of emotions: a contribution from cognitive science to the psychoanalytic theory of therapeutic action. *Journal of the American Psychoanalytic Association, 39S:* 349–382.

Coen, S. (1992). *The Misuse of Persons: Analyzing Pathological Dependency.* London: Routledge.

Cohen, J. A., Deblinger, E., Mannarino, A. P. & Steer, R. A. (2004). A multi-site randomized controlled trial for children with sexual abuse-related PTSD symptoms. *Journal of the American Academy of Child and Adolescent Psychiatry, 43:* 393–402.

Cohler, B. & Galatzer-Levy, R. M. (2000). *The Course of Gay and Lesbian Lives: Social and Psychoanalytic Perspectives*. Chicago, IL: University of Chicago Press.

Colarusso, C. A. (2010). *The Long Shadow of Sexual Abuse: Developmental Effects across the Life Cycle*. Northvale, NJ: Jason Aronson.

Colman, W. (1993). Marriage as a psychological container. In: S. Ruszczynski (Ed.), *Psychotherapy with Couples* (pp. 70–96). London: Karnac.

Cooper, A. M. (1988). The narcissistic-masochistic character. In: R. A. Glick & D. Meyers (Eds.), *Masochism: Current Psychoanalytic Perspectives* (pp. 117–138). Hillsdale, NJ: The Analytic Press.

Da Silva, G. (1990). Borborygmi as markers of psychic work during the analytic session—a contribution to Freud's "Experience of Satisfaction" and to Bion's idea about the digestive model for the thinking apparatus. *International Journal of Psychoanalysis, 71*: 641–659.

Davies, J. M. (2003). Falling in love with love: Oedipal and postoedipal manifestations of idealization, mourning, and erotic masochism. *Psychoanalytic Dialogues, 13*: 1–27.

DeBellis, M. D., Keshevan, M. S., Clark, D. B., Casey, B. J., Giedd, J. N., Boring, A. M., Frustaci, K. & Ryan, N. D. (1999). Developmental traumatology: part II. Brain development. *Biological Psychiatry, 45*: 1271–1284.

Dini, K. (2008). *Video Games: Play and Addiction*. New York: iUniverse.

Dinnerstein, D. (1976). *The Mermaid and the Minotaur*. New York: Harper and Row.

Duncan-Jones, K. (1997). *Shakespeare's Sonnets*. London: Arden Press.

Eagle, M. (1995). The developmental perspectives of attachment and psychoanalytic theory. In: S. Goldberg, R. Muir & J. Kerr (Eds.), *Attachment Theory: Social, Developmental, and Clinical Perspectives* (pp. 123–151). Hillsdale, NJ: The Analytic Press.

Ehrenberg, M. E. (1987). Abuse and desire: a case of father-daughter incest. *Contemporary Psychoanalysis, 24*: 553–604.

Eisenberg, M. E., Ackard, D. M. & Resnick, M. D. (2007). Protective factors and suicide risk in adolescents with a history of sexual abuse. *Journal of Pediatrics, 151*: 482–487.

Election. (1999). Paramount Pictures. A. Payne, director.

Ellmann, R. (1988). *Oscar Wilde*. New York: Vintage.

Erikson, E. H. (1950). *Childhood and Society*. New York: W. W. Norton.

Etchegoyen, R. H. (1982). The relevance of the "Here and Now" transference interpretation for the reconstruction of early psychic development. *International Journal of Psychoanalysis, 63*: 65–75.

Ewens, T. (1976). Female sexuality and the role of the phallus. *Psychoanalytic Review, 63*: 615–637.

Fenichel, O. (1931). Specific forms of the Oedipus complex. In: *The Collected Papers of Otto Fenichel, First Series* (pp. 204–220). New York: W. W. Norton, 1954.

Ferenczi, S. (1926). *Further Contributions to the Theory and Technique of Psychoanalysis*. London: Hogarth.

Fergusson, D., Lynskey, M. & Horwood, L. (1996). Childhood sexual abuse and psychiatric disorder in young adulthood: prevalence of sexual abuse and factors associated with sexual abuse. *Journal of the American Academy of Child and Adolescent Psychiatry, 35*: 1355–1364.

Ferrell, B. R. & Coyle, N. (Eds.) (2010). *Oxford Textbook of Palliative Nursing (3rd edition)*. New York: Oxford University Press.

Finkelhor, D. (1993). Epidemiological factors in the clinical identification of child sexual abuse. *Child Abuse and Neglect, 17*: 67–70.

Fonagy, P., Gergely, G., Jurist, E. & Target, M. (2004). *Affect Regulation, Mentalization and the Development of the Self*. New York: Basic.

Freud, A. (1936). *The Ego and the Mechanisms of Defense*. New York: International Universities Press, 1966.

Freud, A. (1946). The psychoanalytic study of infantile feeding disturbances. *Psychoanalytic Study of the Child, 2*: 119–132.

Freud, A. (1958). *The Writings of Anna Freud, Vol. 5* (pp. 136–166). New York: International Universities Press.

Freud, S. (1895b). Draft "H": Paranoia. *S. E., 1*: 206–212. London: Hogarth.

Freud, S. (with Breuer, J.) (1895d). Studies on hysteria. *S. E., 2*: 1–323. London: Hogarth.

Freud, S. (1896b). Further remarks on the neuro-psychoses of defence. *S. E., 3*: 162–185. London: Hogarth.

Freud, S. (1905a). Three essays on the theory of sexuality. *S. E., 7*: 135–243. London: Hogarth.

Freud, S. (1905e). Fragment of an analysis of a case of hysteria. *S. E., 7*: 1–122. London: Hogarth.

Freud, S. (1906c). Psychoanalysis and the establishment of the facts in legal proceedings. *S. E., 9*: 103–114. London: Hogarth.

Freud, S. (1908c). On the sexual theories of children. *S. E., 9*: 209–226. London: Hogarth.

Freud, S. (1909b). Analysis of a phobia in a five-year-old boy. *S. E., 10*: 5–149. London: Hogarth.

Freud, S. (1912e). Recommendations to physicians practising psycho-analysis. *S. E., 12*: 109–120. London: Hogarth.

Freud, S. (1913c). On beginning the treatment. *S. E., 12*: 123–144. London: Hogarth.

Freud, S. (1917b). A childhood recollection from Dichtung und Wahrheit. *S. E., 17*: 145–156. London: Hogarth.

Freud, S. (1917e). Mourning and melancholia. *S. E., 14*: 237–260. London: Hogarth.

Freud, S. (1918b). From the history of an infantile neurosis. *S. E., 17*: 1–124. London: Hogarth.

Freud, S. (1920g). Beyond the pleasure principle. *S. E., 18*: 7–64. London: Hogarth.

Freud, S. (1923b). The ego and the id. *S. E., 19*: 1–66. London: Hogarth.

Freud, S. (1924c). The economic problem of masochism. *S. E., 19*: 155–170. London: Hogarth.

Freud, S. (1924d). The dissolution of the Oedipus complex. *S. E., 19*: 173–179. London: Hogarth.

Freud, S. (1926d). Inhibitions, symptoms and anxiety. *S. E., 20*: 75–175. London: Hogarth.

Freud, S. (1930a). Civilization and its discontents. *S. E., 21*: 59–145. London: Hogarth.

Freud, S. (1933a). New introductory lectures on psycho-analysis. *S. E., 22*: 5–182. London: Hogarth.

Freud, S. (1940a). An outline of psycho-analysis. *S. E., 23*: 139–207. London: Hogarth.

Gabbard, G. O. (1994). On love and lust in erotic transference. *Journal of the American Psychoanalytic Association, 42*: 385–403.

Gabbard, G. O. & Lester, E. (1995). *Boundaries and Boundary Violations in Psychoanalysis.* New York: Basic.

Galatzer-Levy, R. M. (2002). Emergence. *Psychoanalytic Inquiry, 22*: 708–727.

Galatzer-Levy, R. M. (2004). The death of the analyst: Patients whose previous analyst died while they were in treatment. *Journal of the American Psychoanalytic Association, 52*: 999–1024.

Galatzer-Levy, R. M. (2012). Obscuring desire: A special pattern of male adolescent masturbation, internet pornography, and the flight from meaning. *Psychoanalytic Inquiry, 32*: 480–495.

Galatzer-Levy, R. M. & Cohler, B. (1993). *The Essential Other: A Developmental Psychology of the Self.* New York: Basic.

Garner, S. N. (1989). Male bonding and the myth of women's deception in Shakespeare's plays. In: N. Holland, S. Homan & B. Paris (Eds.), *Shakespeare's Personality* (pp. 135–150). Berkeley, CA: University of California Press.

Gartner, R. B. (Ed.) (1997). *Daring to Remember: A Review of Memories of Sexual Betrayal: Truth, Fantasy, Depression, and Dissociation.* Northvale, NJ: Jason Aronson.

Gawande, A. (2002). *Complications.* New York: Picador.

Geneva Bible. (1570). Geneva, Switzerland: J. Crispin.

Gill, H. S. (1987). Effects of oedipal triumph caused by collapse or death of the rival parent. *International Journal of Psychoanalysis, 68*: 251–260.

Glick, R. A. & Meyers, D. I. (Eds.) (1988). *Masochism: Current Psychoanalytic Perspectives*. Hillsdale, NJ: The Analytic Press.

Goldberg, S., Muir, R. & Kerr, J. (Eds.) (1995). *Attachment Theory: Social, Developmental, and Clinical Perspectives*. Hillsdale, NJ: The Analytic Press.

Green, A. H. (1995). Comparing child victims and adult survivors: clues to the pathogenesis of child sexual abuse. *Journal of the American Academy of Psychoanalysis and Dynamic Psychiatry, 23*: 655–670.

Green, N. (2009). The fall of the House of Oxford. In: R. A. Stritmatter & G. B. Goldstein (Eds.), *Brief Chronicles: The Interdisciplinary Journal of the Shakespeare Fellowship, Vol. 1* (pp. 41–95). Auburndale, MA: The Shakespeare Fellowship.

Greenacre, P. (1956). Re-evaluation of the process of working through. *International Journal of Psychoanalysis, 23*: 439–444.

Grier, F. (Ed.) (2005). *Oedipus and the Couple*. London: Karnac.

Grossman, W. I. & Stewart, W. A. (1976). Penis envy: from childhood wish to developmental metaphor. *Journal of the American Psychoanalytic Association, 24S*: 193–212.

Gruenert, U. (1979). The negative therapeutic reaction as a reactivation of a disturbed process of separation in the transference. *Bulletin of European Psychoanalytical Federation, 16*: 5–19.

Hägglund, T. (1980). Some viewpoints on the ego ideal. *International Review of Psycho-analysis, 7*: 207–218.

Harris, A. (2005). *Gender as Soft Assembly*. New York: Routledge.

Heider, F. (1958). *The Psychology of Interpersonal Relations*. Hillsdale, NJ: Erlbaum Associates.

Holland, N. H., Homan, S. & Paris, B. (Eds.) (1989). *Shakespeare's Personality*. Berkeley, CA: University of California Press.

Holmes, J. (2011). Superego: an attachment perspective. *International Journal of Psychoanalysis, 92*: 1221–1240.

Horney, K. (1924). On the genesis of the castration complex in women. *International Journal of Psychoanalysis, 5*: 50–65.

Horney, K. (1926). The flight from womanhood. In: *Feminine Psychology* (pp. 54–70). New York: W. W. Norton.

Hulsey, T. L. & Frost, C. J. (1995). Psychoanalytic psychotherapy and the tragic sense of life and death. *Bulletin of the Menninger Clinic, 59*: 145–159.

Jaffe, C. (2000). Organizing adolescent(ce): A dynamic systems perspective on adolescence and psychotherapy. *Adolescent Psychiatry, 25*: 17–43.

Joffe, W. G. & Sandler, J. (1965). Pain, depression, and individuation. In: J. Sandler (Ed.), *From Safety to Superego* (pp. 154–159). New York: The Guilford Press.

Jones, E. (1927). The early development of female sexuality. *International Journal of Psychoanalysis, 8*: 459–472.

Jones, E. (1935). Early female sexuality. *International Journal of Psychoanalysis, 16*: 263–273.

Joseph, B. (1989). *Psychic Equilibrium and Psychic Change: Selected Papers of Betty Joseph*. E. B. Spillius & M. Feldman (Eds.). London: Tavistock/Routledge.

Josephs, L. (2001). The seductive superego: the trauma of self-betrayal. *International Journal of Psychoanalysis, 82*: 701–712.

Kaplan, L. (1984). *Adolescence: The Farewell to Childhood*. New York: Simon and Schuster.

Karen, R. (1998). *Becoming Attached: First Relationships and How They Shape Our Capacity to Love*. New York: Warner.

Kazmi, N. (1975). *Pehli Baarish*. Karachi, Pakistan: Urdu Ghar.

Kernberg, O. (1980). *Internal World and External Reality*. New York: Jason Aronson.

Kernberg, O. (1984). *Severe Personality Disorders: Psychotherapeutic Strategies*. New Haven, CT: Yale University Press.

Kernberg, O. (1992). *Aggression in Personality Disorders and Perversions*. New Haven, CT: Yale University Press.

Kieffer, C. C. (1996). Using dream interpretation to work through developmental impasses in group. *Group, 15*: 270–285.

Kieffer, C. C. (2004). Selfobjects, oedipal objects, and mutual recognition: A self-psychological reappraisal of the female "oedipal victor." *Annual of Psychoanalysis, 32*: 69–80.

Kieffer, C. C. (2007). Emergence and the analytic third: working at the edge of chaos. *Psychoanalytic Dialogues, 17*: 683–704.

Kieffer, C. C. (2008). From selfobjects to mutual recognition: Towards optimal responsiveness in father-daughter relationships. *Psychoanalytic Inquiry, 28*: 76–91.

Kieffer, C. C. (2011). Adolescence as a time to play. In: M. Akhtar (Ed.), *Play and Playfulness: Developmental, Cultural, and Clinical Aspects* (pp. 33–50). Lanham, MD: Jason Aronson.

Kisiel, C. L. & Lyons, J. S. (2001). Dissociation as a mediator of psychopathology among sexually abused children and adolescents. *American Journal of Psychiatry, 158*: 1034–1039.

Klein, M. (1937). Love, guilt, and reparation. In: *Love, Guilt and Reparation and Other Works—1921–1945*, pp. 306–343. New York: Free Press, 1975.

Klein, M. (1940). Mourning and its relation to manic depressive states. In: *Love, Guilt and Reparation and Other Works—1921–1945* (pp. 344–369). New York: Free Press, 1975.

Klein, M. (1946). Notes on some schizoid mechanisms. In: J. Mitchell (Ed.), *The Selected Melanie Klein* (pp. 175–200). New York: Free Press, 1986.

Kohut, H. (1971). *The Analysis of the Self*. New York: International Universities Press.

Kohut, H. (1981). *How Does Psychoanalysis Cure?* Chicago, IL: University of Chicago Press.

Kohut, H. (1996). *The Chicago Institute Lectures* (M. Topin & P. Topin, Eds.). Hillsdale, NJ: The Analytic Press.

Kramer, S. (1991). Psychopathological effects of incest. In: *The Trauma of Transgression: Psychotherapy of Incest* Victims (S. Kramer & S. Akhtar, Eds.) (pp. 1–12). Northvale, NJ: Jason Aronson.

Kramer, S. & Akhtar, S. (Eds.) (1991). *When the Body Speaks: Psychological Meanings in Kinetic Clues*. Northvale, NJ: Jason Aronson.

Kroll, J. (1978). Review: Oh, to be in England. *Newsweek*, November 27.

Kulish, N. & Holtzman, D. (2008). *A Story of Her Own: the Female Oedipus Complex Re-Examined and Renamed*. New York: Jason Aronson.

Lab, D., Feigenbaum, J. & Desilva, P. (2000). Mental health professionals' attitudes and practices toward male childhood sexual abuse. *Child Abuse and Neglect, 24*: 391–409.

Lemma, A. (2010). *Under the Skin: A Psychoanalytic Study of Body Modification*. London: Routledge.

Lerner, H. E. (1976). Parental mislabeling of female genitals. *Journal of the American Psychoanalytic Association, 24*: 269–283.

Levy, S. (1987). Therapeutic strategy and psychoanalytic technique. *Journal of the American Psychoanalytic Association, 35*: 447–466.

Lichtenberg, J., Lachmann, F. & Fosshage, J. (2001). *The Clinical Exchange: Techniques Derived from Self and Motivational Systems*. Hillsdale, NJ: The Analytic Press.

Lichtenberg, J., Lachmann, F. & Fosshage, J. (2010). *Self and Motivational Systems: A New Look*. London: Routledge.

Limentani, A. (1989). *Between Freud and Klein: The Psychoanalytic Quest for Knowledge and Truth*. London: Free Association.

Loewald, H. (1951). Ego and reality. *International Journal of Psychoanalysis, 32*: 10–18.

Loewald, H. (1977). The waning of the oedipus complex. *Journal of the American Psychoanalytic Association, 51*: 751–775.

Lowenstein, R. M. (1951). The problem of interpretation. *Psychoanalytic Quarterly, 20*: 1–23.

Lyons-Ruth, K. (1999). Two person unconscious: Intersubjective dialogue, enactive relational representation, and the emergence of new forms of relational organization. *Psychoanalytic Inquiry, 19*: 576–617.

Mahler, M. S. (1967). Discussion of "Problems of overidealization of the analyst and analysis" by Phyllis Greenacre. *Psychoanalytic Quarterly, 36*: 637.

Mahler, M. S. (1972). The rapprochement subphase of the separation-individuation process. *Psychoanalytic Quarterly, 41*: 487–506.

Mahler, M. S. & Gosliner, B. J. (1955). On symbiotic child psychosis: genetic, dynamic, and restitutive aspects. *Psychoanalytic Study of the Child, 10*: 195–212.

Mahler, M. S., Pine, F. & Bergman, A. (1975). *The Psychological Birth of the Human Infant*. New York: International Universities Press.

Mahon, E. J. (1987). Ancient Mariner, Pilot's Boy: A note on the creativity of Samuel Coleridge. *Psychoanalytic Study of the Child, 42*: 489–509.

Mahon, E. J. (2009). The death of Hamlet: An essay on grief and creativity. *Psychoanalytic Quarterly, 78*: 425–444.

Malawista, K., Adelman, A. & Anderson, C. (2011). *Wearing My Tutu to Analysis and Other Stories: Learning Psychodynamic Concepts from Life*. New York: Columbia University Press.

Maleson, F. (1984). Multiple meanings of masochism in psychoanalytic discourse. *Journal of the American Psychoanalytic Association, 32*: 325–356.

Maltsberger, J. & Buie, D. (1974). Countertransference hate in the treatment of suicidal patients. *Archives of General Psychiatry, 30*: 625–633.

Markman, H. (1997). Play in the treatment of adolescents. *Psychoanalytic Quarterly, 66*: 190–218.

Masling, J. (Ed.) (1986). *Empirical Studies of Psychoanalytic Theories (Vol. 2)*. Hillsdale, NJ: The Analytic Press.

McDevitt, J. B. & Settlage, C. F. (Eds.) (1971). *Separation-Individuation*. New York: International Universities Press.

McDougall, J. (1980). *A Plea for a Measure of Abnormality*. New York: International Universities Press.

McDougall, J. (2004). The psychoanalytic voyage of a breast-cancer patient. *Annals of Psychoanalysis, 32*: 9–28.

McLaughlin, J. T. (1992). Nonverbal behaviors in the analytic situation: The search for meaning in nonverbal cues. In: S. Kramer & S. Akhtar (Eds.), *When the Body Speaks* (pp. 131–161). New York: Jason Aronson.

Meadow, P. W. (1990). Treatment beginnings. *Modern Psychoanalysis, 15*: 3–10.

Meissner, W. W. (1997). The self and the body: I. The body self and the body image. *Psychoanalysis and Contemporary Thought, 20*: 419–448.

Meissner, W. W. (1998). The self and the body: II. The embodied self—Self vs. Nonself. *Psychoanalysis and Contemporary Thought*, *21*: 85–111.

Miller, L., Rustin, M. E., Rustin, M. J. & Shuttleworth, J. (Eds.) (1989). *Closely Observed Infants*. London: Duckworth.

Minerbo, V. (1998). The patient without a couch: an analysis of a patient with terminal cancer. *International Journal of Psychoanalysis*, *79*: 83–93.

Mish, F. C. (Ed.) (1998). *Merriam Webster's Collegiate Dictionary (10th edition)*. Springfield, MA: Merriam Webster Press.

Mitchell, J. (Ed.) (1946). *The Selected Melanie Klein*. New York: Free Press, 1986.

Mitchell, S. A. & Black, M. J. (1995). *Freud and Beyond: A History of Modern Psychoanalytic Thought*. New York: Basic.

Modell, A. (1965). On aspects of the superego's development. *International Journal of Psychoanalysis*, *46*: 323–331.

National Resource Center on Child Sexual Abuse (1994). The incidence and prevalence of child sexual abuse. Huntsville, AL: NRCCSA.

Nelson, E. C., Heath, A. C. & Madden, P. A. F. (2002). Association between self-reported childhood sexual abuse and adverse psychosocial outcomes. *Archives of General Psychiatry*, *59*: 139–145.

Nicoli, A. M. (Ed.) (1978). *The Harvard Guide to Modern Psychiatry*. Cambridge, MA: Belknap Press.

Niederland, W. (1968). Clinical observation on the "survivor syndrome". *International Journal of Psychoanalysis*, *49*: 313–315.

Oldham, J. & Liebert, R. (Eds.) (1989). *Psychoanalytic Perspectives. The Middle Years*. New Haven, CT: Yale University Press.

Orange, D. (1995). *Emotional Understanding: Studies in Psychoanalytic Epistemology*. New York: Guilford.

Orange, D. (2002). There is no outside: empathy and authenticity in psychoanalytic process. *Psychoanalytic Psychology*, *19*: 686–700.

O'Reilly, J. J. (1998). The boundaries of the analytic encounter: Clinical and ethical dimensions. A roundtable discussion, January 15. Presenters: Gisele Galdo, PhD, Marilyn Schwartz, CSW, Robin Goldberg, PhD, Michelle Price, CSW, and Kenneth Winnarick, PhD. Meeting chairperson: Joyce Lerner, CSW. *American Journal of Psychoanalysis*, *58*: 339–340.

Paolucci, E., Genuis, M. & Violato, C. (1995). A meta-analysis of the published research on the effects of child sexual abuse. *Journal of Psychology*, *135*: 17–36.

Parens, H. (1979). Developmental considerations of ambivalence: II, an explanation of the relations of instinctual drives and the symbiosis-separation-individuation process. *Psychoanalytic Study of the Child*, *34*: 385–420.

Parens, H., Pollock, L., Stern, J. & Kramer, S. (1976). On the girl's entry into the Oedipus complex. *Journal of the American Psychoanalytic Association*, *24S*: 79–107.

Paz, C. A. & Olmos de Paz, T. (1992). Adolescence and borderline pathology: Characteristics of the relevant psychoanalytic process. *International Journal of Psychoanalysis*, *73*: 739–755.

Person, E. S. & Klar, H. (1994). Establishing trauma: The difficulty distinguishing between memories and fantasies. *Journal of the American Psychoanalytic Association*, *42*: 1055–1081.

Piaget, J. & Inhelder, B. (1958). *The Growth of Logical Thinking from Childhood to Adolescence: An Essay on the Construction of Formal Operational Structures*. A. Parsons & S. Milgram (Trans.). New York: Basic.

Piers, C., Muller, J. & Brent, J. (Eds.) (2007). *Self-organizing Complexity in Psychological Systems (Psychological Issues)*. Lanham, MD: Jason Aronson.

Pine, F. (1997). *Diversity and Direction in Psychoanalytic Technique*. New Haven, CT: Yale University Press.

Pinter, H. (1978). *Betrayal*. New York: Grove Press.

Plaschkes, L. (2005). Affects in development and clinical work—discussion of Blum's chapter "The Language of Affects". In: S. Akhtar & H. Blum (Eds.), *The Language of Emotions: Development, Psychopathology, and Technique* (pp. 19–44). Lanham, MD: Jason Aronson.

Putnam, F. W. & Trickett, P. K. (1997). The psychobiological effects of sexual abuse: A longitudinal study. *Annals of the New York Academy of Science*, *821*: 150–159.

Roe, R. (2011). *Shakespeare's Guide to Italy*. New York: Harper.

Rosenfeld, H. (1964). On the psychopathology of narcissism: A clinical approach. *International Journal of Psychoanalysis*, *45*: 332–337.

Rosenfeld, H. (1971). A clinical approach to the psychoanalytic theory of the life and death instincts: An investigation into the aggressive aspects of narcissism. *International Journal of Psychoanalysis*, *52*: 169–178.

Ruszczynski, S. (Ed.) (1993). *Psychotherapy with Couples*. London: Karnac.

Ruszczynski, S. (2005). Reflective space in the intimate couple relationship: the "marital triangle". In: F. Grier (Ed.), *Oedipus and the Couple* (pp. 31–47). London: Karnac.

Sandler, J. (2003). On attachment to internal objects. *Psychoanalytic Inquiry*, *21*: 12–26.

Sandler, J. & Sandler, A. (1998). *Internal Objects Revisited*. London: Karnac.

Saporta, J. (2003). Synthesizing psychoanalytic and biological approaches to trauma: Some theoretical proposals. *Neuro-psychoanalysis*, *5*: 97–110.

Saywitz, K. J., Mannarino, A. P., Berliner, L. & Cohen, J. A. (2000). Treatment for sexually abused children and adolescents. *American Psychology*, *55*: 1040–1104.

Schafer, R. (1988). Those wrecked by success. In: R. A. Glick & D. Myers (Eds.), *Masochism: Current Psychoanalytic Perspectives* (pp. 81–91). Hillsdale, NJ: The Analytic Press.

Schafer, R. (1999). Disappointment and disappointedness. *International Journal of Psychoanalysis, 80*: 1093–1104.

Schilder, P. (1935). *The Image and Appearance of the Human Body.* New York: International Universities Press, 1950.

Secunda, V. (1992). *Women and Their Fathers.* New York: Delacorte Press.

Segal, J. (2007). The effect of multiple sclerosis on relationships with therapists. *Psychoanalytic Psychotherapy, 21*: 168–180.

Seligman, S. (2005). *Complexity and Sensibility: Non-linear Dynamic Systems Theory as a Meta-framework for Psychoanalysis.* Presented at the Division 39 Spring Conference, New York.

Settlage, C. F., Bemesderfer, S., Rosenthal, J., Afterman, J. & Spielman, P. M. (1991). The appeal cycle in early mother-child interaction: Nature and implications of a finding from developmental research. *Journal of the American Psychoanalytic Association, 39*: 947–1014.

Shakespeare, W. (1596). *The Merchant of Venice.* New York: Houghton Mifflin, 1974.

Shakespeare, W. (1603). *Measure for Measure.* New York: Houghton Mifflin, 1974.

Shengold, L. (1989). *Soul Murder: The Effects of Childhood Abuse and Deprivation.* New Haven, CT: Yale University Press.

Shengold, L. (1999). *Soul Murder Revisited: Thoughts about Therapy, Hate, Love, and Memory.* New Haven, CT: Yale University Press.

Siassi, S. (2007). Forgiveness, acceptance and the matter of expectation. *International Journal of Psychoanalysis, 88*: 1423–1440.

Siegert, R. J. & Abernethy, D. A. (2005). Depression in multiple sclerosis: A review. *Journal of Neurology, Neurosurgery and Psychiatry, 76*: 469–475.

Slade, A. (1998). Representation, symbolization, and affect regulation in the concomitant treatment of a mother and child: Attachment theory and child psychotherapy. *Psychoanalytic Dialogues, 8*: 797–830.

Small Change (French: *L'Argent de Poche*) (1976). M. Berbert, producer. F. Truffaut, director.

Spillius, E. B. & Feldman, M. (Eds.) (1989). London: Tavistock/Routledge.

Stanton, A. H. (1978). Personality disorders. In: A. M. Nicoli (Ed.), *The Harvard Guide to Modern Psychiatry* (pp. 283–295). Cambridge, MA: Belknap Press.

Steinberg, L. & Morris, A. S. (2001). Adolescent development. *Annual Review of Psychology, 52*: 83–110.

Stern, D. (1985). *The Interpersonal World of the Infant*. New York: Basic.

Stern, D., Bruschweiler-Stern, N., Harrison, A., Lyons-Ruth, K., Morgan, A., Nahum, J., Sander, L. & Tronick, E. (1987). The process of therapeutic change using implicit knowledge: Some implications of developmental observations for adult psychotherapy. *Infant Mental Health Journal, 19*: 277–308.

Stoller, R. (1992). *Presentations of Gender*. New Haven, CT: Yale University Press.

Stolorow, R. D. (2007). *Trauma and Human Existence: Autobiographic, Psychoanalytic and Philosophical Reflections*. London: Routledge.

Stolorow, R. D. & Atwood, G. (1992). *Contexts of Being: the Intersubjective Foundations of Psychological Life*. Hillsdale, NJ: The Analytic Press.

Stritmatter, R. A. & Goldstein, G. B. (Eds.) (2009). *Brief Chronicles: The Interdisciplinary Journal of the Shakespeare Fellowship, Vol. 1*. Auburndale, MA: The Shakespeare Fellowship.

Summit, R. C. (1983). The child abuse accommodation syndrome. *Child Abuse and Neglect, 7*: 177–193.

Szasz, T. S. (1963). The concept of transference as a defence for the analyst. *International Journal of Psychoanalysis, 44*: 432–443.

Thelen, E. & Smith, L. (1994). *A Dynamic Systems Approach to the Development of Cognition and Action*. Cambridge, MA: MIT Press.

Thompson, C. (1954). Psychiatry. *Psychoanalytic Review, 41*: 66–92.

Tomkins, S. (1962). *Affect, Imagery, Consciousness*. New York: Springer.

Tronick, E. Z. (2003). "Of course all relationships are unique": How co-creative processes generate unique mother-infant and patient-therapist relationships and change other relationships. *Psychoanalytic Inquiry, 23*: 473–491.

Twain, M. (1874). Old times on the Mississippi. In: *Oxford Dictionary of Quotations, 3rd Ed*. Oxford: Oxford University Press, 1979.

Twemlow, S. W. & Ramzy, N. (2004). The social face of humiliation and the community response to it. *International Journal of Applied Psychoanalytic Studies, 1*: 287–290.

U.S. Department of Health and Human Services (1998). Statistics.

U.S. Department of Health and Human Services (2000). Statistics.

U.S. Department of Health and Human Services: Administration for Children and Families (1995). Child maltreatment statistics.

U.S. Department of Health and Human Services (2011). Children's bureau statistics.

U.S. Department of Justice (1997). Sex offense and offenders study.

Vendler, H. (1997). *The Art of Shakespeare's Sonnets*. Cambridge, MA: Harvard University Press.

Viederman, M. (1989). Middle life as a period of mutative change. In: J. Oldham & R. Liebert (Eds.), *Psychoanalytic Perspectives. The Middle Years* (pp. 224–239). New Haven, CT: Yale University Press.

Von Bertalanffy, L. (1968). *General Systems Theory: Foundations, Development, Application.* New York: George Braziller.

Wallace, E. M. & Amzallag, Y. (2010). Collateral damage: Long-term effects of losing a training analyst for ethical violations. *Canadian Journal of Psychoanalysis, 18*: 248–254.

Waugaman, R. M. (2007). Unconscious communication in Shakespeare: "Et tu, Brute?" echoes "Eloi, Eloi, Lama Sabbachthani?". *Psychiatry, 70*: 52–58.

Waugaman, R. M. (2009a). A psychoanalytic study of Edward de Vere's "The Tempest". *Journal of the American Academy of Psychoanalysis, 37*: 627–643.

Waugaman, R. M. (2009b). The psychology of Shakespearean biography. *Brief Chronicles: The Interdisciplinary Journal of the Shakespeare Fellowship, 1*: 34–48.

Waugaman, R. M. (2009c). The Sternhold and Hopkins "*Whole Book of Psalms*" is a major source for the works of Shakespeare. *Notes & Queries, 56*: 595–604.

Waugaman, R. M. (2010a). Echoes of the "*Whole Book of Psalms*" in Shakespeare's "*Henry IV, Part 1*", "*Richard II*", and "*Edward III*", *Notes & Queries, 57*: 359–364.

Waugaman, R. M. (2010b). The bisexuality of Shakespeare's sonnets and implications for De Vere's authorship. *The Psychoanalytic Review, 97*: 857–879.

Waugaman, R. M. (2010c). The discovery of a major new literary source for Shakespeare's works in the de Vere Geneva Bible. *Brief Chronicles: The Interdisciplinary Journal of the Shakespeare Fellowship, 2*: 109–120.

Waugaman, R. M. (2011a). The Sternhold and Hopkins "Whole Book of Psalms" offers crucial evidence of de Vere's authorship of the works of Shakespeare. *Brief Chronicles: The Interdisciplinary Journal of the Shakespeare Fellowship, 3*: 213–234.

Waugaman, R. M. (2011b). Shakespeare's "Sonnet 80", Marlowe, and "Hero and Leander". *Shakespeare Matters, 10*: 1, 27–30.

Waugaman, R. M. (2012). The psychopathology of Stratfordianism. *The Oxfordian, 14* (in press).

Waugaman, R. M. & Stritmatter, R. A. (2009). Who was "William Shakespeare"? We propose he was Edward de Vere. *The Scandinavian Psychoanalytic Review, 32*: 105–115.

Weiss, E. (1934). Bodily pain and mental pain. *International Journal of Psychoanalysis, 15*: 1–13.

Whole Book of Psalms. (1569). T. Sternhold & J. Hopkins (Trans). Geneva, Switzerland: J. Crispin.

Wilde, O. (1897). De profundis. In: *The Complete Works of Oscar Wilde.* New York: Harper Collins, 1948.

Widom, C. S. (1999). Posttraumatic stress disorder in abused and neglected children grown up. *American Journal of Psychiatry, 156*: 1223–1229.

Widom, C. S. & Ames, M. (1994). Criminal consequences of childhood sexual victimization. *Child Abuse and Neglect, 18*: 303–318.

Williams, M. (1987). Reconstruction of an early seduction and its aftereffects. *Journal of the American Psychoanalytic Association, 35*: 145–163.

Winnicott, D. W. (1953). Transitional objects and transitional phenomena. *International Journal of Psychoanalysis, 34*: 89–97.

Winnicott, D. W. (1960). Ego distortion and the terms of true and false self. In: *Maturational Processes and the Facilitating Environment* (pp. 140–152). New York: International Universities Press.

Winnicott, D. W. (1965). *Maturational Processes and the Facilitating Environment.* New York: International Universities Press.

Winnicott, D. W. (1971). *Playing and Reality.* New York: Basic.

Wolf, E. S. (1988). *Treating the Self.* New York: Guilford.

Zetzel, E. R. (1958). Ernest Jones: His contribution to psycho-analytic theory. *International Journal of Psychoanalysis, 39*: 311–318.

INDEX